DAS BOOK On Growth and Development

DAS BOOK
On Growth and Development

Dan Silva

© 2017 Dan Silva

Some rights reserved

Rights and Permissions

This work is available under the Creative Commons Attribution 3.0 IGO license (CC BY 3.0 IGO) https://creativecommons.org/licenses/by/3.0/igo/. Under the Creative Commons Attribution license, you are free to copy, distribute, transmit, and adapt this work, including for commercial purposes, under the following conditions:

Attribution – Please cite the work as follows: Dan Silva. 2017. *Das Book: On Growth and Development.*

10 9 8 7 6 5 4 3 2

"Truth and love will overcome lies and hatred."
VACLAV HAVEL

CONTENTS

INTRODUCTION/1
Defining Economic Growth and Development/4

IT'S THE PEOPLE, STUPID!/9
How to Create a Middle-Class/13

ENABLERS and DISABLERS of GROWTH and DEVELOPMENT/27

BEFORE DEVELOPMENT:
Why Some of Us Live in Developed Countries and Others in Undeveloped Ones/37
Geography 101: Who Won the Geography Lottery/42
Institutions 101: The First to Organize were the First to Dominate/49
Markets 101: From Primordial Times to Adam Smith/59

UNDEVELOPED:
The Plight of the Bottom Billion/65
Geography 102: Being Stuck between a Rock and a Hard Place/68
Institutions 102: Building Leadership for the Leaderless/74
Markets 102: The Big Bang Theory or How to Make Something out of Nothing/80

DEVELOPING:
How to Overcome the Middle Income Trap/87
Geography 1.0: Mastering Nature to Master the Economy/90
Institutions 1.0: Stability and Foundations for Long-Term Growth/101
Markets 1.0: Modernizing the Economy/110

DEVELOPED:
How to Invent the Future/119
Geography 2.0: Winning the Lottery Does not Mean Eternal Bliss/122
Institutions 2.0: The Innovative State/130
Markets 2.0: The Bedrock of the Economy/139

RECOMMENDATIONS: What to Do and What Not to Do to Grow and Develop/147

TOWARDS A DEVELOPED WORLD/151
People and the Pursuit of Happiness/152
The Good Big Brother/156
The Shrinking Middles Class/170
The Super-Productive Companies/176
A Flexible and Motivated Workforce/179
Large Unified Markets – Make It Easy to Move Goods around the World/185
A Global Lingua Franca – Make it Easy for Ideas to Move around the World/189
The Importance of Hope, Vision and Trust/192
Concentration, Spillovers, and the Re-birth of the Renaissance Man/195
The Importance of Connectivity/198
The Importance of Access to Financing/202
Help People to Educate Themselves/204
Create Big Data Storage/206
Playing with the Status Syndrome/208
How Can We Achieve More of Our Dreams/210
The Iceland Response to the Renaissance Man/211

WHAT CAN COUNTRIES DO?/213
Solutions for Undeveloped Countries/215
Solutions for Developing Countries/232
Solutions for Developed Countries/252

MUSINGS on the ECONOMY of TOMORROW/267
Limits to Growth or Space the Final Frontier/269
The End of Countries/271
Mayors will Rule the World/272
Strong Universities will be a Critical Success Factor for Cities/273
The Transport Revolution/274
The End of the Tower of Babel/278
The World Currency and the Disappearance of Banks/279
The Death of Intermediaries and Repetitive Jobs/281
Global Cadaster/282
Faster and Faster Knowledge Acquisition/282

Instead of Conclusions/285

Notes/290

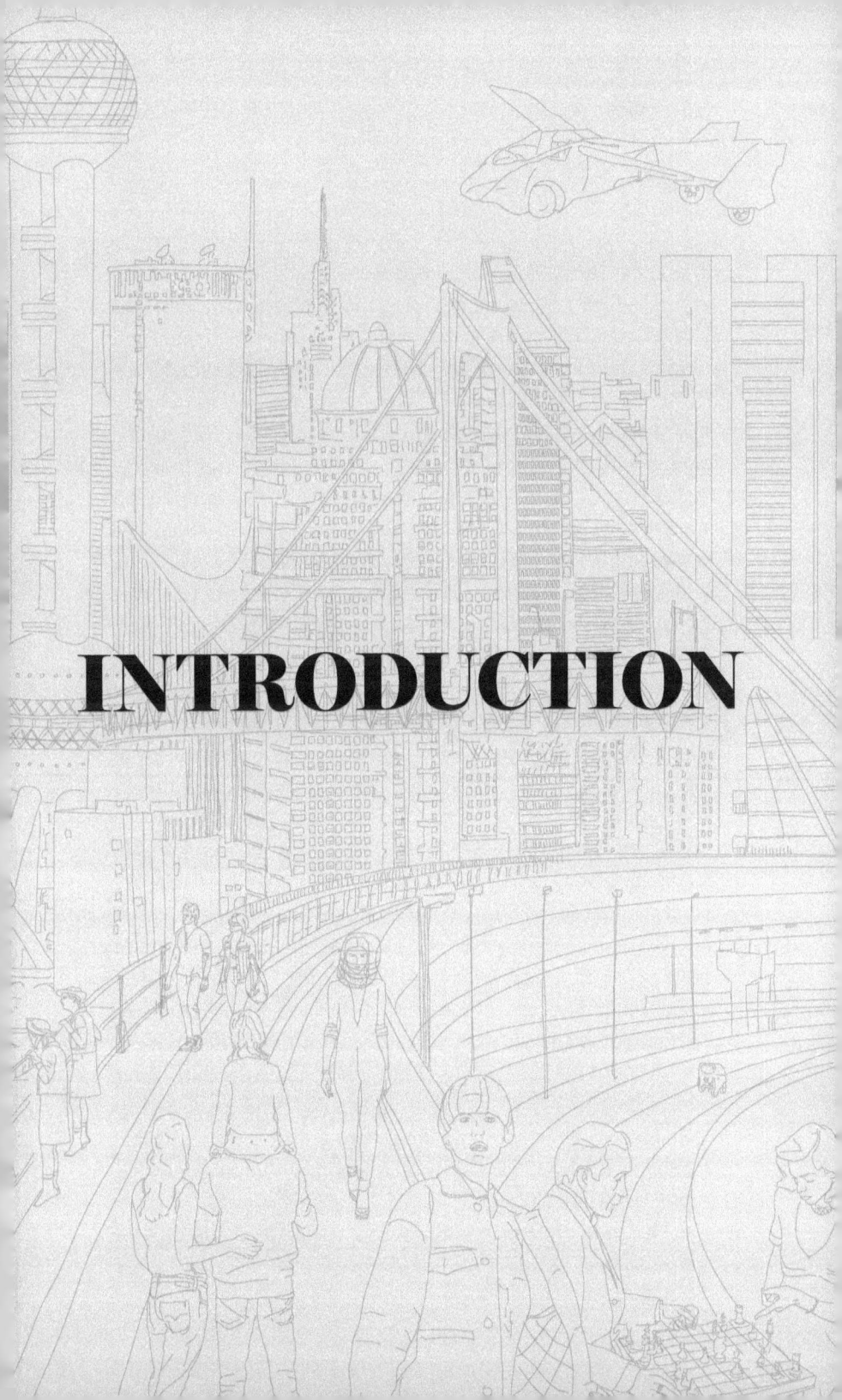

INTRODUCTION

"December 19th, 1989. Romanians were marching on the streets, crying out for freedom and hoping that the revolution they just started would offer them a better life. The gunshots and the sound of tank caterpillars eating away the asphalt were the last barks of a dying system. On Christmas Eve, Communism turned its last page and democracy started writing its first chapter. As many of the people in Romania, I didn't know what that meant, but from my father's tears, I could tell it was something big." This is how I began my graduate school admissions essay in the Spring of 2003. The essay did impress every admissions commission I submitted it to, with the exception of the one I was most anxious to impress – the one at UC Berkeley. I eventually went on to do a masters at Cornell, with the plan to reapply for a Ph.D. at Berkeley the following year. My second try was also a failure, but this time around I was more interested in getting into Cornell's Ph.D. program, as I have grown to love the place. Luckily I managed to make enough of an impression on the professors in my department and got them to keep me for another three years. I have not regretted one day of my time spent there. As the almighty Rolling Stones quipped, sometimes "you don't get what you want, but you just may get what you need."

While my soppy essay was primarily a means to an end (getting me in a grad school program in the US), it ultimately ended up defining my life. Forcing myself to tell an admissions committee what I wanted to do once I grew up, ultimately became the blueprint for my life hence forth. I have thus spent the better part of the past 14 years trying to understand what countries like Romania can do to encourage long-term growth and sustainable economic development. This book is a humble summary of what I have learned so far.

The soppy tale of a kid growing up in the dying days of

INTRODUCTION

Communism and coming of age during a tough and cumbersome transition did a good first impression on the folks at Cornell. My good performance in my first year there did the rest. In many respects my personal story of growth and development follows a similar logic to the growth and development of full-blown economies – it involved lots of work, a good dollop of luck, and unexpected twists and turns. The purpose of this book is to outline (a version of) the story of economic growth and development, with an in-depth look at the lucky breaks, the hard work, and the unexpected twists and turns that have allowed some countries to move ahead, while keeping some behind.

The story of economic growth and development deserves to be told time and time again. It is a story that will likely never get old, and a story that could potentially improve the life of millions. One of the most important takeaways for any student of economics is that economic performance impacts almost every aspect of our lives. By and large, places that are more economically developed tend to have a higher life expectancy, generate more art and culture, provide better education and better opportunities than places that are less developed.

In many respects, economics is just as important today as medicine was in Medieval Times. But, just as healers in Medieval times had a spurious knowledge of what made a sick person better (e.g. blood-letting was considered a cure-all for diseases for quite some time), so do economists today have a spurious knowledge of what makes a sick economy better. The very foundation of economics, up to a few years ago, was built on the fallacious premise that humans are rational beings, and economists have been more pre-occupied with developing fancy mathematical models rather than trying to understand the world around them. Fact is, a lot of the key lessons of economics are common sense and have been known for quite a while. At the same time, the field of economics is advancing very rapidly, and new insights are brought to the fore every year. Unfortunately, a large majority of economists focus on fringe topics rather than big questions.

This book tries to focus on the big topics. It primarily aims to bring together some of the key lessons of economics we have learned so far, and tries to provide some new lessons. As such, the book is as much a compilation of existent major growth and development theories and ideas, and an attempt at an original contribution to this large field. You will be the judge of whether this task was actually achieved or not.

But before we delve into the lessons learned so far, it is important to define some of the economic jargon that will be used in the book. I have tried to keep fancy economic terms to a minimum. Technical jargon is the codex that enables people in a specific field to communicate in an easier and more efficient manner. However, it also poses a significant challenge when the people in the field try to communicate their ideas to a wider audience. Just think how you felt the last time you looked at a complex mathematical formula. I even have problems to communicate economic ideas in Romanian, because many of the English technical terms I've learnt don't have an equivalent in Romanian (or I don't know the equivalent).

Defining Economic Growth and Development

Economic growth and economic development are two similar and intertwined concepts, and they are often taken to mean the same thing. One cannot have one without the other (i.e. development is difficult without economic growth, and growth is not sustainable without economic development), but there are important nuances to these two concepts, and these deserve a more in-depth analysis.

INTRODUCTION

In very simple and simplistic terms, one could say that growth is quantitative, whereas development is qualitative. An analysis of economic growth is most often an analysis of hard numbers and facts. What is a country's GDP performance? Have wages gone up? Is productivity increasing? These are the typical questions one would ask when studying economic growth. And, these are the types of questions economists are most often asking. Since economic growth can be measured more precisely, and since economics has been driven in recent years by econometrics and mathematical models, economists have largely preferred to focus their attention on economic growth, and this is the area where economics has made most progress in the past 70 years or so.

Economic development focuses more on soft issues. Has welfare improved? Are social inequalities widening? Is economic progress sustainable? These are some of the questions posed by students of economic development. And, it is usually people outside the field (e.g. sociologists, urban and regional planners, environmentalists) that usually pose these questions. Such questions do not beget easy answers, nor answers that can be placed in a neat mathematical formula.

Economic growth and economic development have to be studied jointly though. Without sustained growth, one cannot have proper development, and without sustainable development, one cannot have long-term growth. For example, Alexander the Great and Genghis Khan managed to grow huge empires in a short time, but were not able to employ the proper development tools to hold these empires together for the long-term. Similarly, Communist countries managed to bring millions of people out of poverty and offer them a higher standard of living, but they unraveled when they failed to sustain economic growth.

Identifying ways to encourage and sustain economic growth and economic development is the Holly Grail of our era – the most important quest of humanity for years to come. If we manage to figure out how to make economies tick, we will directly or indirectly solve some of the most important issues humanity is facing (hunger, poverty, social injustice). Luckily, for the first time in human history, we have had a large group of middle-income countries make the transition to high-income, and this transition has happened in a data abundant environment that enables the analysis of growth and development from different vantage points.

However, clues to what makes economies tick can come from different fields and from unlikely places, not just from reams of economic data. Such an unlikely place is a masterpiece of the sci-fi literature. In 1951, at the tender age of 31, Isaac Asimov, a young Russian writer, finished the first book of the "Foundation" trilogy, which ended up defining a genre and provided some ideas on how economic growth and development could be analyzed. In essence, the "Foundation" deals with the long-run evolution of societies and civilization at large. The book is a pleasure to read (if you haven't read it yet, it is well worth putting it on your reading list), but the genius of Asimov lies not only in his writing style, but also in the way he chose to look at societies, and implicitly at economies.

Asimov took the long view, or rather the very long view, in the analysis of societies and economies, and tried to posit how civilizations would transform over very long periods of time – 30,000 years in this case. Such a focus on the long-run dynamics of economies, is critical. Unfortunately, the history of economic growth and development is a very short one (up to the Industrial Age, economic growth has been relatively flat), and the recorded history is even shorter. Reliable and detailed data on the World's economies is only available for the past 70 years or so. And, in order to understand long-term trends, one has to take a long-term view. Several of those who have taken a long-term view to study humanity will be discussed in this book – most of them are not economists.

In trying to imagine how a sophisticated human civilization

could evolve over 30,000 years, Asimov came up with a theory that is a blend between Adam Smith and Nassim Taleb. Three major ideas evolve from his writing:

1. ***You cannot fight the tide of evolution.*** Civilizations are molded by the decisions taken by a myriad of people, and when a civilization sets course on a certain path, everybody will follow suit. At a smaller scale, think of how the decision of a few countries to allow women to vote, eventually led to universal suffrage in developed countries; or how the decision of a few countries and states to allow gay marriage, is now gradually spreading to most mature economies.

2. ***Black Swan events trigger the progress or regress of societies.*** The tide of evolution is usually broken by what Nassim Taleb calls "Black Swan events" – unexpected occurrences, which are usually foreseen by only a few people, and which permanently alter societies and the course of history. Humanity has, and will continue to be defined by disruptive events that either send it in a downward spiral (as has happened during the Dark Ages), or on an upward swing (as has happened after the Industrial Revolution).

3. ***It is people who decide whether a Black Swan event triggers progress or regress.*** Black Swan events may be generated by people, or they could be exogenous, but how we respond to such events ultimately decides our fate. An economic downturn can force people to look inward and close up, or to look outward and figure out how to learn from this event and build a better society. The First World War saw much of the countries in the World look inward and close-up, which ultimately gave rise to Hitler

and triggered the Second World War. In turn, the Second World War saw countries look outward, in an attempt to learn from past mistakes, ultimately giving birth to global entities, such as the United Nations, and regional entities like the European Union. It is people, and how they react to life-altering events, that ultimately shape history and economies.

Consequently, the story of economic growth and development is the story of people's growth and development, with all its multi-faceted aspects. An economy will not perform well if its people do not perform well. This is why the title of the book is "On Growth and Development", not "On Economic Growth and Development". The next chapters will discuss in more detail why people are important and under what circumstances people perform well.

IT'S THE PEOPLE, STUPID!

> "The reasonable man adapts himself to the conditions that surround him... The unreasonable man adapts the surrounding conditions to himself... All progress depends on the unreasonable man."
> GEORGE BERNARD SHAW

Economic growth is the product of two things: 1) population growth; and, 2) productivity growth. Not only is the economy the product of these two things, but for much of our history, population growth and productivity growth have went hand in hand – in essence, the more our numbers have grown, the more productive have we become. And, conversely, the more productive we have become the more have our numbers grown.

The historical data collected by Angus Maddison highlights this dynamic nicely (see figure below). Basically, the average annual growth rate of the population (a.k.a. the compound annual growth rate) between 1700 (before the start of the Industrial Revolution) and 2001 was almost the same with the annual productivity growth rate – 0.77% and 0.76% respectively.

Population growth goes hand in hand with productivity growth

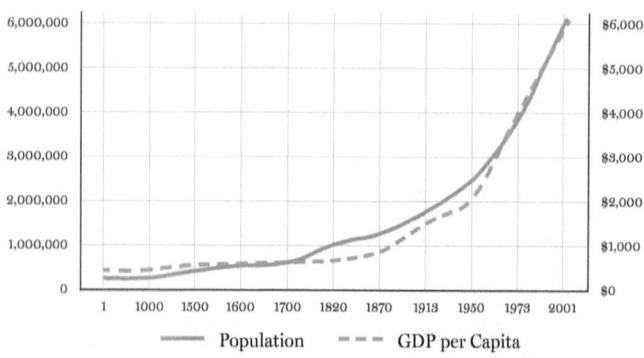

Source: Maddison, Angus. 2003. The World Economy: Historical Statistics. OECD Publishing.
Note: Population is in 1,000 people. GDP/Capita figures are in million 1990 International Geary-Khamis dollars

Knowing what we know about our economy today, this dynamic is a bit puzzling. It makes intuitive sense to assume that the World Economy has grown faster than the growth of the population, given all the things we see around us. What has happened in effect though is an uneven development of the World, with some countries developing much faster than others.

In fact, unevenness is a key defining feature of development, and in many case it is a precondition for development. As we will see later, development requires the concentration of resources (people, knowledge, capital), primarily in cities, and the combination of these resources to generate innovation and higher productivity. And, the more people there are, the more such concentrations (i.e. cities) can take shape, and the more productive the World becomes. However, as the historical data shows, the economy has not yet managed to outperform demography. An economy is only as strong as its markets are, and markets are ultimately represented by people. If population numbers don't grow, it will also be difficult for the economy to sustain growth.

A growing population is critical for an economy, for two important reasons. On the one hand, a larger population means a larger market for all the goods, services, knowledge and ideas that are produced in an economy. On the other hand, a larger population enables more diverse markets and a more diverse offering of goods, services, knowledge and ideas. For example, if you are a bread maker, you will likely do only small scale barter if there are only 10 people you could provide bread for. However, you could start an actual business if you have a market of 10,000 people. Similarly, if you are a tattoo artist, you have a higher likelihood to find clients in a market of 10,000 people than in a market of 10 people.

Population growth, which was enabled by medical advances in medieval times, has been absolutely critical for economic growth and development, and the exponential rate of growth of the Global Economy has gone hand in hand with the explosive population growth. In essence, an economy is the sum of transactions between buyers and sellers. The more people there are, the more (potential) buyers there are, and the larger an economy can grow. And, the better some sellers are at producing something that a lot of buyers want, the better off everybody is. So far, developed countries, which amass only around 16% of the World population, have been most astute at producing what other people in the World wanted.

A large population does not necessarily translate into large and diverse markets. China and India are the most populous countries in the World (together they account for around 36% of the world population), but they have productivity levels below the World average, and they largely cater to outside rather than internal markets. Thus, in 2014, China and India were together responsible for around 10% of World consumption. China actually consumed less than Japan, and India consumed less than Italy. In fact, while developed countries had only around 16% of the World population, they accounted for 68% of global consumption.

This discrepancy can be explained by individual productivity. On the one hand, productivity growth is equivalent to more goods, services, knowledge and ideas being produced by the individual in an economy – the textile mills enabled their textile workers a dramatic rise in individual productivity (they went from producing 1 shirt per day to producing 1,000). On the other hand, more productive individuals tend to have higher earning and afford more of the goods, services, knowledge and ideas offered in the economy. Individual productivity is made possible when a person knows how to do things that few other people in the World know how to do. When you have skills that many other people possess, the competition will be larger, and there will be a larger downward pressure on costs and profit margins. Of course, good skills are not enough – you also need a market interested in what you have to offer.

In essence, an economy cannot sustain its long-term growth if it does not manage to maintain population and productivity growth. Basically, to prosper, an economy needs a growing middle-class – people that both have the right set of skills (i.e. skills that few other people in the World have) and significant buying power.

Without a strong middle-class, no economy can prosper.

The fact that most developed countries now have a shrinking middle-class is a trend that is already having a deep impact on the global economy. It is enough to look at world sales of a staple good that targets the middle-class – new passenger cars. In the EU, the US, and Japan, the sale of new cars has stagnated in the past 10 years – with an average of 25 million cars sold in these large markets every year. On the other hand, the sale of new passenger cars in Asia has more than doubled from around 14 million in 2005 to over 35 million in 2015.[1]

In many respects, the Global Financial Crisis of 2008 is a result of the shrinking of markets (i.e. the middle class) in the developed world. With these traditional markets shrinking, companies have tried to look for "un-tapped" markets. The result we know all too well. The "un-tapped" markets were the lower middle-class and poor people in the US, who were offered easy access to subprime mortgages in an attempt by financial companies to generate growth anyway possible.

Later in the book, I will discuss in more detail the importance of the shrinking middle-class for growth and development, as well as some options for addressing this issue. In the next section I will discuss how a middle-class can be created. Or, in more technical terms, what can be done to encourage individual productivity growth. To a large extent, it is this particular issue that most economists directly or indirectly focus on.

How to Create a Middle-Class

Economic growth theory is a burgeoning field that largely focuses on what is required to trigger productivity growth. It is a field peppered with many relevant insights and several Nobel prizes. Each breakthrough in this field brings to light a step on the path to making people more productive; each step is in turn a chapter in the story of economic growth – a story that is still very much unfolding.

STEP 1: Give People Tools

Roy Harrod and Evsey Domar have, independently of each other, laid the foundation of economic growth theory – Harrod was the first to write on this issue; Domar was better at popularizing his ideas. They both received a Nobel Prize for their contribution to the field of economics.

The idea Harrod and Domar came up with is brilliant in its simplicity and is considered common-sense by most people today. They basically posited that the performance of an economy is directly related to the amount of factors of production (i.e. tools) available in an economy, as well as the amount of money available to purchase or create these factors of production. They have also indicated that in order to encourage economic growth, a higher share of existent savings in an economy should be allocated to the purchase or creation of factors of production.

This idea is of course an outgrowth of the times Harrod and Domar were living in, and their theory merely organized on paper empirical insights that were abundant at that point. By the time they finished their articles, Russia had already registered significant economic growth (it grew faster than Western European countries between the two World Wars) by (unfortunately, forcefully) moving people from the country side to factories, while starving the population so that funds would be made available for the construction of more factories.

This approach to economic growth was subsequently adopted by most communist countries after the Second World War. And it worked! In the first two decades after the War, countries in Eastern Europe registered economic growth rates that were higher than those registered by Western European countries. Paul Samuelson, the father of modern economics, even famously predicted that the GDP of the Soviet Union might outstrip that of the United States sometime between 1990 and 2000[2].

It is easy to understand why this strategy has worked – at least in the short-to-medium term. If you move someone from the country side to a factory that produces, say tractors, not only do you raise that person's productivity (a tractor assembled in a day, may be worth the crop produced previously by that person in an entire year), but you can also raise productivity levels in other sectors. For example, the tractor may be used to replace animal powered tools and increase productivity in certain agricultural sectors.

However, by the late 1970s this strategy has come undone for Communist countries, and by 1990s most communist regimes have been toppled – contrary to what Nobel Prize winner Samuelson had predicted. To a large extent, the Soviet Block lost the Cold War because it did not manage to sustain economic growth rates, and have thus lost the economic race with the West. Basically, blue jeans and pop music proved a stronger force than tanks and missiles.

But why did communist countries have this fate while market economies continued to thrive? The answer to this question was provided by another Nobel Prize Laureate.

Step 2: Give People New Technologies

Bob Sollow, considered by most economists to be the father of economic growth theory, looked at the US economy after the Second World War and tried to understand how it manage to find the resources to sustain growth over the long term. He expected the US economy to hit a plateau as soon as the large majority of the population made the transition from agriculture to industry and services.

Around the time Sollow wrote his seminal work on economic growth, only around 5% of the work force in the US was still engaged in agricultural activities. Given that most of the people that could have made the transition from agriculture activities to higher value-added activities have done so, one would expect the economy to hit a plateau. For example, a person who assembles tractors (regardless of where they do this), may over time get better at their job (e.g. they may be able to assemble two tractors in a day instead of just one), but eventually they will hit a productivity plateau – there's only much you can do with only two hands and good labor regulations. Similar to the tractor guy, Sollow though that at some point, all the workers that have made the transition from agriculture to industry will eventually hit a productivity plateau in their new jobs, which would ultimately lead to the entire economy hitting a plateau.

And this is indeed what happened in Communist countries in the late 1970s. One by one, they hit a growth plateau. However, the US, Germany, France, the UK, and Japan continued to grow. How? The details of the how is what got Bob Sollow a Nobel Prize, while also laying the foundation for the burgeoning field of economic growth theory.

What Sollow noticed in the US was how individual companies made decisions. Thus, when a company hit a productivity plateau, it had two options: 1) go bust and be replaced by more productive companies; 2) innovate and change the way of doing things. Companies in market economies go bankrupt all the time if they don't manage to keep up productivity levels, and they are allowed to go bankrupt. This was virtually unheard of in Communist countries – no matter how bad a company was doing, it kept alive and running at all cost. The central government preferred technical unemployment (i.e. keeping people employed although they did nothing or did little) to bankruptcy.

The companies that manage to endure in market economies

are those that manage to improve their productivity, or those that enjoy some sort of monopoly or oligopoly. For example, many industrial plants have modernized their production facilities by mechanizing work flow processes. This has enabled them to cut costs and raise the productivity of their workforce. Thus, instead of having 1,000 people manning the assembly line, they could have 1 managing the mechanized assembly system. In essence, these companies took advantage of new technologies to improve their performance.

Sollow considered these new technologies to be primarily "exogenous" – i.e. generated by universities and research centers, and then integrated by companies in their productions flows. To a large extent, developing countries modernize their economies through the transfer of technologies from developed countries – either through foreign direct investment, or by modernizing existing production facilities. Almost all developing countries modernize by ways of exogenous technological transfers, of the type described by Sollow.

This is also how Communist countries modernized their economies – they transferred technology from abroad to create new industries. For example, Communist Romania developed its main car manufacturing plant, Dacia, using technology from Renault, and even copying one of Renault's car models. However, while Renault continually modernized its production facilities, Dacia failed to follow suit. In 1989, when Communism drew its last breath in Romania, Dacia produced a marginally improved version of the old Renault car model, whereas Renault had an entire array of substantially improved car models. Few people outside Romania were willing to buy a Dacia, whereas Renault had a global clientele.

And, this is what happened in every sector in Communist countries – the economy simply did not modernize quick enough to keep pace with the technological advances in the West. For one, poorly performing industrial plants were not allowed to perish – they were simply subsidized, to keep the workforce employed. Even for the relatively well performing state companies, there were few incentives to promote technological change. Given that companies were not allowed to go bankrupt (so there were few downsides to a poor performance), and given that a better performance of the company did not translate into higher pay, most managers did little to modernize their companies. Even if they wanted to modernize, they were to a significant degree dependent on technological breakthroughs produced in the West. Consequently, in the late 1980s, most Communist countries had an obsolete and poorly performing industrial base. Many of the state-run companies were in fact a significant burden on national budgets. For example, in the Valea Jiului mining area in Romania, for every $6 spent on extracting coal, only $1 of actual revenues was generated. Multiply this over several companies and sectors, and you understand why these economies went bust.

Nonetheless, it is not only Communist countries that have shifted massive amounts of people from agriculture to industry and services. Latin American countries have largely undergone a similar process. Latin America now has some of the most urbanized countries in the World. Moreover, many of the Latin American that have made the transition had functioning market economies in which private companies competed with each other. In these systems, poorly performing companies were allowed to go bankrupt, and the ones that survived continuously modernized.

Despite this, few of the Latin American countries have managed to sustain economic growth and catch up with their Western counterparts. This of course begets the obvious question: why? Part of the answer to this question is provided by one of the biggest contributors to economic growth theory and a very likely candidate for the Nobel Prize – Paul Romer.

Step 3: Enable People to Innovate

Having access to a continuous stream of technological innovations is not enough. Companies in Latin America had easy access to Western technologies, but they produced few of their own. As such, Latin American countries have always been one step behind, and their economies remained to a large degree dependent on the markets of developed countries. They would have to wait for a technology to be developed somewhere else, and then wait for the patent protection to expire before they could use that technology in their own production processes. In essence, they were always one or a few steps behind the developed countries.

And this is where Paul Romer's theory comes in. What Romer concluded in his landmark article "Endogenous Technological Change" is that long-term growth requires home-grown innovation. For a country or company, to stay on the cutting edge of technology, and thus create the premises for its sustained growth, it has to generate its own innovations. For it to generate its own innovations, a country needs to have a large enough pool of human capital – i.e. people who innovate.

Where Sollow saw technological change as a primarily exogenous process, Romer considered that endogenous technological change is a sine-qua-non condition for long-run growth. In simple terms, if companies or countries are not able to generate their own innovations (i.e. be the ones who push the technological frontier), they will be always dependent on the innovations generated somewhere else. And those who innovate, are those who dictate the course the economy will take. Everybody else will follow in the footsteps of the innovators. Thus, although countries like China grow at a very rapid pace now, unless the Chines economy will shift from copying and improving Western technologies to generating disruptive technologies of their own, they will always be one step behind innovators like the US.

Romer's contribution to economic growth theory has spawned a whole literature and public policy work focused on ways to attract, retain and nurture human capital, as a way of creating the conditions for endogenous technological change. It is thus considered that if you only have enough well educated people in one place, innovations will be generated seamlessly. That, of course, is not necessarily the case.

In order to fit human capital in a neat mathematical formula (the type that economists insist, for some reason, on using), Romer took human capital to mean people with higher education. As anyone who has been in a university knows, simply graduating from higher education does not turn one into an innovating genius. In fact, many claim that breakthrough innovations usually require a break with the norm and the reshuffling of entire fields. This in essence means thinking things differently than they are presently thought. Universities, by definition, teach that which has already been invented – most teach students to follow, *not* break the mold. It is thus not surprising that some of the people that have revolutionized the World in recent years (Bill Gates, Steve Jobs, Mark Zuckerberg, Sergej Brin) are university drop-outs. They had tacit knowledge of the particular field they worked in, and relied less on acquired knowledge – they embody well the principle according to which the best way to predict the future is to invent it. The former Communist countries had excellent technical schools, but their graduates have primarily generated innovations in the military field.

And thus we come to our third major question in the series: if a highly educated population is not enough to generate productivity increasing innovations, what else is required? The answer to this question comes not from a growth economist, but from a development economist.

Step 4: Enable People Easy Access to Opportunities

Bill Easterly has worked for the World Bank for 18 years. He is unlikely to win a Nobel Prize, but the time he spent working in different countries around the World has made him much more attuned to the nuances and fickleness of development. He has tried to put neat theories and beautifully drafted public policies in practice, only to see them come undone because the real world does not conform to neat theories and mathematical formulas.

In "The Tyranny of Experts" Easterly indicates that one of the key preconditions for development is a functioning democracy that enables as many people as possible, preferably all, easy access to opportunities (jobs, education, healthcare, culture, entertainment, etc.). A similar argument, although not as clearly argued, was made by Amartya Sen – who did get a Nobel Prize for his work.

The statement that economic growth is ultimately about enabling as many people as possible access to opportunities may seem a platitude upon first reading, but it is not if we look at the real state of affairs in the World. Although developed countries and international institutions preach democratic values, they are often hard-pressed to take a clear stance in their dealings with autocratic governments. Moreover, even in developed countries there have been slippages in recent years, while more and more power gets concentrated in a few private hands, at the expense of the middle-class and the Average Joe.

However, Easterly did not take his argument further than overall implications for development. Access to opportunities can also refer to how different age groups access opportunities. For example, young people in Europe and Japan enjoy less upward mobility than young people in the US. Given that disruptive innovations are disproportionately generated by young people, this reality has series implications for some countries. In the US, young people do not only have better upward mobility than in other countries, but they also have more levers for generating and maturing innovations, and easier access to financing.

Obviously, before a country can generate disruptive innovations it has to undergo a number of development steps. In essence, an economy has to reach a certain level of maturity before it can innovate on a wide scale. Opportunities are overwhelmingly located in developed countries. So, what do you do if you are a bright kid from the developing world trying to make a dent in the Universe?

The next section tries to answer exactly this question. Three major factors that have a significant impact on how people access opportunities will be discussed. These three factors are:

1) **Geography - which has been hard for people to alter;**
2) **Institutions - which represent the purposeful action of a few people;**
3) **Markets - which represent the uncoordinated actions of a lot of people.**

GEOGRAPHY has for the most part been ignored by economists. Paul Krugman revived the field of economic geography with a brilliant little book ("Development, Geography, and Economic Theory"), which has marked an inflection point in my studies in the field. Krugman followed this work with a joint effort with Masahisa Fujita and Tony Venables ("The Spatial Economy"), where concepts that have been in use for over 50 years, were formalized in a set of mathematical models. The key tenant of this work is that geography is important – more important than you might think. Think only of the consequences for humanity if Earth was only a few kilometers closer or further from the sun. Similarly, whether you are born in the Gobi Desert of Western Europe, or whether you are born in a rural area or an urban area, has a big influence on how you will do in life. Geography can also influence people's lives in funny ways. Following the Korean War, the US and the USSR decided to split Korea on the 38th parallel because the line stood out on an officer's map. People's destinies took completely different turns because of a line on a map.

INSTITUTIONS and the talk about institutions is all the rage today. Ever since Daren Acemoglu and James Robinson's "Why Nations Fail", it has become trendy again to talk about how to build and sustain stronger institutions. But the talk about institutions is not new. Douglas North, himself a Nobel Prize winner, has an impressive body of work dealing with institutions, but the topic was also tackled by classical greats, such as John Maynard Keynes and Adam Smith. North defines institutions as the "humanly devised constraints that structure political, economic and social interactions" and considers these to consist both of "informal constraints (sanctions, taboos, customs, traditions, and codes of conduct)" and "formal rules (constitutions, laws, property rights)"[3]. One could say that institutions are tools that have been created by communities to protect both community interests (e.g. rule of law) and individual rights (e.g. the right to the pursuit of happiness). Throughout history, institutions have continuously evolved and have been refined to allow a balance between the community's interest and those of the individual.

MARKETS are the pooled effects of our past decisions shaping our present and future decisions. Markets are the "invisible hand" that enables economies to function and flourish. Markets are as omnipresent in the economic literature as love is in poetry books and cheesy pop songs. Just as with love though, we don't really know how to properly define them. We simply know they are there and they play a very important role.

These three factors have a different relevance, depending on where you happen to find yourself in terms of development – i.e. in a developed; developing; or undeveloped country. As I will discuss later in the book, geography (particularly proximity to markets) is of particular importance to undeveloped countries. In developing countries, the development of strong institutions plays a critical role in strengthening their economies. While, in developed countries it is markets, and in particular continued market integration, that are critical for sustained long-run growth.

Before we go into a detailed account of the importance of geography, institutions, and markets to growth and development, it is important to re-state, forcefully, that an economy is the sum of its people. An economy will be only as strong as its people are, and it is people and the actions they take or fail to take, which make or break an economy. And, the one thing we know about people is that they are unpredictable. New advances in behavioral economics show that people are much less rational than we thought, and this has deep implications for classical economics.

Another important point to remember is that the only thing we know about the future, is that it will be different from the present. Much of the economic literature develops models that are supposed to tell us ow the world of tomorrow could/should look. However, in a brilliant treatise[4] Karl Popper makes a wonderful case for why the future is murkier than we think. He indicates that any prediction of the future would also presuppose a knowledge of the technologies that will define that future age. However, a knowledge of future technologies now, would mean that these could be developed presently – there would be no need to wait until some point in the future to invent them. The truth is that we don't know what technologies will define our future. No economist in the early 1990s foresaw the importance of the internet in the economy of the New Millennium. We do know however that there are a number of factors that enable or disable the growth and development of countries/regions/communities. These key factors will be the subject of the next section.

ENABLERS and DISABLERS of GROWTH and DEVELOPMENT

> *The idea that any concrete sequence or succession of events [...] can be described or explained by any one law, or by any one definite set of laws, is simply mistaken. There are neither laws of succession, nor laws of evolution.*
>
> KARL POPPER

People are the foundation of growth and development. A country is only as strong as its people are. However, having a pool of highly productive people is easier said than done. Geography, Institutions, and Markets play a key role in enabling people to reach higher productivity level, and this section will discuss how these factors can enable or disable growth and development.

I will start the story of the enablers/disablers of growth and development with the prequel – i.e. what happened before there was growth and development (roughly before the Industrial Revolution). This is important as it sets the stage for understanding why some countries had a leg up in the growth and development race, when growth and development actually started.

Next, I will look at three types of countries: **undeveloped countries** (where not much is happening in terms of growth and development); **developing countries** (countries where a growth and development process is underway); and, **developed countries** (countries that set the tone and pace of growth and development for the rest of the World). This categorization, albeit quite basic, is needed for a better understanding of growth and development dynamics.

The point of departure for this categorization are the four income categorizations used by the World Bank: Low Income; Lower Middle-Income; Upper Middle-Income; High Income. The World Bank, while the most pre-eminent development institution in the World, has refrained from using actual development indicators to categorize countries, and has instead focused on the actual income generated by individual countries.

The World Bank Categorization of Countries by Income Level, in 2015

Level of Development in 2015
- High Income
- Upper Middle-Income
- Lower Middle-Income
- Low Income

Data Source: World Bank

The income indicator used for this purpose is the Gross National Income (GNI) per Capita, using the Atlas Method.[5] A number of thresholds are then used to determine in what category a particular country falls. For example, in 2015, countries with a GNI of less than $1,025 were considered to be Low Income; those with a GNI falling between $1,026-$4,035 were Lower Middle-Income; those in the $4,036-$12,475 were Upper Middle-Income; while those above $12,475 were High Income. This categorization of countries has been in use since 1987.

In 2015, there were 79 High Income Countries, 56 Upper Middle-Income Countries, 52 Lower Middle-Income Countries, and 30 Low Income Countries. These statistics paint a rather rosy picture, with an overwhelming number of countries in the High Income category. However, among the 79 High Income countries, 33 had less than 1 million people (these are primarily small countries, such as San Marino, Andorra, or the British Virgin Islands), and 61 had less than 10 million people.

There were overall, 1.2 billion people living in High Income countries, 2.6 billion living in Upper Middle-Income countries; 2.9 billion living in Lower Middle-Income countries, and 0.6 billion living in Low Income countries. Thus, a majority of the World population lives in relatively well developed countries.

Nonetheless, the number of people that have made the transition to higher income is impressive, and nothing short of spectacular. In 1987, 56% of the World Population lived in Low Income countries. By 2015, this share dropped to 8%. Most significant in this dynamic is China's transition from Low Income to Upper Middle-Income and India's transition from Low Income to Lower Middle-Income. Consequently, the success of growth and development measures World-wide, is to a significant degree dependent on what the governments of China and India will do in the future. These two countries amass together 36% of the World's population, and getting the fundamentals right there, is critical for the future of humanity as a whole.

Breakdown of Countries by Income Level

	Countries (number)		Population (in billion)	
	1987	2015	1987	2015
High Income	53	79	0.8	1.2
Upper Middle-Income	37	56	0.6	2.6
Lower Middle-Income	76	52	0.8	2.9
Low Income	51	30	2.8	0.6

Data Source: World Bank

The share of people living in High Income countries has remained relatively stable over the entire period between 1987 and 2015, at around 16%. This indicates that overcoming the middle-income trap is a tough cookie to crack. Of the 26 countries that have managed to make the transition to High Income between 1987 and 2015, only 6 had in 2015 a population of over 10 million. Most of the larger countries that have managed to overcome the middle-income trap are EU Member Countries, and we will come back to the EU model of development later in the book.

What is important to note here is that the fact that a country is High Income, does not mean it is also developed. Similarly, the fact that a country is Upper Middle-Income, does not necessarily mean it is developing. There are countries that may be High Income, but don't have the fundamentals for sustained growth and development. The lack of a functioning democratic system, people's difficult access to opportunities, or deep social inequalities, may all affect a country's future growth prospects.

However, these factors are easier to address if there is a clear will. What is less easy to address is countries' dependence on resource exploitation. While countries like the US built an economy making smart use of all the resources found within their territory, and while there are countries that have been reasonably good as managing their natural resources (e.g. Norway or Australia), an over-reliance on resource exploitation directly translates into the under-development of a country's main resource – its people.

Later in the book I will discuss in more detail several of the perils of resource dependence. These perils more or less boil down to forgone opportunities to grow individual productivity. The reasoning is quite simple. Obtaining resources and selling them, does not require a lot of people (the mining sector rarely is a large employer in resource dependent countries), and neither does it require any specialized skills (with a few exceptions). This means that countries that are overly reliant on resource exploitation, do not have a population that can compete globally in the real market (i.e. productivity is low in high value-added sectors). For example, if resource exports (e.g. gold, iron ore, coal briquettes) are not taken into consideration, Australia exports less than Romania does – although it has a GNI per Capita that is 6 times larger, and 3 million extra people. Similarly, if resource exports are taken out, Norway exports less than half of what Denmark exports, although they are about the same population, and Norway has a GNI per Capita that is almost double that of Denmark.

Resource dependence is from my point of view one of the major disablers of growth and development, and economies that are dependent on resource exploitation lack a key fundamental required for sustained growth and development.

To determine the countries that are resource dependent I have used a simple measure. Using the amazing trade database put together by the MIT Observatory of Economic Complexity, resource dependent countries are considered to be those where at least 51% of goods exports are resource exports. The measure is of course imperfect, but it provides a quick and dirty way of assessing a country's potential to sustain growth and development. When your economy depends on global resource prices and the continued availability of resources, it is likely that it will sooner or later behave erratically.

The map below provides an overview of the resource dependent countries. The interesting thing is that quite a high number of countries are dependent on resource exports – ranging from developed ones like Norway and Australia, to developing ones like Chile and Colombia, to large ones like Russia and Iran, to poor ones like Nigeria or the Democratic Republic of Congo. Overall, around 1.2 billion people live in such resource dependent countries.

The World's Resource Dependent Countries

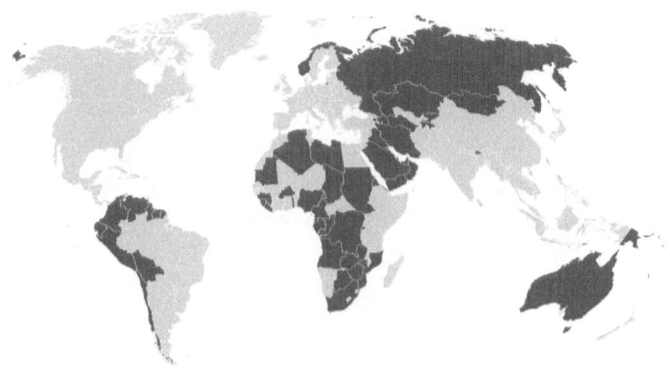

Data Source: MIT Observatory of Economic Complexity

This book primarily targets the countries that are non-resource dependent (i.e. the ones in the map below). It is these countries that stand the best chances to sustain growth and development in the long term.

Categorization of Countries by State of Development

Level of Development in 2015
- Developed
- Developing
- Undeveloped
- Resource Dependent Countries

Economies that are resource dependent behave erratically, because they do not depend on the skills and expertise of their population, but on the availability of resources and on global resource prices. The figure below, shows the behavior over a long period of time of two types of High Income countries: non-resource dependent (in this case, France, Germany, the UK, and the US), and resource dependent (in this case, Kuwait, Qatar, Saudi Arabia, and the United Arab Emirates). What this figure makes immediately obvious, is that non-resource dependent countries behave in a predictable upward manner – i.e. they get better and better at what they do. On the other hand, resource dependent countries seem to be subject to the vagaries of global resource prices.

The Economic Performance of Two Types of High Income Countries: Non-Resources Dependent and Resource Dependent

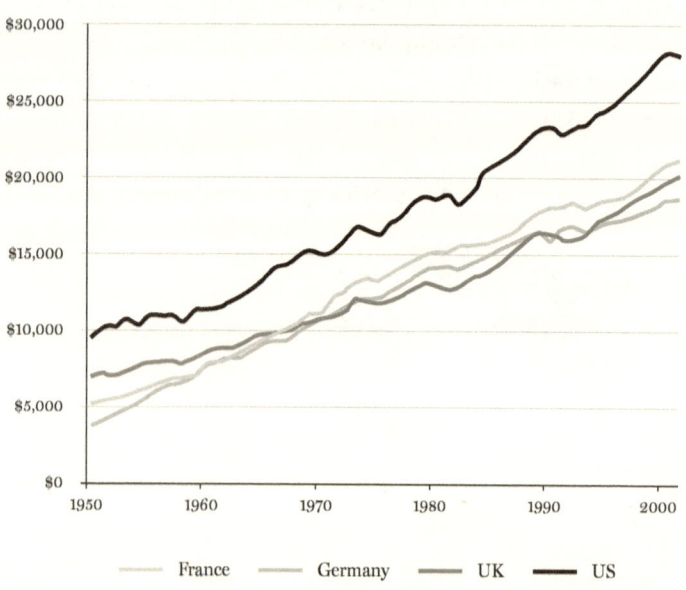

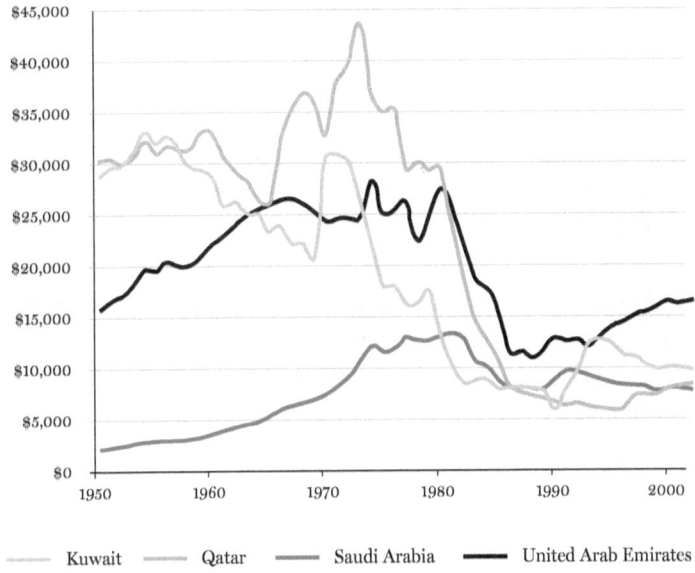

Data Source: Maddison, Angus. 2003. *The World Economy: Historical Statistics.* OECD Publishing.
Note: GDP/Capita figures are in million 1990 International Geary-Khamis dollars

It is interesting to note that in 1950, Kuwait and Qatar generated a GDP per Capita that was three times higher than that of the US, four times higher than that of the UK, six times higher than that of France, and around eight times higher than that of Germany. However, by the start of the new millennium, the GDP per Capita values of Kuwait and Qatar were half those of France, Germany, or the UK.

Generally, the countries that display the most erratic growth are largely those dependent on the export of resources. Many of them have a high GDP per Capita, but their economic performance is subject to global resources prices and global demand. These economies often turn into rentier economies, where the State plays an overwhelming role in ensuring the welfare of the people, and where individual enterprise and resourcefulness end up playing a small role. Given that the majority of the population is not engaged in high-value added sectors, competitive on international markets, one could say that these countries are missing the skill-base required for long-term growth. Without their natural resources, these countries would have to basically build from scratch internationally competitive sectors (and such an undertaking is neither quick, nor easy).

The key focus of this book is to determine how to enable countries to embark on a growth and development path that resembles that of France, Germany, the UK, and the US. But, first, we will first see how the UK, France, Germany, and the US got to becomes the World's economic growth engines.

BEFORE DEVELOPMENT: Why Some of Us Live in Developed Countries and Others in Undeveloped Ones

> "From the earliest times of which we have record back, say, two thousand years before Christ down to the beginning of the eighteenth century, there was no very great change in the standard of life of the average man living in the civilized centres of the earth. Ups and downs certainly. Visitations of plague, famine, and war. Golden intervals. But no progressive, violent change. Some periods perhaps 50 per cent better than others – at the utmost 100 per cent better - in the four thousand years which ended (say) in AD 1700 (...) At some epoch before the dawn of history – perhaps even in one of the comfortable intervals before the last ice age – there must have been an era of progress and invention comparable to that in which we live today. But through the greater part of recorded history there was nothing of the kind."
>
> JOHN MAYNARD KEYNES

I started the book with a soppy description of my experience of the Romanian 1989 Revolution. That was the moment I started thinking about development, and particularly about the developed West, and how Romania could achieve the same level of development. Before 1989, the only interaction people in Romania had with the West was through bootlegged Chuck Norris and Bruce Lee movies. We were otherwise fed an incessant stream of propaganda news, largely resumed to how bad and foul the West was.

After 1989, we got easy access to all of the Western media channels, and some of us managed to also travel abroad. I remember my first experience with the West. Together with a bunch of students from my middle-school I spent a few weeks with a family in Austria, through a program sponsored by the Austrian Government. The Austrians wanted to expose us to the West and enable us some pleasurable moments after a bloody revolution.

My first impression of the West was that of color. The Austrian towns were pretty and clean (in sharp contrast to the grey that dominated most towns in Romania), the people looked happy and relaxed, and the grass looked greener than at home. Yes, the grass was a bright and exuberant green – I remember that vividly. To this day, I use the greenness and upkeep of the grass in a city, as a proxy for that city's development.

The days I spent in Austria had the effect the Austrian Government probably intended when they sponsored our sojourn – it gave us a taste and a longing for a better life. Soon thereafter, my head started to fill with questions – questions without easy answers. Why was the grass greener in Austria than in Romania? Why did they have such beautiful and clean buildings, and we did not? Why did their roads have no potholes? Why were all of the people so relaxed and sure of themselves? Austria was only a throw-stick away, but we seemed to be ages apart.

The only explanation I found for the development gap that separated Austria from Romania, was that Austrians were some sort of **übermenschen** – people that were smarter, more disciplined, and harder working than we were. I was not alone in this assessment. For a long time, I looked to Westerners with deference and a deep and troubling complex of inferiority. Chances are that if you're coming from a developing country, you also had to deal with something similar.

The purpose of this section is to dispel such a feeling, by showing how it happened that developed countries became developed. I don't believe we are all born equal, but neither do I think that people from a particular culture or country have innate abilities that other people don't have. Each culture has smart and stupid people, hardworking folks and lazy fellows, talented individuals and space cadets.

Why are then some countries and cultures more developed than others? I will argue here that it is because over the millennia some people have benefited from better geographic conditions, which helped them create functional and sustainable institutions, which in turn have encouraged the appearance of functional markets.

Up until the Industrial Revolution, around the mid-18th century, one cannot really speak of growth and development, and economics did not yet play a leading role in shaping the destiny of regions and communities. The figure below shows this quite nicely. It draws on historical estimates developed by Angus Maddison, the World's leading expert on historical statistics. Somewhere around 1750, economics started to become important, and some regions in the World have started to develop much faster than the rest – first Western Europe, then the US, and following the Second World War, Japan. Eastern Europe and Latin America have been hovering around the World average, while China, India, and Africa have registered productivity rates below the World average. Thus, we come back to the unevenness theme, which is a corner-stone of the development process. More specifically, and we will see this dynamic within countries too, development usually means that some regions will over-perform, some will hover around the mean, while some will under-perform.

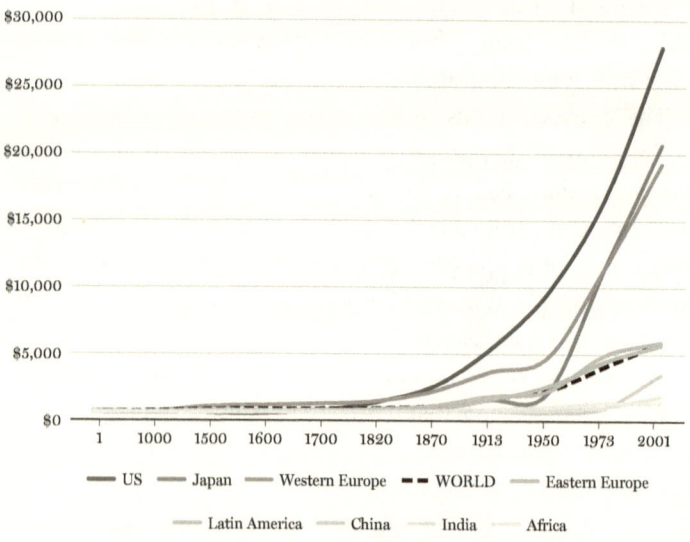

Historic GDP per Capita in Selected World Regions

Source: Maddison, Angus. 2003. The World Economy: Historical Statistics. OECD Publishing.
Note: GDP/Capita figures are in million 1990 International Geary-Khamis dollars

ENABLERS AND DISABLERS: BEFORE DEVELOPMENT

When the data is analyzed for the 1 AD – 1700 AD period, that is "before development", it becomes evident that for the longest time in human history, economic output was relatively uniform across the globe - somewhere in between $400 and $600. In the Medieval Ages however, Western Europe took off. From Western Europe, development has leap-frogged to the US, Canada, and Australia, and an opening of the US market to Japanese products, has enabled Japan's, and subsequently Taiwan's and South Korea's, phenomenal economic performance.

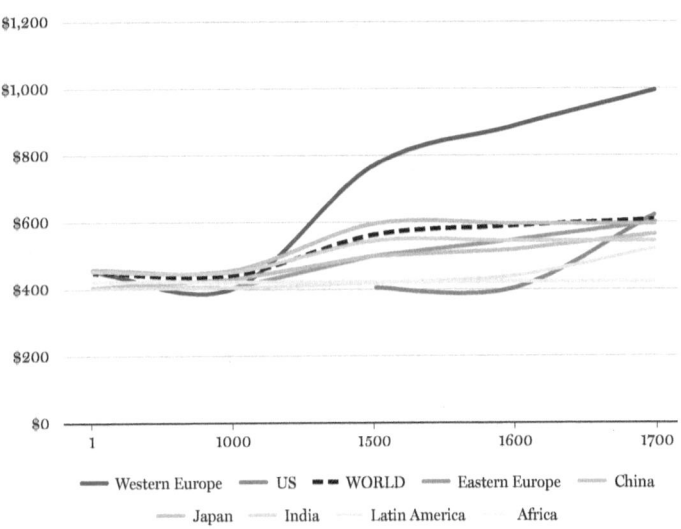

Historic GDP per Capita in Selected World Regions

Source: Maddison, Angus. 2003. *The World Economy: Historical Statistics*. OECD Publishing.
Note: GDP/Capita figures are in million 1990 International Geary-Khamis dollars

It is Western Europe that has written the first chapter in the growth and development of the World Economy, and the following sections will discuss in more detail what enabled Western Europe this initial advantage, and why some countries and regions have underperformed.

GEOGRAPHY 101:
Who Won the Geography Lottery

History followed different courses for different peoples because of differences among people's environments, not because of biological differences among people themselves.
JARED DIAMOND

People are incredible beings. Over the years, we have managed to colonize every piece of land on the planet. Driven by hunger, war, love, adventure, or pure curiosity, people have established settlements in freezing areas of the North Pole, the scorching deserts in the Gobi or Sahara, or remote and foreboding places like the Easter Islands. There is almost no environment that we haven't manage to bend to our needs.

However, in the grand scheme of things, and over the long term, some people have made more fortunate choices than others. We will discuss how these choices have impacted the development of different groups of people over the long term.

Water, Food and Climate

Water, food, and climate are essential for our existence. A person can survive 5 days without water and up to 8 weeks without food. Similarly, extreme weather conditions such as extreme cold, extreme heat, or extreme humidity, can make people more prone to disease and premature death.

Consequently, the places where early communities of people have flourished are those that offered abundant sources of fresh water, plenty of food, and milder climates. Even today, when technology allows easy access to water and food virtually everywhere, there are large tracts of land that remain poorly inhabited or uninhabited. The map below is quite evocative in this sense.

The Area in Black has the Same Population as the Areas in Gray

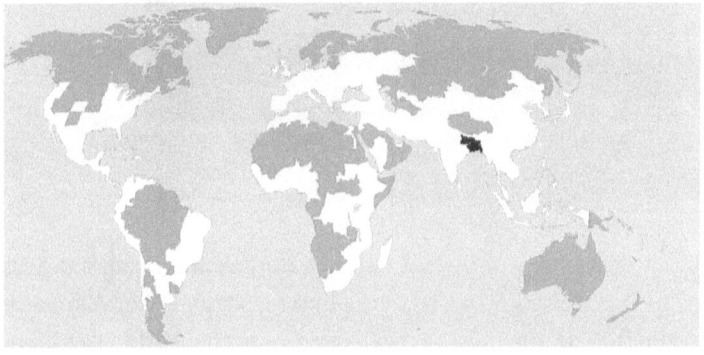

Source: Roser, Max. 2016. Retrieved on-line from: *http://waitbutwhy.com/2015/07/theres-an-equal-number-of-people-in-the-blue-and-red-areas.html*

Cold places, like much of Siberia and Canada, scorching deserts, like the Gobi, Sahara, or much of Australia, rain forests, like the Amazon or West Africa, were and continue to be inhospitable for human settlement. These areas have made the growth of large communities difficult and in many cases they continue to be an important barrier to growth and development. The most populous places today, China and India, used to dominate the World economy up to the time of the Industrial Revolution. Before individual productivity became a factor in determining economic strength, the largest economies were inevitably those with the largest population.

China and India used to dominate the World Economy

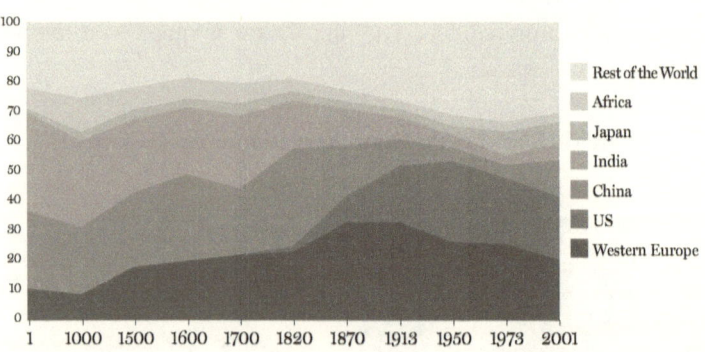

Data Source: Maddison, Angus. 2003. The World Economy: Historical Statistics. OECD Publishing.

Conversely, many of the poor areas today are areas with a dearth of fresh water, poor quality agricultural land, and harsh climates. Around 1 AD, the most populated places in the World were those that provided the best living conditions for people. These include Wester Europe, the Fertile Crescent Area in the Middle East, China, and India. We will discuss in what follows some of the key characteristics that enabled a population "boom" in these areas.

Domesticated Plants and Animals

For much of our history, we were hunter-gatherers. We lived of what the earth, forests, and water bodies offered to us. This dependence on the bounties of nature was a great equalizer. To a large extent, people were organized in small groups, close to sources of fresh water, continuously foraging for food, and constantly fighting for survival. Life was pretty harsh.

Then came a game changer – the first domesticated plants and animals. At a certain point in our history, a brilliant person (a Bill Gates of those times) realized that it is inefficient to move from place to place in search of carbohydrates and protein. It made more sense to grow those around oneself. Independent of each other, groups of hunter-gatherers around the globe have become sedentary, with one piece of land they started to call home, rather than roaming from place to place. This did not happen everywhere though, and success rates differed from place to place.

In one of the most brilliant books ever written, "Guns, Germs, and Steel" (if you don't own a copy, get one now), Jared Diamond shows that geography played a key role in the early stages of human development, and it offered some communities a competitive edge. The first civilizations were those that managed to domesticate plants that provide a reliable source of carbohydrates.

The first larger communities formed in the Fertile Crescent (an area that largely covers present day Israel, Lebanon, northern Syria, and eastern Iraq), along the course of the rivers Tigris and Euphrates. The advantage of the Fertile Crescent was its distinct climate, characterized by mild, wet winters, and long, hot dry summers. Such a climate favored annual plants that invested much of their energy into producing large seeds able to resist the long, hot summers, and able to sprout quickly when the rainy season came. Annual plants, as their name suggests, only last a year (they die off after producing their seeds), and as such don't waste their energy on producing inedible wood or fibrous stems, as is the case with the body of trees and bushes.

The Fertile Crescent is unique in that it included an unusually high number of plants that were suitable for domestication, and it was particularly suitable for the domestication of plants that pack a lot of calories. The staple foods in most cultures are such high-calorie plants that offer sustenance with as little effort as possible. For example, people in the Fertile Crescent could simply collect wild growing wheat, and spend only one calorie for every 50 calories in grain collected. This is what has enabled the first large settlements, like Uruk, Byblos, Jericho, Damascus, Aleppo, or Jerusalem to take shape.

Other crops have enabled communities elsewhere to take shape (e.g. rice in China, corn and beans in Mesoamerica, potato in the Andes, manioc in Amazonia, sunflower in the Eastern United States, yams in West Africa, or the banana in New Guines), but none pack as much calories and are as easy to grow as grains. From their place of origin, domesticated plants eventually made their way to other areas. Most notably, agriculture practices and the seeds of domesticated plants have spread from the Fertile Crescent to the Eurasian landmass – all the way from present day France to Siberia. Other areas of the globe, particularly those that faced major geographical barriers and inhospitable climates, were less fortunate. Thus, agriculture was introduced relatively late to places such as Australia, Sub-Saharan Africa, or the rain forests of South America.

The Rough Area Covered by the Fertile Crescent

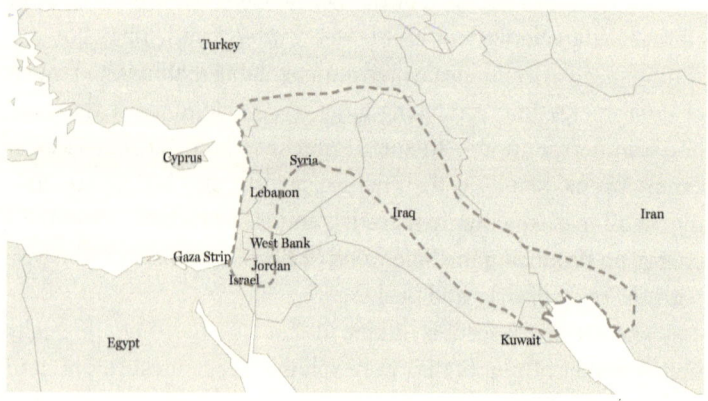

However, the biggest game changer in the making of human civilizations were not domesticated plants, but domesticated animals – which are in essence a portable source of protein. The communities that had reliable sources of protein, were also those that had more time to invest in other activities than savaging for food. They had time to think, plan, and invent. And gradually, they spread their dominance over other communities.

Jared Diamond notes that domesticated animals share a common trait – they are a wonder of human civilization. With all the advances of technology, out of over 5,400 mammal species, only 14 large mammals have been domesticated so far (i.e. sheep, goats, cows, pigs, horses, camels, dromedaries, the llamas, donkeys, reindeer, water buffaloes, yaks, Bali cattle, and the mithans). Four of these mammal species (sheep, goats, cows, pigs) have been domesticated early in the Fertile Crescent, while 13 were originally domesticated in Eurasia, and were subsequently spread across the Eurasian landmass. Eurasia, and in particularly Europe, offered the perfect conditions that allowed both the cultivation of many domesticated plants and the raising of a large number of domesticated animals. No major mammal was domesticated in Sub-Saharan Africa, in North America, or Australia. The only mammal that was domesticated in South America is the llama, and even it is a finicky beast and hardly an easy companion of human communities.

Reliable sources of carbohydrates and protein were critical in enabling European communities to grow and thrive. Europeans formed stable settlements, cities, and then ventured out to conquer the rest of the World. Virtually every corner of the World was at one point or another under European rule or influence. And it is pigs, cows, and chickens that Europeans have to thank for this early advantage. I bet you won't look at bacon the same way now!

East-West vs. North-South Orientation

Jared Diamond came with another brilliant insight in "Guns, Germs, and Steel". He looked at the World map and observed a fact that has eluded many people before him. Namely, the Eurasian landmass enjoys an advantage that other landmasses and continents don't enjoy – it has an East-West orientation, as opposed to a North-South orientation. This has conferred the early settlers of Eurasia an advantage. Plants and animals that were domesticated in one area spread easily from East to West, and from West to East, because the climates were relatively similar and the domesticated plants and animals could adapt quickly to the new conditions.

By around 7,000 BC, the crops domesticated in the Fertile Crescent have spread to the Anatolian Peninsula (present-day Turkey), by 6,000 BC to present-day Greece and Italy, by 5,000 BC to much of Central, Eastern, and Western Europe, and by 2,500 BC all the way to Scandinavia. Similarly, rice domesticated in present-day China around 7,500 BC spread all over Asia. Horses, first domesticated in the Eurasian steppes of present-day Kazakhstan, spread all over Eurasia; as did pigs, which were first domesticated in the Fertile Crescent.

Eurasia has a Clear Geographical Advantage over the Americas and Africa

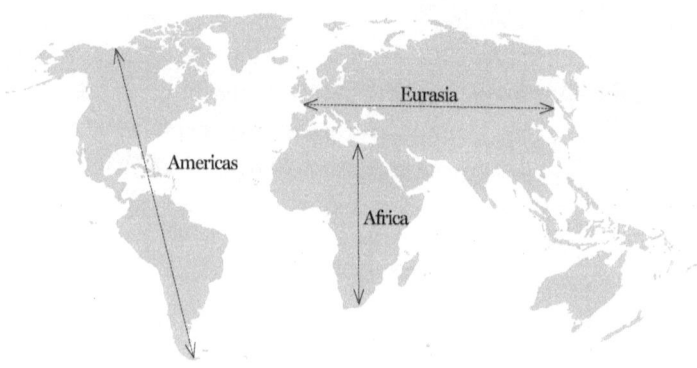

From the areas where they have been first domesticated, the staple plants and animals that make much of our diet today, spread to the rest of the World. In the process, crops have been mutated and improved to enable larger harvests and better resistance to varying climates. Still, as big as the World is, there are only a few places where high agricultural yields can be generated without significant human intervention. The places with the best agricultural land are also the places that now have the highest population density. Moreover, these are the places that have given birth to the first human civilizations.

So, the next time someone tells you that geography is not important for development, tell them to search for a map with the most fertile and productive soil and a map with the highest population densities – there is a direct correlation between the two. And, of course, a high population density is a very important element for development, as we will see later in the book. It is enough to mention that even around 1 AD, the regions in the World with the highest economic output where those with the highest population density – the Fertile Crescent, Europe, China, and India. Geography played a critical role in giving these regions a competitive edge.

INSTITUTIONS 101: The First to Organize were the First to Dominate

When two tribes of primeval man, living in the same country, came into competition, if (other circumstances being equal) the one tribe included a great number of courageous, sympathetic and faithful members, who were always ready to warn each other danger, to aid and defend each other, this tribe would succeed better and conquer the other.

CHARLES DARWIN

Any ruler whose power grew significantly would eventually find that it was in his interest to subvert his neighbor's realm.

HENRY KISSINGER

If you're reading this book, there is a high likelihood that you've also read Acemoglu and Robinson's "Why Nations Fail". It is a brilliant tome that makes a case for institutions that safeguard democracy and people's access to opportunities, as opposed to extractive institutions that concentrate and aim to conserve power in the hands of a few. They make an excellent case, and provide plenty of evidence to support it. The one drawback of the book is the fool-hearted attempt to discount the importance of geography in development. Sometimes, smart people put reason aside for the sake of a good argument.

Institutions provide one key ingredient for growth and development – stability. When you know you don't have to worry for your safety and well-being, when you are living in an environment with clear rules and regulations, you are more likely to pursue higher goals than just a simple existence.

However, the type of stability institutions provide, matters a great deal. As Acemoglu and Robinson show, extractive institutions that concentrate power in a few hands, eventually wither and die. Even when the leaders in charge of those institutions have the best interests of their people in mind, they are often overwhelmed by the sheer amount of decisions and choices they have to take for a large number of people.

The most resilient institutions are those that offer as many people as possible, preferably all, access to power and opportunities. The future of a country is brighter when all of its citizens have a stake in it, then when only a handful do. The same is relevant for companies. But, while companies go bankrupt on a regular basis, and are replaced by other companies, countries do not – the weak ones are simply dominated by the strong ones. This relative permanence of states, or rather the notion of the state, means that strong institutions, institutions that continuously undergo change and reform, are critical. You can replace a company with another, but you can't exactly replace a country with another.

In what follows, I will discuss three of the key institutions that have played a role in giving some countries a competitive edge.

War and the Birth of the World's Second Oldest Profession

Institutions are a relatively early creation of humankind, but they are the bedrock required for the growth and development of human civilization. These institutions have not evolved however out of people's drive to be better organized, but out of need.

In "War in Human Civilization", Azar Gat shows that war has been a constant in human affairs, from the early beginnings of humanity. Contrary to popular belief that people have lived in connection with nature and with each other, evidence shows that people have lived in a continuous state of warfare, and they have depleted resources around them (e.g. entire species of animals have vanished at the hands of humans), when they had the proper conditions to grow and prosper.

War was waged then, as it is waged today, for more serious or more trivial reasons, such as: access to resources (e.g. water, arable soil, grazing grounds, gold and other precious metals); strategic considerations (e.g. growing the territory and population to discourage potential enemies from attacking); personal ambitions of group leaders; love interests; envy; or simple inertia (i.e. war was waged for the sake of war).

Gat even points to evidence that our species, the Homo Sapiens, has wiped out cousin species like the Neanderthals. And from the Neanderthals onwards, there are probably very few people that have not witnessed human conflict at least once in their lifetime. However, as Steven Pinker argues in "The Better Angels of Our Nature", war is not only a force for evil, but also a force for good, and it has prompted several leaps forward in human evolution.

War and conflict of course significantly reduce a person's life expectancy, and everybody will do whatever is within their power to increase their chance of survival. Across time, people have hedged their bets with life by adhering to larger and stronger groups. There is safety in numbers, and, by and large, bigger groups of people have dominated over smaller groups of people.

Of course, a big group of people, as civil society movements learn anew today, require proper organization and clear rules and regulations – i.e. institutions. Without such institutions, big groups of people end up being ruled by anarchy, and are quickly dismantled or conquered by other, better organized groups of people. In "Grooming, Gossip, and the Evolution of Language", one of the most cited books in popular literature today, Robin Dunbar shows that it is almost impossible to have functional groups of more than 150 people, without having a clear set of rules and regulations governing their interactions. It is simply too difficult for human beings to maintain and entertain meaningful relationships with groups larger than 150 – the human brain simply does not have the computing power to process all the information.

At a minimum, a large group of people requires a leadership structure (someone who calls the shots) and some basic norms for how a leadership position can be obtained. From that position, leaders have went on to build bureaucracies, and usually the more efficient a bureaucracy was, the more efficient was that group of people at ensuring its survival and development. By and large, the more efficient a bureaucracy is, especially in relation to other bureaucracies, the more willing are people to pay to be part of that bureaucracy.

And thus, as a way of mitigating the effects of war, people have formed institutions and have given birth to the second oldest profession in the world – the public official. And just as prostitution (the oldest profession in the world) has never gone out of fashion, neither will public administration. This is something to consider when you're looking for a stable job. Public administration has, and continues to offer some of the most stable career prospects for a job seeker (groups of people will always needs to be administered), but it is only slightly more attractive than the oldest profession.

The good thing about institutions is that when they are good, they can permanently alter humankind for the better. Some of institutions created by the Ancient Greeks and the Romans (democracy, the legal system, city planning, water systems and plumbing, military strategy) have shaped humanity henceforth, and continue to be in use today. Moreover, as institutions become stronger, people's lives become safer. Steven Pinker shows that while war and conflict continues to be a reality of day-to-day life, the share of people dying in armed conflict has gone down the more sophisticated the institutions have become. In essence, the most efficient institutions have made life safer for the communities they were created by, without requiring a lot of individual sacrifice to safeguard the safety of the group.

And, of course, some of the most efficient institutions were created in Europe. These institutions have enabled European Countries not only to conquer and populate much of the unknown world (e.g. the Americas and Australia), but to also subjugate other communities (e.g. much of Africa was part of one or the other European empire) and impose trade deals with much larger countries (e.g. China). Because of their stronger institutions, Western European countries virtually controlled much of the rest of the World before the dawn of the Industrial Revolution.

Language, Religion, and Culture

The first groups people have formed were organized around blood lines. We are genetically programmed to like our own kin (Richard Dawkins posited that this is part of our DNA programming aimed to increase the chances of its survival), and are naturally more protective, caring, and inclusive of our family members. Thus, for a significant part of our history, people have primarily banded in family clans.

Over time however, as group size has started to play an increasingly important role in the fight for survival, people have started to look for other common denominators to bond them together, beyond blood-lines. Language has proven a powerful instrument in this respect. When you are not connected to somebody by blood, language provides an excellent binding glue. Understanding someone else is an essential pre-condition to getting along with that person, and speaking the same language dramatically increases the chances that this will happen. The large majority of modern states are made up of people that by-and-large speak the same language. In the same vein, speaking a different language, which often pushes people to define a different identity for themselves, is one of the chief reasons minority groups seek independence from a larger group.

Religion is another major institution that has played a significant role in how communities have formed and evolved. In "Darwin's Cathedral", David Sloan Wilson indicates that "religions exist primarily for people to achieve together what they cannot achieve on their own". If language was devised by people to explain everything that was known about the World, religion was devised to explain that which was not known. We are not the humblest species, and we assig everything that we don't understand, especially those things that can kill us, to a higher power. Storms, thunders, droughts, blizzards, were for a long time seen, and in many parts of the Globe they are still seen not as fits of nature, but as the wrath of the gods. And, the way people have chosen to interpret this wrath of the gods, has significantly impacted their destiny.

Religion is one of the most powerful and influential institutions with respect to the growth and development of economies, and more often than not it has acted as a barrier to development, not as a catalyst. Moreover, religion was, and continues to be one of the main catalysts for war and conflict, with the World's major religions (Christianity, Islam, Hinduism, Buddhism) having all but wiped out smaller religions. Today roughly 33% of the people on Earth are Christians; around 20% are Muslims; 13.5% are Hindus; 6% are Buddhists; 14% are agnostic or atheists; with the rest of the population adhering to other religions (e.g. Judaism, Shintoism, Confucianism).

As with all other institutions, religion poses a significant barrier to growth and development when it becomes primarily an extractive institution. The religious institutions that have not gone through a reform process have either withered away, they have become weaker over time, and where they have become stronger they also acted as a barrier to sustainable growth and development.

The reform of religious institutions has in several cases provided an impetus for the development of individual initiative and the development of the economy as a whole. Max Weber makes a wonderful case in "The Protestant Ethic and the Spirit of Capitalism" about the importance of Protestantism in building the foundations for the modern market economy. In essence, Protestantism represents a reform of the Catholic Church. A number of clerics from Central Europe have gotten fed-up with the greed, corruption, and incompetence of the leaders of the Catholic Church, and have decided to split up and form their own brand of Christianity. This new brand did not centralize Church power in a few hands, did not tax people as much, and enabled an easier access to Heaven. While the Catholic Church was literally selling seats in Heaven, with the best seats going to those willing to pay the most, the Protestant Church indicated that the way people carry themselves in this life will have a strong bearing on how they do in the after-life. Thus, the prime sports in Heaven were reserved for the most industrious and hard-working individuals. Protestants lived with the knowledge that they could pull themselves up by their own boot-straps – all the way to Heaven.

The countries that have undergone this religious reform, have also undertaken reforms in other areas – most notably they have reformed their economic systems. The Industrial Revolution was started in the UK and has spread the fastest in other Protestant countries or areas, such as the Netherlands or Germany. (Full disclosure here: I am neither a protestant, nor a very religious person.)

Religion and language have come together and have given birth to another important institution – culture. Culture was, and continues to be a fuzzy concept. It is nonetheless a powerful force in the growth and development game, and it has become increasingly important, with religion taking more of a back-seat. We speak today of the culture of the developed West and the culture of the less developed South, of market economies and autocracies, of liberalism and socialism or communism. A country's prevalent culture and societal norms play a significant role in that country's economic performance, and is a subject that has been discussed and analyzed at length – see, for example, "Riding the Waves of Culture" by Alfons Trompenaars.

Writing, Literacy, and Books

Writing is probably humanity's grandest invention. Like most inventions that have changed the World, it has humble beginnings. It has evolved more out of need than purposeful tinkering. The first writings were generated by traders and merchants who needed better accounting tools. When you are a successful trader, you are likely to have a lot of customers, and if you want to continue to be a successful trader you need to be able to keep track of who owes you what. From small etchings on clay (the cuneiform alphabet), writing has continuously evolved into the diversity we know today.

Over time, writing has become the natural counterpart to language and the receptacle of our thoughts and musings. It is the one institution that has transformed all other institutions – it is the tool that has given eternal life to ideas. Up to the invention of writing, rules, norms, religion and culture were passed on orally from generation to generation – *memes* that were kept alive only if they happened to be memorable enough. Given that the human brain cannot hold and process too much information, the stuff that was passed on orally was limited to the essentials. Writing has changed all that. All of the sudden, people had a tool that enabled them to pass all their ideas on to the next generations. Many of these ideas were nothing more than a waste of good paper and ink, but others have changed humanity profoundly.

The basic concepts of democracy have survived from Ancient Greece to today. The way we organize our legal and political systems continues to be influenced by ideas and institutions generated by the Ancient Romans. The Bible, the World's undisputed bestselling book, has dramatically altered and shaped the World we know today.

Those that have not managed to put their ideas on paper, have largely seen those ideas go to the garbage bin of history. And we don't know how many good ideas lie in this landfill. Failing to put ideas on paper can also lead to the dismantling of great achievements. Alexander the Great and Genghis Khan have been great leaders and history's greatest conquerors. They were however not as astute at building a bureaucracy as they were at conquering other people. Consequently, their empires have fallen apart soon after they died.

An alphabet however is not enough to ensuring growth and development. You also need people who can decipher it. For a long time, literacy was however a privilege of the wealthy and powerful.

And those that could read controlled the information, and by controlling information they managed to keep their grip on power.

Information was of course codified in books, and following the Dark Ages, books were primarily written, read, and maintained by monks. Stephen Greenblatt talks in "The Swerve" about the world of books in medieval times. He indicates that books were not only rare and extremely expensive, but their elaboration and dissemination was tightly controlled by the institutions of the Church. People had no access, even if they had the means, to those books that were considered a heresy by the Church.

The great equalizer came when Guttenberg invented the printing press. It is after the invention of writing probably the most important invention of humanity. If writing allowed the codification of knowledge and ideas, books enabled their wide-spread dissemination. They have democratized access to information, and they have enabled key institutions to survive the test of time. The first countries to benefit from the printing press, and from cheap books, were of course those in Western Europe. Cheap books allowed Western Europeans to codify good ideas and pass them to the next generations, which spared those next generations the pain and energy of coming up with those ideas anew – they could spend their time improving those ideas.

The spread of literacy has been one of the great equalizers when it comes to growth and development. According to OECD data[6], only around 12% of the World population was literate. By 1900, this share only went up to 21%, and by 1950 it rose to 36%. Since 1950, literacy had gone up by heaps and bounds, and by 2014, 85% of the World population was literate.

MARKETS 101:
From Primordial Times to Adam Smith

Complete chaos is ironically a kind of perfection.
LEONARD MLODINOV

The first step to thinking clearly is to question what we think we know about the past.
PETER THIEL

For a large share of economists, markets are the only thing that matter for growth and development. And indeed, markets are important, but not the only driver of growth and development, and often not the most important one. Markets have existed ever since the first hominids have learned to walk, but they have started to play a serious role only with the dawn of the Industrial Revolution. As discussed earlier, before the Industrial Revolution, the size of an economy was largely a factor of the size of the population. Following the Industrial Revolution, individual productivity has started to play a more significant role, and so did markets.

The time of the Industrial Revolution is also the time Adam Smith discovered markets (which he described using the metaphor of the "invisible hand") and codified his theory in "The Wealth of Nations". Now markets play an overwhelming importance for growth and development, particularly in countries that have managed to master their geography and build strong institutions.

In what follows I will discuss some of the most important early markets. As said, markets played less of an important role before the Industrial Revolution, and they are often dysfunctional and weak in countries with poor geography and weak institutions.

PROPERTY or How Your Self-Interest is in Everyone's Best Interest

The concept of property is innate to most of us. It is something we learn from an early age, the same way we learn to speak. However, the concept is not as self-evident as we might think. Following the fall of Communism in 1989, I saw all sorts of people in Romania talk on TV about the need for private property, as a foundation for a true market economy. I owned a bunch of stuff at the time, but the notion of private property was new to me. The Communist regime did not allow people to own land or properties; and, if you did, the State made sure to let you know that these could be taken from you at any time. Like the Romanians, there were millions of people around the globe that had only a spurious idea about the notion of private property.

Most interesting is the fact that to this day there still are groups of people around the World for which the notion of property is foreign – largely they are hunter-gatherer communities that live from what nature offers, and the little they have is jointly owned by the community. There are also people who think property is innately bad, a theft, and a sad display of mindless consumerism. They may be true, but just as true is the fact that without property, they would not have had a venue to complain about it, but would have most likely been now chased by a saber tooth tiger.

Property is at the foundation of a market economy, and one of the tools that has allowed humanity to evolve. Adam Smith explains why. Basically, our desire to own things is what helps turn the wheels of growth and development. If people were completely disinterested in owning things, the World today would be inhabited by pack of hunter-gatherers. Without a desire or interest to own things, there is no need to trade, and without trade, no economy can develop – because everybody is self-sufficient.

Hernando de Soto, in a lecture given upon receiving a prize for his land-mark book "The Mystery of Capital", gives a wonderful account of the importance of property. He talks about trust (which I will touch upon later in the book) as a key building block for a functioning market economy, and he sees trust as being intimately related to property. He gives a vivid account of him going to a hotel in the West that he has visited many times before. Upon getting to the reception, he tells the gentleman there that he has visited the hotel many times before, and his data should be in the system. The gentleman finds him indeed in the system, but requests a credit card none-the-less, as this credit card provides an assurance that Hernando can actually pay for his stay. A piece of plastic, which is an indication of what you own, thus helped build trust between two strangers. It is not that people in that particular Western country are more trusting, but that they have the mechanisms that encourage trust, and property (and the proof of property) is one of those key mechanisms. Without trust, there is less trade, and without trade, one cannot speak of economic development. Thus, when someone calls you a consumerist, don't take it to heart – your self-interest is in their best interest too.

TRADE or How to Turn the Wheels of Growth and Development

If our desire to own things gives birth to the wheels of growth and development, trade is what helps turn those wheels around. Trade is what turns productivity into profitability. In "The Rational Optimist", Matt Ridley shows how trade has played a crucial role in shaping human civilization. Let's take the example of an early farmer, for example. If the farmer just produces enough to feed himself and his family that is the end of the story of trade. Subsistence farming was not and will never be conducive to growth and development. If, however, the former produces a surplus and is interested to exchange that surplus for something he desires (e.g. a plow to help him tend his field), he will engage in trade. This in turn allows the emergence of specialization and helps drive productivity growth. By focusing only on manufacturing plows, the plow-maker gets better and better at his craft, and he can produce more and better plows than he can subsequently trade for other things he desires (e.g. a vacation in the Alps). Similarly, countries can specialize in producing a certain set of things, and engage in trade to obtain the other things they need. For example, most large countries have air carriers, but airplanes are primarily produced by two companies, Boeing and Airbus. Romania used to produce planes, but nobody wanted to buy them, so that sector eventually went bust.

Another fringe benefit of trade is that it forces people to be nice to each other. If my ability to put bread on the table hinges on me being nice to the bread-maker, I will make sure to keep her on my good side. Similarly, countries that have strong relationships with each other and deeply intertwined economies, will think twice before starting a conflict with each other.

Trade figures have gone up continuously, in tandem with population growth. The more people there are in the World, the more trade there is, as there are more needs to fill. Thus, we come back to the importance of population growth to economic growth and development. An economy is intimately connected to trade, and trade is intimately linked to population numbers.

MONEY or How to Grease the Wheels of Growth and Development

Money is instrumental for economic growth and development. It is an essential tool that makes trade between people easier, and its invention actually enabled the rapid growth of global trade. The earlier example of the farmer and the plow-maker is evocative in this sense. The farmer has provided the plow maker with grain in exchange for the plow. He is interested in continuing his trade with the plow maker, but does not need an extra plow. In turn, the plow maker is interested to get the grains from the farmer, but is conscious that a plow won't do. This is the point where another genius of humankind thought of using an intermediary good (e.g. a rare metal) for completing the trade. Thus, instead of giving the farmer another plow, the plow maker would pay with such an intermediary good, which the farmer could subsequently use to buy some of the things he needed (e.g. a knife from the smith).

In "The Ascent of Money", Nial Ferguson provides an excellent exposition of the history of money, and explains why money is the crucial element that helps grease the wheels of growth and development. He shows how the development of Italian Merchant cities in the Renaissance period (as a side-note, the Renaissance would not have been possible without the economic boom of the times) was intimately linked with the availability of money and credit. It is these Italian Merchant cities that have laid the foundation for the modern banking system (bank comes from the Italian "banca", which are the benches of Florence on which credit agreements were often completed), and they have given birth to credit and bond instruments. Credit instruments arose out of the need of Italian merchants to finance large trade expeditions, while bonds emerged out of the need of cities to finance wars with other cities. Both private and public actors in Florence realized that expanding a business or financing large public needs requires large amounts of cash now, which could be paid back over several years. The emerging lenders and banks have thus developed more and more sophisticated tools to determine the capacity of borrowers to pay back loans. By the end of the 14th century, there were a dozen major bankers in Florence (the Medici being actually one of the smaller banking enterprises) who generated significant interest from the money they lent to private merchants and various foreign kings. The wealth thus generated financed the artistic and cultural boom in the region, making possible everything from Leonardo da Vinci's discoveries and art, to Brunelleschi's dome.

Money is often demonized (called the eye of the devil), but it would be very hard to imagine our modern economy, any economy for that matter, function without it. For it to serve its purpose however, money should be used judiciously. In essence, money is really worth the paper it is printed on. Its exchange value is given by the goods, services, and knowledge existent in the economy, and by the value markets give to these goods, services, and knowledge. If there is an over-supply, value usually goes down.

For money to actually work, we need to trust that the value printed on the money is the actual value. This trust is often shattered by greedy speculators or incompetent politicians, who either play on the market with a particular currency or print too much of it. Of course, the value of money can also fluctuate in response to a global event. For example, a drop in oil prices can debase the value of currencies in oil dependent countries.

In many respects, money are the embodiment of an economy, so the trust we put in a particular currency is equivalent to the trust we put in the respective economy. Without widespread trust, and economy cannot function.

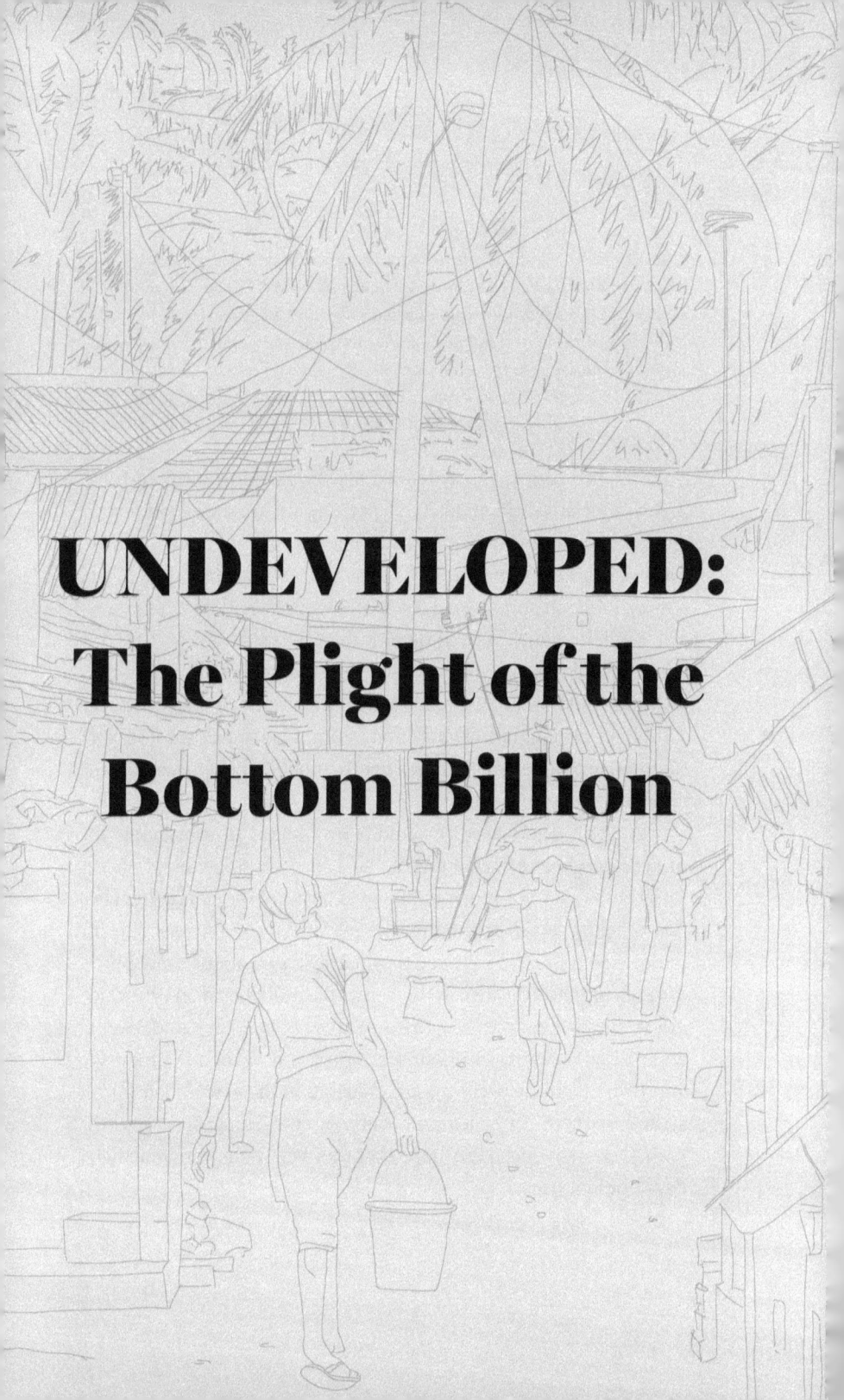

UNDEVELOPED: The Plight of the Bottom Billion

> *Suppose a country starts its independence with the three economic characteristics that globally make a country prone to civil war: low income, slow growth, and dependence upon primary commodity exports. It is playing Russian roulette. That is not just an idle metaphor: the risk that a country in the bottom billion falls into civil war in any five-year period is nearly one in six, the same risk facing a player of Russian roulette.*
> PAUL COLLIER

Undeveloped countries are defined here as Low Income countries (following the World Bank GNI per Capita Atlas methodology) that are non-resource dependent. The number of Low Income countries has decreased from 51 in 1987 to 30 in 2015. The most remarkable transformation is of course China's, and its population of 1.3 billion, which moved quickly from Low Income in 1987 to Upper Middle-Income in 2010. Just as remarkable is the transition of India, Indonesia, Pakistan, Bangladesh, and Vietnam, with a combined population of 2 billion, from Low Income to Lower Middle-Income. There is consequently much to be optimistic and hopeful about.

In 2015, there were around 440 million people living in **undeveloped countries**. One of the key characteristics of these countries is that not much happens in terms of development. The figure below, which highlights the performance of a selection of undeveloped countries (selected primarily based on the availability of data), is quite evocative in this sense. Basically, between 1962 and 2000, their economies remained relatively flat – they underwent almost half a century without any significant economic progress, and with an erratic performance. Starting in the new millennium, several of these countries gave signs of embarking on a growth path – a trend which gives hope that they will soon overcome their development trap.

GNI per Capita (Atlas Method), in Selected Undeveloped Countries

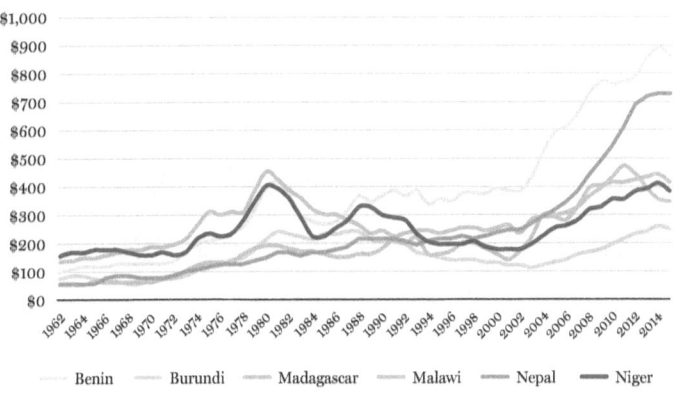

Data Source: World Bank

The purpose of this section is to identify the triggers that can enable undeveloped countries to set out on a sustainable development path. I will draw on a lot on work that has already been completed on this issue, and Paul Collier, a former World Bank staffer, is probably one of the best resources on this issue. In "The Bottom Billion", he goes on to explain why certain countries and regions are perpetually stuck in a rut. The book deserves to be read cover to cover. Here, I only touch on some of the ideas Collier and others have developed.

One of the key characteristics of undeveloped countries, as I discussed above, is slow growth and/or erratic growth. The countries that register slow or no growth are the type of countries that require an outside jolt (i.e. external assistance from developed countries) to set out on a development path. They simply don't have the resources (capital and qualified labor force) to kick-start their economies, although in the long term it is ultimately up to the people living there to set the foundation for growth and development.

In what follows, I will discuss how geography, institutions, and markets influence the growth and development of undeveloped countries, and what some of the key challenges undeveloped countries face are.

GEOGRAPHY 102: Being Stuck between a Rock and a Hard Place

Geography is not destiny in development, but to say geography plays no role in how a country develops, is like saying that growth can happen without capital. Geography is in fact a strong predictor of a country's development, especially for undeveloped countries. Some of the ways in which geography affects undeveloped countries will be discussed below.

Distance from Markets

To set a country on a development path, it is important to produce something that others are willing to buy. For undeveloped countries, it is critical to have access to more mature markets. Without exports to these mature markets, undeveloped countries have to rely on relatively poor and stable internal markets – i.e. they have to rely on markets with a small growth potential. There is virtually no country that has set on a development path, without a concomitant growth in exports. The figure below shows nicely that economic growth in Developing Countries has gone hand in hand with export growth. Basically, without access to more developed markets, developing countries could not have sustained the growth they registered in the past years.

The Link between Economic Growth and Exports in Developing Countries

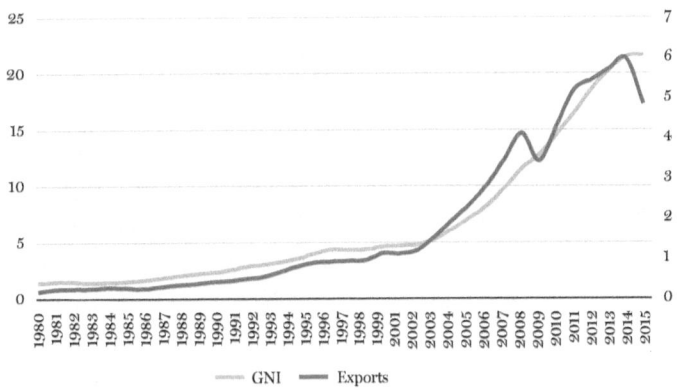

Data Source: World Bank
Note: Exports and GNI are in Trillion Current US$

Boosting external trade is paramount to setting undeveloped countries on a growth path. But, to have trade, one has to have something that others are willing to acquire. The problem is that undeveloped countries have little of everything. And, the little they have is usually uncompetitive on outside markets.

Ricardo Hausmann, Cesar Hidalgo, and a group of researchers from Harvard University and MIT maintain an excellent database on exports – the MIT Observatory of Economic Complexity. The database shows how much countries export, what they export, and where they export. What the database shows is that undeveloped countries primarily export resources (e.g. oil, diamonds, wood) or agricultural products (e.g. bananas, nuts, cocoa). This affects their economic performance in several ways.

Undeveloped countries rarely export staple agricultural products that developing and developed countries are good at producing. Farms in undeveloped countries tend to be uncompetitive (they are usually more labor intensive than capital intensive), and even when they are competitive, the cost required to ship those products to outside markets are too big to surmount.

Geographic distance is a barrier, and, as Paul Collier has shown, landlocked countries face another hurdle – they have to overcome not only barriers posed by distance and bad infrastructure in their own country, but also barriers posed by customs taxes, regulations, and bad infrastructure in their neighboring countries. Undeveloped and landlocked countries, are literally stuck between a rock and a hard place.

Thus, the agricultural products that undeveloped countries do export, are usually the products that are hard to grow in developed countries (e.g. bananas, mangos, coffee, cashew nuts, cocoa, coconuts). Moreover, agricultural products take up a very small share in global trade. For example, in 2014, vegetable product exports (e.g. wheat, corn, rice, soybeans) represented only 2.5% of global exports.

On the other hand, the countries that have natural resources, often think these resources are a way to develop their economies. More often than not, they learn that resources are rather a curse than a boon – particularly for the least developed countries. The next section will discuss why.

The Resource Curse

Resource-rich nations aren't innovative for a simple reason: they don't have to be.
ERIC WEINER

One of the most common misperceptions people have about the world of economics is that every plus is a positive. Thus, if a country discovers it is rich in one or more resources (e.g. oil, gas, coal, gold, diamonds) than it is automatically better off. Resources however are almost never good for an economy, and this for several reasons.

The Dutch Disease is the most well known and most discussed resource curse. The term was coined in an *Economist* article, which analyzed a weird phenomenon the Dutch economy underwent in the 1950s. Around 1959, the Dutch discovered significant gas resources within their territory. Like almost all of us would do, they took this to be a great gift from God. Being industrious and highly industrialized, they didn't wait too long to start exploiting these gas reserves. And of course, the money started pouring in. Up to this point, all was good and dandy. However, as more and more money was earned from the sale of the gas, other sectors of the Dutch economy, most notably the strong industrial base, started to suffer. At first, the Dutch did not know what hit them. Upon closer inspection though, they realized that it was actually the gas extraction that was at fault – in a rather subtle way. In essence, all the extra revenue the Dutch economy earned from selling the gas, drove the value of the Dutch currency (the Guilder) upward. For example, the Dutch would sell their gas to the Germans, who would pay a certain amount of Deutsch Marks for the gas. These Deutsch Marks would then be converted by the Dutch into Guilder, which would enable them to spend those extra funds on the local market. This additional demand for Guilder, above what the real economy would demand, drove the value of the Guilder up. However, an appreciated Guilder had a negative impact on exports – particularly the exports produced by the industrial sector. And of course, the more gas was exported, the less did the Dutch export what the real economy produced. The Dutch Government realized pretty quickly that continuing this practice risked running their real economy into the ground, so they gradually reduced the export of natural resources to a more sustainable level. Virtually every developed country now has a stockpile of resources which they conserve for strategic reasons and to avoid a Dutch Disease effect.

Undeveloped countries however, don't have the luxury of being strategic with their resources. Since they don't have an industrial base to begin with, the export of resources is the only way they can ensure the relative welfare of their population. Even in countries that have an industrial base, but allow themselves to remain reliant on resource exploitation, the industrial base is gradually eroded. Russia is a prime example in this respect. While other countries in Eastern Europe have embarked on a tough transition to market economies, Russia has kept much of its old and obsolete industrial base on life support, by subsidizing it from revenues generated from oil and gas exports. Thus, if in 1995 oil and gas represented 34% of Russian exports, by 2014 this share rose to 67%.

The experience of oil rich Middle Eastern countries indicates why undeveloped resource rich countries don't necessarily have a bright future. In addition to the Dutch Disease, a second risk resources bring with are rentier economy risks. More specifically, the revenues generated from resource exports allow governments to subsidize the salaries of many of the people in the economy, which reduces people's incentive to be more productive or excel in their particular field. And indeed, most countries that over-rely on resource exports have failed to develop a diversified economic base.

But by far the most damaging effect of resource dependence is the erosion and lack of development of people's productivity potential – a country's most valuable asset. Resource extraction companies often scoop up the most qualified people in the country, as they often offer the best salaries. The rest of the people are left working either in low salary jobs or in sectors that are uncompetitive at the international level.

In sum, if you are the leader of an undeveloped country and you happen to discover important resources within your administrative boundaries, pretend they are not there. Focus instead on the true resource in your country – its people, and how to enable as many of the people, preferably all, access to opportunities (not access to easy money). This is, of course, easier said than done, but it is the only solution to set your economy on a sustainable growth and development path.

Bad Neighbors

Proximity to a developed country has its benefits. Central and Eastern European countries have profited fully from being close to Western Europe. Mexico and Canada are better off for being close to the US. South Korea and Taiwan took advantage of their proximity to Japan.

The reverse is unfortunately also true, being close to countries with weak economies can be contagious. For one, trade economics shows that developed countries primarily trade with their immediate neighbors. If your neighbors however have weak and/or unstable markets, you have to rely on more distant markets, which ultimately make your exports more costly and less competitive.

Bad neighbors also create a climate of instability. Undeveloped countries are by definition fragile states, susceptible not only to the vagaries of nature (e.g. droughts, floods, famines) and of the global economy, but also to shifting dynamics within the region. For example, a civil conflict started in a country can easily spread to neighboring countries. Similarly, a famine in one country can strain the economies and social systems of surrounding countries.

Unfortunately, the same way people can't chose their parents, countries can't chose their neighbors. They have to play the cards they have been dealt and identify ways of gaining easier access to developed markets – even if these markets are some distance away.

INSTITUTIONS 102: Building Leadership for the Leaderless

*[I]t's no puzzle to understand why people want to lead.
The real puzzle is why people are willing to follow.*
JONATHAN HAIDT

Institutions are critical for development. They are however a reflection of the state of the economy and society. In countries with strong economies and an active civil society, people demand and build strong institutions. However, in countries where a large share of the population lacks formal education and gainful employment, it is hard to build and sustain strong institutions.

For institutions to function properly, a few ingredients are required. For one, you need a democratic system that allows people to oust underperforming governments. You also need a large enough pool of experts that can ensure the proper functioning of the bureaucracy. In addition, you have to pay these bureaucrats high enough salaries so you can attract qualified people (which will not be tempted by corruption). At the same time, salaries in the public sector cannot be too high, because they will discourage private sector development and might encourage corruption. If it is more attractive to work for the public sector, few people will chose to work for private companies – people will primarily compete for the higher salaries in the public sector.

Ensuring that right ingredients are in place is a challenge even for developed countries, and a Herculean task for undeveloped countries. You don't only need a strong administration, but also a functional and fair legal and judicial system, an effective education system, and a health system that is equipped to face the many challenges undeveloped countries face on a regular basis. This is no small feat, and there are very few undeveloped countries that have managed to ensure these basic pre-conditions by their own means.

The following sections include a discussion on three institutions that play a critical role for jolting undeveloped countries on a growth and development path.

The Teacher Gap

A country is only as developed as its people are. And, when your population is largely un-educated, the country does not have too sunny prospects. There are mountains of empirical research that show that an improvement in education outcomes is one of the strongest predictors of future economic growth and development. However, it is hard to talk about educational outcomes in undeveloped countries, especially in the frequent instances where less than 50% of the population is literate, and where only a fraction of people move beyond primary education.

And, the mounting challenge undeveloped countries and regions face in surmounting the education gap, can to a large extent be attributed to the teacher gap. In simple terms, if you don't have enough qualified teachers to educate the new generations of people, there is no hope of making fast progress in this sector. And, unfortunately, this is a simple mathematics game. Assuming, according to international standards, that you need around one teacher for a class of 30 students, it means that for 300,000 people of school age, a country would need at least 10,000 teachers; for 3,000,000 people of school age, 100,000 teachers would be needed. And indeed, according to UNESCO data, the pupil-to-teacher ratio is quite high in Low Income countries – 42, as opposed to 24 in Middle Income countries, and 19 in Upper Middle-Income countries. In countries like Rwanda, Chad, or Malawi, the pupil-to-student ratio is over 60.

Ensuring such a large number of qualified teachers is outside the means of most undeveloped countries. Even if the number of teachers would be available, there are a number of other hurdles undeveloped countries have to overcome. Given that these countries are largely rural, their population tends to be fragmented in a myriad of small communities, where economies of scale are hard to achieve – e.g. the communities may be too small to warrant the development of a school. Another problem is the fungibility of skills qualified teachers bring with them. Since they are educated, these teachers find it easier to get a job in more developed countries – and many actually leave for better opportunities elsewhere. Lastly, teaching positions are often unattractive for qualified people, given the relatively low salaries for these positions.

I will not discuss here the challenge that stems from a dysfunctional education sector, the lack of a developed and viable curricula, or the other activities that vie for the attention and time of people of school age (e.g. helping the parents put food on the table by helping with farming activities or doing other jobs).

Solving the teacher gap is one of the most important for undeveloped countries, and recent advances in technology (e.g. tele-teaching) may help overcome this challenge. Even so, though, it takes 18 years to prepare a new generation of educated people – a time-span that is discouraging for politicians that have to undertake such reforms.

Lastly, an educated population is not a sine-qua-non condition for development, as the experience of former Communist countries shows. Unless educated people can find gainful employment (which is pre-conditioned on having easy access to large markets), benefits coming from education cannot be accrued by the economy. Similarly, in countries where resources exploitation and export plays a significant part in the economy, education does not bring many benefits to the economy, because mining sectors rarely are competitive.

From Leaders to Autocrats

Since about 400 B.C., no leader until [George] Washington who had assumed such vast power had ever relinquished it voluntarily.

JAMES O'TOOLE

In "The Dictator's Handbook", Bruce Bueno de Mesquita and Alastair Smith, dissect the chain of events that transform a leader into an autocrat. The analysis is quite interesting as it shows that throughout history, many autocrats started out as true leaders, eager to make a positive change, but somehow managing to get lost along the way. That "somehow" almost always follows a similar pattern.

As soon as a budding politician has found himself/herself in a position of power, he/she realizes that there are two types of constituents he/she will need to satisfy: 1) the citizens as a whole, which may have put the leader in his/her position of power; and, 2) special interests, such as army and police leaders, large companies, other politicians.

Responding to the multitude of citizen needs is a very difficult task even in developed countries, but this is made almost impossible in undeveloped countries. To respond to the needs of all the citizens, a leader cannot only rely on personal charm and hard work – a fully functional and effective public administration system is needed. Even if an excellent administration apparatus would be in place, the lack of a real economic base means it is very hard to make a lot of people happy in a 4-5 years electoral cycle.

Consequently, undeveloped countries with democratic systems are usually plagued by political instability. The norm however in undeveloped countries are autocratic forms of government. Autocracies basically are the result of politicians' thirst for power. As politicians find themselves in a position of power, they realize quite quickly the limited real change they can actually engender, and they start focusing less on promoting change and more on securing their position in power. And, of course, securing this position is easier to achieve if these politicians curry favors to special interest groups than if they try to respond to the needs of citizens.

The special interest groups are in turn interested in preserving the status quo, and keeping an autocrat in power that provides stability and predictability to their enterprise.

Even if such a country would have an active civil society that demanded regular elections, one would need a large enough pool of enlightened leaders, to help promote ambitious reforms. However, enlightened leaders are often in short supply even in developed countries, and their success hinges on having a large enough and effective team to complete these ambitious reforms. Add on top of that the fact that hard reforms take years to show meaningful impact, which basically means that most reformers don't have a long political life, and you have the basic ingredients that often turn an enlightened leader into an autocrat. Most of the time, leaders-turned-autocrats genuinely think that they are doing what is best for their country/community, and are quick to trade the needs and demands of the people for their own needs.

An analysis of undeveloped countries indicates that the large majority of them had, at some point in their past, an autocratic government or are presently ruled by one. This may provide stability and predictability for the short and medium term, and it will certainly serve the purpose of a small interest group, but over the long term this is very detrimental to a country's growth and development prospects, and ultimately to its people. The Economist Intelligence Unit computes the Democracy Index, arranging countries in four categories: *full democracies; flawed democracies; hybrid regimes; authoritarian regimes.* None of the Low Income countries in 2015 had a full democracy or even a flawed democracy. Moreover, of 30 Low Income countries, 20 had authoritarian regimes.[7]

Freedom of Movement for People

There is no country that offers all the opportunities that its people are looking for. For some loonies and dreamers, not even the World is big enough. Generally, the smaller the country and the less developed, the fewer opportunities it has to offer. For example, if you are born in Luxembourg, although you are living in one of the most developed countries in the World, there are a limited number of opportunities to your disposal. If you want to study behavioral economics or become a film actor, Luxembourg may not be the best place to do this. A country, like Guyana, offers even less opportunities to its people, unless you are interested in sugar cane or rice plantations, or in the gold and aluminum mining business.

Even if you happen to be one of the over 180 million citizens of Nigeria, the opportunities you have are quite limited. While Nigeria is one of the most populous countries in the World, its economy is rather homogenous. Thus, over 90% of Nigerian exports are represented by oil sales. There are relatively few opportunities for people interested in other professions, with the exception of subsistence agriculture.

And this is one of the toughest challenges undeveloped countries face. If a significant share of people can't access the opportunities they are interested in at home, than public authorities should create the premises and institutions that would enable these people to access opportunities elsewhere. Reality shows that this is rarely the case. Of course, not all of the World's gifted consultants can get a job in Luxembourg, but greater freedom of movement for the World population ensures a better matching of people and opportunities.

Being skilled but stuck in a country that offers few opportunities is a significant loss not only for the country, but for the world as a whole. It's like having a fast race car, but no track to run it on.

Creating the national and international institutions that enable a larger freedom of movement for people, is one of the key preconditions for triggering growth and development in undeveloped countries. People that have sought better opportunities elsewhere often chose to come back to their home country. When they do, they also bring back capital, knowledge, and connections from abroad. It is often these people that play a key role in helping undeveloped countries make a turn for the better. Even if the people chose not to come back, the World is better off, as these people have reached higher productivity levels and have helped grow the World economy.

MARKETS 102: The Big Bang Theory or How to Make Something out of Nothing

Undeveloped countries have relatively little to offer – little for their citizens and little for potential foreign investors. They try to bank on the natural resources they have, but, as we have seen earlier, these efforts more often than not backfire. To have a chance at real growth and development, undeveloped countries, as all other countries, should focus on the one thing that can enable them long-term prosperity – their people.

The critical challenge for undeveloped countries is to enable their people to become more productive. This can be achieved in several different ways. We will discuss here three possible approaches.

Access to Capital

In undeveloped countries, the active labor force is to a large extent focusing on small scale, largely subsistence farming. According to World Bank Development Indicators, around 70% of the population of Low Income countries lives in rural areas, eking out an existence from small size individual farm plots. A few people may be working for the mining companies that have come to take advantage of natural resources, or for the few industrial plants operating in the country. The rest are usually engaged in low-value added service jobs (e.g. retail) or working in the public sector.

One of the key tasks for policy makers in undeveloped countries is to create the proper conditions to ensure that present day farmers go through the steps that farmers from developed countries have gone through many years ago – i.e. becoming more productive by taking advantage of existent technological advances. To be able to take advantage of these technologies though, farmers need access to capital. Capital, however, is in short supply in undeveloped countries, so farmers get stuck in a vicious cycle.

Access to capital is one of the biggest market dysfunctions. There is business to be made with the poor – one only has to undergo a change mindset. We commonly believe that the poor, given their state of impoverishment are not credit worthy. In "Banker to the Poor", Muhammad Yunus, the founder of Grameen Bank (the first micro-lending institution in the World), shows, by power of example (an inspirational example) that the poor are actually credit worthy. Not only that, but they are also good business. The Grameen Bank now has provided billions of dollars in micro-loans to millions of people.

These micro-loans will not necessarily put an economy on a sustainable growth path, but they can ensure that a larger share of the population has a better livelihood and a more predictable future. For example, Bangladesh, which is where Grameen Bank is doing a significant share of its business, managed to make the transition in 2014 from Low Income country to Lower Middle-Income country, and it virtually doubled its GNI per Capita over the 2007 value – from around $600 to around $1,200. However, much of this growth was fueled by foreign direct investments, particularly in the textile sector, and continued textile export growth.

Micro-loans cannot sustain long-term growth, but they can help improve the condition of the poor in undeveloped countries, and create a pre-requisite for future growth. When people have some more stability and predictability in their life, they can also spend more on creative and higher productivity pursuits.

Cheap Labor

In order to modernize their economies, in a quick fashion, undeveloped and developing countries are reliant on technological transfers from developed countries. The alternative would be for the people in those countries to reinvent technologies that are already existent. Such a task is almost impossible to achieve in a short time-frame.

Thomas Thwaites ingeniously shows why this is the case. In "The Toaster Project", he tells the story of how he attempted to build a $3 toaster from scratch – i.e. Thwaites had to mine and get all the basic materials required to build every sub-component of the toaster. What at a first glance may seem as a trivial and simple enough task, turned out to be an almost impossible feat. This bland and ubiquitous appliance is made of hundreds of different parts and a myriad of materials sourced from all over the world. Basically, to produce a simple appliance, which costs less than a loaf of good bread, dozens of countries had to trade with each other, and thousands of people contributed labor and knowledge to help fabricate this toaster.

Consequently, in order to modernize, undeveloped countries are almost by default dependent on technological transfers from abroad, which most often come in the form of foreign direct investments.

Of course, attracting foreign direct investment is easier said than done, and a key measure of success for any government. The one thing undeveloped countries can offer to foreign investors is cheap labor. Labor intensive industrial enterprises from developed countries often move to places with cheaper labor, to ensure higher profit margins and respond to growing labor costs at home. Typical enterprises that undertake this migration are light industry companies (e.g. textiles or footwear).

And indeed, when one looks at the countries that have made the transition from undeveloped countries to developing countries, light industries have played an overwhelming part in that transition. For example, 90% of Bangladeshi exports came from the textile sector in 2014. Similar high figures were registered in other countries that have managed the transition to a developing state: Cambodia (68% of exports from textiles); Pakistan (55%); Morocco (18%); Vietnam (16%); and India (14%).

However, foreign direct investors often shy away from places with difficult geography (e.g. landlocked and with bad neighbors), unstable and weak institutions, and distorted markets (e.g. markets where labor costs are artificially inflated by natural resource exploitation). It is up to undeveloped country governments and the international community to provide the enabling conditions for attracting investors. Without foreign investors, the path to growth and development will be long and arduous for undeveloped countries.

Access to Markets

Proximity to markets matters – it matters a lot. 70% of Canadian exports and 75% of Mexican markets go to the US. East European countries export around 70% of what they produce to Western Europe. 43% of Chinese exports, 57% of Japanese exports, and 61% of South Korean exports go to other Asian countries – primarily those closest to them. Worldwide, 37% of global exports go to Europe, 36% go to Asia, 18% go to North America, 3.5% got to Africa, and 3.2% got to South America. If you're not close to large markets in Europe, Asia, or North America, you may be sheer out of luck.

And of course, undeveloped countries have one common trait – their relative distance from these large markets. Since trade with their neighbors does not generate a lot of extra revenue (since their neighbors tend to be poor too), undeveloped countries engage in wide distance and relatively costly trading. For example, around 80% of Sudanese exports go to Asia – primarily China. 72% of Nigerian exports go to Europe and Asia. In fact Europe and Asia are the main export markets for most countries in Africa.

Access to the rich markets in Europe, East Asia, and North America is important for undeveloped countries, but this access is also costly. Moreover, exports are resumed for the most part to natural resources and exotic fruits and vegetables that can't be grown in these developed markets.

To achieve higher rates of competitiveness, it is important for undeveloped countries to trade more with their neighbors. Large, regional trade spaces (as those provided by the EU or NAFTA) have a number of key advantages. They provide a large labor pool investors can chose from, they provide larger markets for selling goods and services, and they enable knowledge flows for product improvement.

Where Countries Export Most

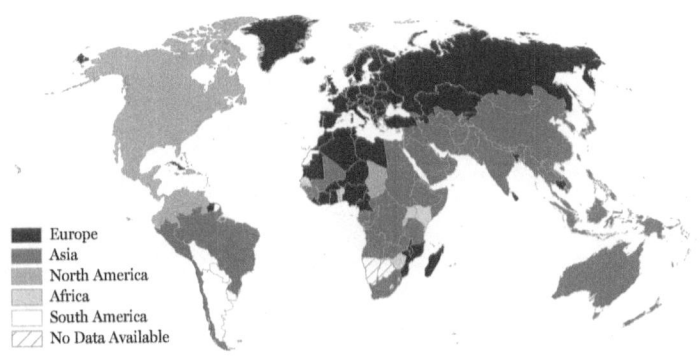

Data Source: MIT Observatory of Economic Complexity

Undeveloped countries should therefore try to take full advantage of the rich markets close to them, and they should try to band together with other undeveloped countries. This can help them pool resources and create a larger, common market.

DEVELOPING: How to Overcome the Middle Income Trap

For the purposes of this book, developing countries are understood as being Lower Middle-Income and Upper Middle-Income countries (as defined through the World Bank GNI per Capita Atlas Method) that are non-resource dependent (i.e. where less than 50% of exports are resource exports). The vast majority of people on Planet Earth, currently live in a developing country – around 4.6 billion of us (or 63% of the World Population). If you are reading this book, chances are you were born in a developing country. Thus, this may be one of the chapters you are most interested in.

One of the characteristics of developing countries is sustained growth over a longer period of time. Between 1995 and 2015, the average compound annual growth rate for developing countries was around 6%, with the poorest performers growing at around 2% per year, and the best performers growing at around 10%-14% per year. Most significantly, large countries like China, India, Indonesia, Brazil, Pakistan, or Bangladesh, have grown at rates above 5% - positively impacting their around 3.5 billion people. It is a global growth trend that is likely to define the economy of tomorrow.

Before we continue talking about developing countries, and their good performance in recent years, let me however plug a piece of economic literature that changed my life and may well change yours. You know, when people ask you what's your favorite book, you probably struggle, like most people, to name that ONE book. I'm no different when it comes to books in general – I love George Orwell, Hermann Hesse, Nassim Taleb, Panait Istrati, and a few dozen other writers. When it comes to economics thought, there is one book that, in my book, towers over them all. It is a book that in all likelihood you have never heard of. It is a book you should get as soon as you finish reading this paragraph (especially since it's free on-line). It is... drum roll please... "The World Development Report

2009: Reshaping Economic Geography", written by a World Bank team coordinated by Indermit Gill – a dude who deserves the Nobel Prize for economics more than most economists I know of, save for Ronald Coase and Daniel Kahneman (neither of which is actually an economist).

The World Bank does not always get the credit it should get. It generates an amazing volume of ideas on development, but it is incredibly inept at actually popularizing those ideas. Although the vast majority of research produced by the Bank is free for download, fewer than 3,000 people accessed the Bank's most popular report[8]. Less than 3,000! Let that sink in. 31% of World Bank reports are never downloaded, and the average number of downloads is 87. Most of my blog posts, which target the population in a small city in Romania get more readers than that. In fact, big names in development such as Paul Collier, Bill Easterly, or Alain Bertaud, have become much more famous after leaving the Bank than when working for it. Their books sell like hotcakes. People are more willing to pay for what these guys write post-Bank, and less willing to download freely similar work produced by the Bank.

Unfortunately, "The World Development report 2009" (WDR'09) has had a similar fate as most Bank reports. I am hoping however this will not stay this way for too long. If you are lazy and only have time to read one book on economics in your life, read this Bank report. You won't regret it – it's the best tome I know on development issues. You can, with a free conscience drop this book now and start reading the WDR'09. I won't hold it against you.

Should you chose to hang in though, I promise I will make it worth your while.

GEOGRAPHY 1.0: Mastering Nature to Master the Economy

For a developing country like Romania, geography has been both a blessing and a curse – as it is the case for a vast majority of developing countries. In 1945, it was close enough to Russia to fall within its sphere of influence. Although the Communist Party in Romania at the time was weak and had almost no popular support (as opposed to Greece, where it was a major political force), the geographical position of Romania put it within the sphere of influence of the Soviet Union, and that's where it stayed for over 40 years.

Following 1989 and the fall of the communist regime, Romania's position became a boon – the country now was under the sphere of influence of the EU, and it has joined the Union with bells and whistles in 2007.

Within Romania, geography continued to be a development molding force. In 1989, Cluj, a city in the West of Romania, and Iasi, a city in the East of Romania, the two largest university centers outside Bucharest, had about the same population (Iasi was slightly larger) and the same economic output. Within a few years however, Cluj was generating more than twice as much as Iasi. Although the cities were similar in almost every aspect, Cluj took off and Iasi didn't. Cluj had a natural advantage – it was closer to Western Europe, where 70% of Romania's exports go to. Iasi had the misfortune of being stuck on the other side of the Carpathian Mountains, with poor connections to the West.

But the story does not end here. Cluj is one of the fastest growing cities in the EU, but its development has not come without challenges. While the vast majority of people in Cluj have benefited from the city's development, some did not do so well. Cluj has a number of pockets of poverty and a slum neighborhood, all located in peripheral areas with difficult access to the city.

This section discusses in more detail how geography impacts the fate of developing countries, the same way it has impacted Romania's development – at all levels, from macro to micro.

The Many Benefits of Good Neighbors

There are three major poles of development in the World: the EU, the US, and Japan. The map below nicely shows their economic footprint at the global level.

The World's Largest Markets (GDP Output in Constant US$)

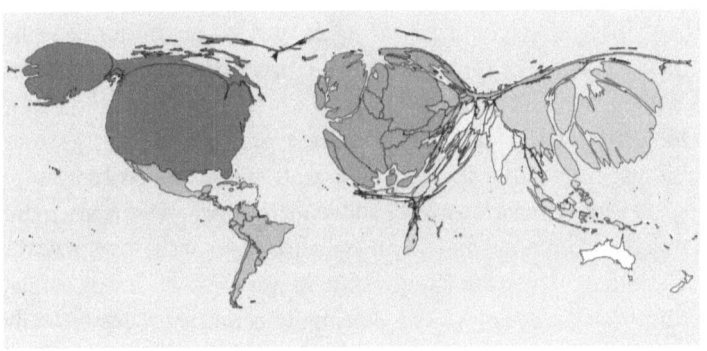

Source: World Bank. 2009. World Development Report 2009: Reshaping Economic Geography

If your country happens to be near one of these development poles, and if you happen to have few or no trade barriers with these developed countries, you've hit the jackpot. As indicated earlier in the book, around 70% of Central and Eastern European exports go to the EU; around 75% of Mexican exports go to the US; and, China exports more to Japan, South Korea, and Hong Kong, than it does to the US.

Having strong neighbors helps a developing country in several different ways. Most importantly, good neighbors also represent large markets. Depending on how porous the boundaries with the developed neighbors are, trade can bring significant benefits. Obviously, being part of the EU and firmly embedded within a common market, has a more significant positive impact than being part of a free trade agreement with the US, as is the case of Mexico, but not having a fully functional common market. In addition to a free movement of goods, a common market also enables the free movement of people, knowledge, and ideas.

Proximity to good neighbors also enables the spill-over of good institutions and the nurturing of stability. By and large, countries with good neighbors have a lower incidence of slippages of democracy. A healthy society is just as contagious as a sick society. Of course, here too there are nuances. Being part of the EU comes with obligations. New Member States commit to strengthening their market economies and their public institutions, while enabling the civil society and regular citizens more access to power. Vietnam benefits from being close to the booming markets of Hong Kong and Guangzhou, but there are no outward pressures to improve its public institutions and strengthen its civil society.

Obviously, countries with stable democratic systems are more attractive to investors and they benefit from significant foreign direct investments. These foreign investments are, as we have seen earlier, critical for undeveloped and developing countries. They basically enable the developing countries to make a technological and productivity leap that would be hard to accomplish in an autarchic fashion. Just imagine how much time, effort, and capital would be needed so that developing countries develop the technologies that have been refined over the decades in developed countries. Moreover, think how long it would take a company from the developing world to build a reliable and stable logistics and distribution network in the developed world (where most stuff is consumed).

One of the key benefits of the EU is that it provides its members with a cloak of stability, and it provides access to the largest market in the World. An investor knows that although the market system and the public institutions in Romania are not perfect, his/

her interests have a high likelihood of being guarded, given that Romania is a member of the EU. The EU is in fact humanity's most efficient "convergence machine", having managed to either enable all of its Member Countries to overcome the middle-income trap, or having set them on a path to achieving this desiderate.

Before commencing accession talks with the EU, Spain, Portugal, and Greece were developing countries. Upon entering the EU, they quickly became developed countries. On the other hand, countries like Argentina, Chile, Uruguay, or Peru, which in 1950 had a higher GDP per Capita then these Southern European states, have had a slower convergence towards development and they are still trailing behind the EU Member Countries. Between 1950 and 2006, Southern European countries converged at an average of 1% per year, while South American countries at around 0.3% per year[9].

Moreover, in 1990, countries like Argentina, Chile, or Uruguay, had productivity levels similar to or higher than those of their Eastern European peers. However, upon joining the EU, the Czech Republic, Slovakia, Poland, Hungary, Slovenia, Lithuania, Latvia, Estonia, and Croatia have become high-income countries. An impressive feat by any standard.

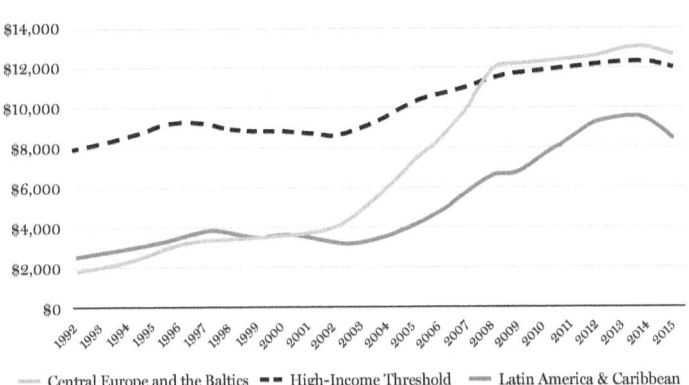

Diverging Fortunes in Latin America and Central Europe

Central Europe and the Baltics — — High-Income Threshold — Latin America & Caribbean

Data Source: World Bank
Note: Data represents GNI per Capital Atlas Method, in Constant US$.

One does not need to engage in a too complicated imagination exercise, to realize that Latin American countries would have been much better off had they been part of the EU, or something similar to it.

Density

For a long time, economists did not factor geography in their analyses. Too many of them, the economy was a black box in which you threw a few ingredients, and you would get growth and development. However, as the collection of data at the sub-national level got better, it quickly became obvious that economic development absolutely never is spatially even – absolutely never. Just as some countries are more developed than others, some regions within individual countries are more developed than others. There are always some areas, most often metropolitan areas or urban agglomerations that develop much faster than the rest. These areas do not only make up a significant share of the economy, but they are also responsible for an overwhelming share of economic growth. In the EU, primate cities (the largest city in the respective country) and secondary cities amass around 10%-30% of the total population, but generate around 50%-70% of economic output. In the US, the 16 largest metropolitan areas generate over 50% of the national GDP. In Japan, Tokyo and Osaka alone generate around 33% of national output. Manila, Cairo, and Buenos Aires generate over 60% of the GDP in the Philippines, Egypt, and Argentina respectively.

Tokyo and New York are the 14th and 15th largest economies in the World; Los Angeles is the 20th largest economy; Chicago, London, and Paris are the 24th, 25th, and 26th largest World economies. Among the 100 largest economies in the World, 45 are individual metropolitan areas. These metropolitan areas are basically the World's economic growth engines.

Cities matter! They matter a lot and a sound urban

development policy is critical for any developing country. It is a handful of cities that decide the pace of growth for developing countries, and the proper management of these cities' growth is critical for the countries' growth.

The reason cities are a country's main development engines are manifold. First and foremost, cities benefit from a density of people, firms, and institutions. A large number of people is equivalent to large markets and a large labor pool. Consequently, firms like big cities both because they can find there a large enough and diverse labor pool, and because cities offer large and dense markets (i.e. goods and services can reach more cost effectively a large number of customers).

In turn, people like big cities, because big cities offer a large number and array of opportunities (jobs, higher education, specialized healthcare, national and international transport connections, culture, art, entertainment, shopping). Cities are also attractive to people because of the other people living there – particularly more people that are similar to us. We are social beings and naturally like to be around similar people.

But cities are not only places where you find a lot of other people and firms, they are also places where you can be more productive. There is a plethora of studies that show that people are more productive in cities. One such study finds that for a two-fold increase in city size, productivity grows by 2%-5%[10]. The reason is quite simple. In bigger cities, there is a higher likelihood to identify people that are better than us at what we do. And it is these people that drive us to be better and more productive. That is why it is better to be a small fish in a big pond than a big fish in a small pond. In the big pond you have many more opportunities for growth.

This is also why a talented individual in a developed city has better opportunities for development than an individual in a developing city. Basically, those, those that have more receive more, benefiting from a virtuous circle, or positive circular and cumulative causation (as the process was dubbed by Nobel Prize Laureate Gunnar Myrdal).

Companies are driven by market forces to co-locate close to other companies. In tune with the proverb "keep your friends close and your enemies closer", companies frequently do a counterintuitive thing and move closer to their competition. Part of this process represents a strategic choice companies make – being close to similar companies enables them to take advantage of a large skilled labor pool, to quickly learn and adapt innovations in the field, and to continuously be on their toes in a competitive game and sector. Part of the process simply represents natural selection – the companies that do not stay competitive by continuously innovating and learning from their peers, eventually get flushed out of the market.

Yet another advantage cities offer is diversity of options. A young entrepreneur wishing to open a tattoo shop, will have a hard time finding clientele in a small village. In fact, you have a hard time finding a clientele for almost any business in rural areas, apart from small retail and service shops.

In almost every country, the largest and most dynamic cities are the country's main economic growth engines. When these cities do well, so does the economy as a whole. When these cities do poorly, the economy usually does poorly too. The figure below shows the economic performance of the main economic centers in Romania. As can be seen, the capital, Bucharest, has not only outperformed by a wide margin the Romanian economy, but it is now also outperforming the EU economy. The secondary cities Timișoara and Cluj-Napoca are also growing at rates that surpass the EU growth rates, and may soon be more performing than the EU average. They are even now technically "developed" cities – i.e. they have an estimated GNI per Capita (Atlas Method) above the High Income Threshold. Thus, while Romania still is a developing country, its main economic cities are already developed. The rest of the country will likely follow suit if current growth dynamics are maintained.

The Economic Performance of the Most Dynamic Cities in Romania

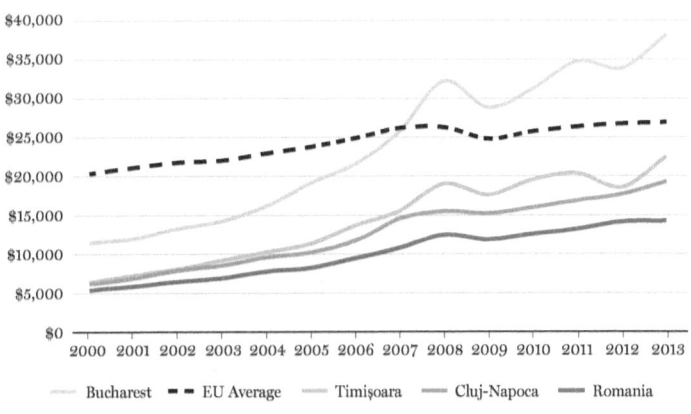

Data Source: EuroStat
Note: Data represents GDP per Capita (Purchasing Power Standard), in Euro

This dynamic is also encountered in every other country around the World. In Poland, dynamic cities like Warsaw, Poznan, Crakow, Gdansk, or Wroclaw, outperform the national economy, and pull it forward. The same is the case for Prague in the Czech Republic, Sofia in Bulgaria, Budapest in Hungary, Buenos Aires in Argentina, Sao Paulo and Rio de Janeiro in Brazil, and so on.

For developing and developed countries, growth and development is intimately connected to urban growth and development. If your main cities don't do well, neither will your economy as a whole. This is a lesson many policy makers have not yet learned.

Proximity to Density

For a developing country, the highest dividends to development come from being close to one or more developed countries and from the level of integration in those developed markets. Slovenia is a small country with no large urban center, but it borders Austria and Italy and is well integrated within the EU common market. This proximity has allowed it to develop quite fast.

Next in terms of importance is the presence of density – e.g. metropolitan areas, urban agglomerations, or conurbations. Within a country, the primate city is usually also the main economic engine. The larger the city is and the closer it is to other developed markets, the more developed it tends to be. Prague and Bratislava have a higher GDP per Capita than Warsaw or Bucharest, although the latter are bigger.

Geography is relevant at a third major level – proximity to density. More concretely, the closer an area is to one of the country's economic engines (usually the primate city and the secondary cities), the more developed it tends to be. The areas that are distant both from large markets and from density, tend to be the least developed.

These territorial dynamics can be observed in almost every developing and developed country. The World Bank did an in-depth analysis of such territorial dynamics in several countries across the globe. In country after country, from Vietnam to India, Colombia, or Sri Lanka, one can observe these territorial development patterns.

The maps below highlight these patterns in Romania, indicating how individual localities have performed from 2002 to 2011. Three major patterns emerge immediately. One, almost every locality in Romania has seen an improvement in this time period. EU accession has basically been a boon for the entire economy. The localities in the West of the country, within the arc of the Carpathian Mountains, have developed faster than the East and the South of the country. Basically, being closer to Western and Central Europe, where 70% of Romanian exports go to, has favored the Western localities. The fastest growth has been registered by localities close to dynamic cities. The larger and more developed the city, the larger the functional urban zone that formed around it.

Territorial Development Patterns in Romania (2002 and 2011)

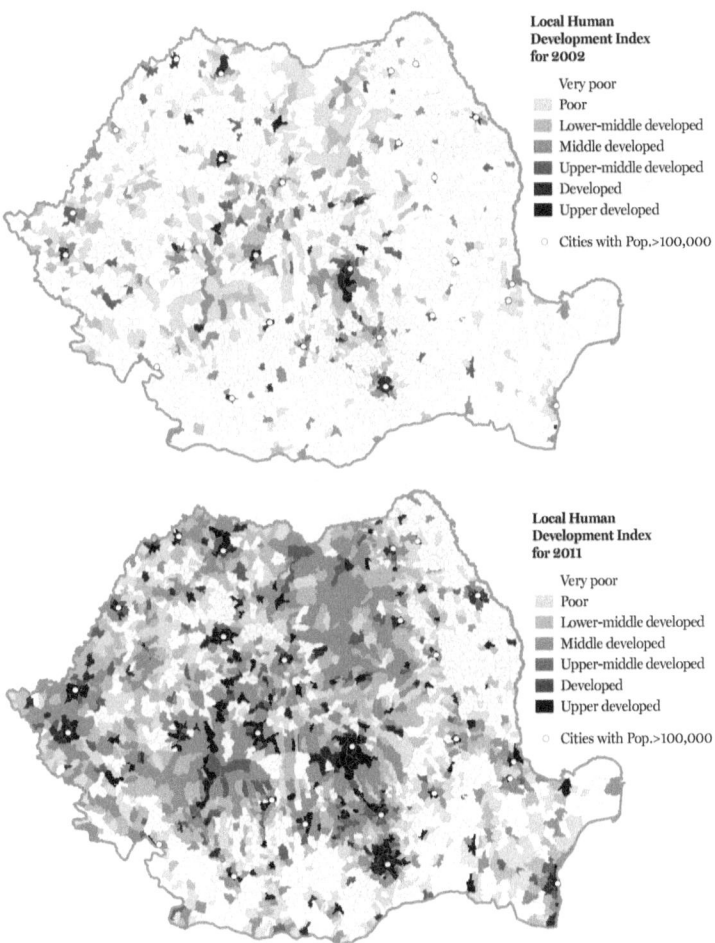

Source: *World Bank. 2013. Competitive Cities: Reshaping the Economic Geography of Romania*

Of course, the more dynamic urban regions, and the area around them, grow much quicker than the rest of the country. They are the country's economic engines. As they grow at a fast pace, they also grow apart from the rest of the country. In 1995, 38 out of

41 counties in Romania had a GDP per Capita above 50% of Bucharest's GDP. By 2010, only two counties managed to stay above the 50% mark. This dynamic is more often than not worrisome for politicians and policy makers. They see the growing gap between leading and lagging regions as a problem. However, this is a pattern that every developing country goes through, a pattern that every developed country has went through already.

A growing disparity between leading and lagging regions is a sign the country's actually developing, and should not necessarily be a cause for concern. While leading regions grow faster than the rest, a rising tide raises all boats and usually no region is left behind. Basically, everybody is growing, but at different speeds.

Moreover, a poor performance of leading regions has negative repercussions for lagging regions too. Since leading regions often represent an overwhelming share of the economy, if they perform poorly, the whole economy suffers. If they do well, they also generate extra revenues that can be redistributed to help lagging regions develop at a faster pace (e.g. by transferring national funds for investments in local public infrastructure).

Over time, differences in life standards between leading and lagging regions tend to flatten, and people manage to access in almost every corner of the country quality education, healthcare, public administration and public utilities. In essence, the growth of leading areas gradually spills over to wider and wider areas, to finally encompass the whole of the country. Those areas that are closest to these epicenters of development, grow earlier and faster than the rest.

INSTITUTIONS 1.0: Stability and Foundations for Long-Term Growth

Social cohesion is a necessity, and mankind has never yet succeeded in enforcing cohesion by merely rational arguments. Every community is exposed to two opposite dangers: ossification through too much discipline and reverence for tradition, on the one hand; and on the other hand, dissolution, or subjection to foreign conquest, through the growth of individualism and personal experience that makes cooperation impossible.

BERTRAND RUSSEL

Institutions are critical for growth and development. This point deserves repeating time and time again, because it is important. For developing countries, strong institutions provide two key ingredients for development: 1) stability for people, firms, and investments; 2) in-built mechanisms that ensure a continued evolution and modernization of national systems, and guard that the needs of the few do not negatively affect the future and interests of the many.

Institutions in developing countries also have to develop in-built mechanisms that prevent their atrophy. Private companies that are badly managed go bankrupt. Institutions that are badly managed receive more funding to fix existent problems.

The same way developing countries need technologies from developed countries to modernize their economies, so do they require modern institutions. The problem is that developing countries not only require wide-ranging institutional reform, but they also deal with tougher challenges than developed countries deal with. By and large, undeveloped and developing countries have a larger number of poor people they have to provide for, they have less people that are gainfully employed, and they have to provide social services to a population that by and large has meager earnings.

Not only do developing countries have bigger problems than developed countries, but they have fewer tools to deal with those problems. Land transactions are hampered by a lack of functional cadaster systems; urban development is hampered by the lack of spatial planning tools, rules and norms; access to opportunities is hampered by dysfunctional housing institutions; private sector development is discouraged by regulatory vacuums and unpredictability.

Institutional development is critical for developing countries, but not for the sake of having good public institutions. Institutions are important insofar as they help the efficient and sustainable development of the private sector. Without a strong private sector, one cannot have a strong economy, and without a strong economy it is impossible to have long-term growth and development. As we will see later however, a strong private sector is not necessarily equivalent to a high share of the population working in the private sector. Only around 56% of the population of High Income countries is gainfully employed – as opposed to around 60% in Middle Income countries, and 73% in Low Income countries[11]. Moreover, many of the High Income countries have a high share of their employed population working in the public sector – 35% in Denmark; 29% in Sweden; 24% in the UK; 20% in France[12]. Comparably, public sector employment is under 10% in countries such as the Philippines, Zimbabwe, Ghana, Cameroon, Bangladesh, Colombia, or Senegal[13].

An overwhelming share of economic output is generated in almost every country by a handful of companies. These companies employ a smaller share of the population, but ensure sustained economic growth. One of the key roles of public institutions should be to create an environment that is attractive for such large companies. When the countries are developing, public institutions should provide the environment and tools for attracting investors. When the countries are already developed, it is important that they create an environment that allows companies to grow sustainably.

The sections below discuss three institutions that are particularly important for the growth and development of developing countries.

Stability and Predictability for People and Investors

Institutions have originally evolved as mechanisms employed by people to bring stability and predictability in a volatile, dangerous, and perpetually changing environment. They largely play the same role today, although the array of institutions has grown exponentially, in tune with the growth of the population.

While change is essential to growth and development, people generally do not like change. We are conservative by nature. Even when we are stuck in a situation that does not favor us, such as a dictatorship, it is hard for us to mobilize and change things.

As such, stability and predictability is a two-edged sword. If we are part of a system with good institutions, than a healthy dose of conservativism is OK (albeit, there's always room for improvement). If we are part of a system with bad or worsening institutions, than change is absolutely necessary.

Nonetheless, stability and predictability are some of the key things investors are looking for before deciding to invest in a developing country. Investors often want to take advantage of cheaper labor in developing countries, but before they invest they want to make sure that their interests are protected. Most investments in recent years have flown to the places that have provided the strongest guarantees for investors. Two models have emerged in this respect: 1) the East Asian model; 2) the EU model.

The East Asian model draws its strength from autocratic or quasi-autocratic institutions that are relatively stable over time. China has a one-party system that has evolved to cater to the interests of foreign direct investors by providing a stable, consistent, and favorable system of rules and regulations, as well as a system of incentives. China has rapidly made the transition from Low Income, to Lower Middle-Income (in 1999) and the Upper Middle-Income (in 2010). Between 1995 and 2015, China has grown at a compound annual growth rate of 14.3% - a staggering rate (the highest of any developing country). In 1995, it had a GNI per Capita of $540. By 2015, the GNI per Capita grew to $7,820 - 14 times larger than in 1995.

Even in countries with regular elections, some institutions become entrenched and ensure continuity over the years. Lee Kwan Yew has been Prime Minister of Singapore for over 30 years, and has seen his country's dramatic rise from Third world to First. The "chaebol" system dominates the functioning of the South Korean economy, the same way the "keiretsu" model dominated the Japanese economy, and provides stability and predictability to businesses even when governments change.

The EU model offers stability and predictability in a different way – by means of a para-state structure. While all New EU Member Countries have to undertake major institutional reforms upon accession, their institutions cannot become strong overnight. Moreover, free elections can provide a source of instability, especially when national institutions are not strong enough (a change in government often comes with a change in priorities and a reform of existent institutions). Despite these relative volatile systems (in the EU, prime ministers don't last for 30 years, as Lew Kwan Yew has in Singapore), investors are willing to take a risk on these countries because of the security provided by the EU umbrella. More specifically, an investor knows that in case national institutions fail, there is a safety hatch higher up the chain, represented by the EU institutions.

Stability and predictability however, can only take you so far though. The next section will discuss a few more ingredients required for long-term growth and development.

A System of Checks and Balances

A recent article on Facebook (where I take most of my wisdom these days) posited that the strength of a democratic system lies not only in the free and open electoral process, but also in a system of institutions that provide checks and balances – i.e. institutions that address the failures/blunders of other institutions. Thus, when a particular institution slips or makes mistakes, there is a proper mechanism in place to address it.

In "Leading Change", James O'Toole indicates that almost every institution is subject to atrophy, because those who lead the institution, no matter how enlightened and open minded they might be, eventually become complacent and comfortable in their position, and by extension they become conservative – i.e. reluctant to change and reform. Moreover, those that are in power naturally want to conserve their position and the status quo.

In the private sector, when the leadership of a company fails to adapt to change, the company usually goes bankrupt. In the public sector, when the leadership of a public institution atrophies, the public institution does not go bankrupt. Consequently, for the public institution to reform, there is a need to have outward pressure. In most functional democracies, there is a division of power and responsibilities between the legislative, the executive, and the judicial. However, as economies have become more complex, so has the system of institutions providing checks-and-balances (e.g. anti-corruption and integrity agencies). Moreover, this system has to continuously evolve to meet ever evolving needs.

A case in point is the 2008 Housing Market and Financial Sector Crises in the US, which has triggered a global crisis. In the

"Big Short", the brilliant Michael Lewis provides a vivid account of how the institutions in the World's most powerful economy and democracy, failed to see the crisis coming and respond to early signs of trouble. The rating agencies (S&P, Moody's, Fitch) were more interested in keeping the big financial companies happy than in downgrading financial instruments that in hindsight proved to be toxic. The US Securities and Exchange Commission, whose role is to be a watchdog of the financial sector, failed completely in this instance, with its employees being more interested in getting a job with the big financial corporations than with making sure these corporations behaved rationally and ethically.

If you only have institutions that provide stability and predictability, but don't have institutions that provide adequate checks-and-balances, you sooner or later get to situations where the system ossifies around the interests of a few to the detriment of the many. And, an ossified system comes undone sooner or later.

A potential example of an ossified system is Japan. Japan has for the longest time been the poster-child example of how to bring a country from underdevelopment to development. In 1900, Japan had a GDP per Capita that was three times lower than that of Western Europe, and 4.5 times lower than that of the UK. However, sustained growth ensured that by 1995 Japan had the second highest GNI per Capita of all developed countries (i.e. High Income non-resource dependent countries) – second only to Switzerland. The year 1995, however, was also the start of Japan's relative decline. Between 1995 and 2015, Japan is the only developed country to have registered a negative compound annual growth rate (-0.6%). It has thus went from having the second highest GNI per Capita among developed countries to having the 17th highest GNI per Capita. It was in the interim overtaken by countries such as New Zealand, Hong Kong, Finland, Ireland, or Singapore.

The explanation of Japan's economic decline can be a subject for a stand-alone book. It is however widely known that the choice of Japanese institutions to hermetically close the country to immigration, have worsened demographic decline and aging dynamics, and have ultimately led to a slow-down of economic innovation and reform. In essence, institutions in Japan have failed to adequately respond to a negative trend, and this has had, and will likely continue to have negative repercussions on the economy.

The Pursuit of Happiness for All

In the "Tyranny of Experts", Bill Easterly brings to the fore the critical importance of democracy and of market systems that enable all citizens access to power and opportunities. Achieving a fully functional market system and a working democracy is not easy. Quite the contrary – it is incredibly hard! But unless developing countries start from this premise, it will be very hard for them to sustain long-term growth and development.

A working democracy is however not enough for a good economic performance, and some countries without democratic systems manage to do quite well from an economic point of view. Over the long-term though, it is virtually impossible to sustain a positive economic performance without devolving access to power to all your citizens.

I have seen first-hand how the hubris of a leader who thought himself enlightened, eventually led to the demise of a system. Even if you have a group of brilliant people at the helm, an economy and society are far too complex to be administered by only a handful of people – no matter how brilliant they are. When a country has hit a rough patch, you want everybody in the country to be looking for a solution out, not just a handful of people. And people will only be looking for a solution if they feel there is a stake in for them – if they don't stand to lose or gain anything from getting involved, they simply won't do it. The more people in a country, preferably all, have a stake in the country's future, the better off the country is likely to be – it's simply a matter of the country hedging its bets.

That is why history's biggest leaders tend to be those that have guided their country through tough times or times of drastic change (war, revolution, deep reform), and their leadership qualities are based on the ability to be decisive and wise with primarily binary decisions – i.e. decisions between two major courses of action (e.g. go to war or not). When decisions are not binary, it is much harder to exercise enlightened leadership. That is what Churchill learned the hard way, promptly losing the election after the Second World War was over.

For me, one of the best and vivid examples of how decisions taken by many people are better than decisions taken by a handful of people, are the cities we live in. When people feel they have a stake in the future of their country, they are more likely to invest in a good home for themselves. If they fear that a nice home may be taken away from them, they will be reluctant to over-invest. During Communism, the regime in Romania built housing units throughout the country in a functionalist and utilitarian way. Basically, they created a few apartment block designs, and then went on to build thousands of units using these designs. I grew up in one of those neighborhoods, which is many things, but not pretty. On the other hand, in democratic systems, city neighborhoods are diverse and interesting, and more closely reflect the multitude of choices of the people living there. They also reflect the financial capacity of various households and existent social divisions, but this will be discussed later on.

Authoritarian or quasi-authoritarian governments are attractive because of the clear direction and purpose they provide to a country (things that people universally crave), and in the short and medium-term they are more attractive than democratic systems, and often times more efficient and effective. A democracy is by nature and design messy and it is by no means foolproof.

Hitler came to power by popular vote, and politicians with extreme views often get a significant share of votes, even in well developed countries.

Jonathan Haidt brilliantly discusses in "The Righteous Mind" how our genes, our upbringing, and the system of moral values we grow up with, all come together to define who we are as a person and what things we chose to believe in. Thus, in most societies, you will always find a group of people that are more conservative in nature, a group of people that is more progressive and open to new things, and a group of people that are somewhere in the middle. Inevitably, when someone from an opposing party wins, people get antsy, angry, and defensive. When George W. Bush won his second term in office, half of the Cornell Campus pledged to move to Canada.

Depending on the strength of the existing political parties and their political leaders, democratic countries tend to meander between periods of conservativism and periods of reform. This flip-flop creates uncertainty and angst among the people that happen to find themselves at the extremes of the political spectrum, but it is ultimately critical for the health of society. If a country ends being perpetually dominated by a party on the right, or on the left, a part of society will perpetually feel dispossessed. Obviously, this is not a path to a healthy society.

No matter how messy democracies are, over the long-term they provide much better outcomes than any of the other systems people have created. You will always be better off when the entire population of your country is engaged in helping the country grow and develop, than when only a handful of people are working towards this goal. People that feel dispossessed and unrepresented will hardly commit their energy and resources to strengthen a country's economy.

MARKETS 1.0: Modernizing the Economy

If the geography is unfavorable and the country lacks strong institutions, all the markets in the World cannot change things for the better. Without functioning markets however, no economy can modernize. These are critical, and it is important for developing countries to provide the proper institutions that enable markets to flourish, while also guarding against possible negative market externalities. In what follows, we will describe some of the most important market forces for developing countries.

Trade Specialization

One of the most important lessons in development is that no developing country can make the transition to high-income on its own. Development requires access to large markets, and developing countries simply don't have large enough markets of their own. If they would, they wouldn't be developing countries anymore – they would be already developed. Just to put things into perspective, Low Income countries (with a combined population of around 635 million), consume less than Belgium (with only 11 million people). Developing countries, as defined here, and which combined have around 4.6 billion people, consume less than the US does, with its 0.32 billion people.

In fact, not even developed countries have large enough endogenous markets to power to power their own economies independently. Only the US economy comes close to a self-sufficient market system, but even there full advantage is taken of the benefits provided by trade.

In simple terms, markets are largely equivalent to the middle-class – i.e. the people with the expendable income to buy the goods, services, and ideas produced by developing countries. As countries develop, they do so by enlarging their own middle-class. Without a strong middle-class, a country cannot develop. However, until developing countries develop their own middle-class, they are at the whim of the middle-class in developed countries. Thus, while high-income countries amassed only 16% of the World's population in 2014, they consumed 69% of all the goods and services generated in the World. As a point of comparison, India, with a population of around 1.3 billion, consumed less than Italy, with a population of around 60 million. It is thus clear that without access to the markets of high-income countries, it is quite difficult for developing countries to sustain growth.

The World's Largest Markets, in 2015

	Population		Consumption		
	(in billion)	% of World Population	(in trillion)	% of World Consumption	Consumption per Capita
World	7.26	100%	$55.04	100%	$7,581
United States	0.32	4.4%	$13.77	25.0%	$42,835
European Union	0.51	7.0%	$13.70	24.9%	$26,946
Japan	0.13	1.7%	$4.47	8.1%	$35,242
China	1.37	18.9%	$4.34	7.9%	$3,169
India	1.31	18.1%	$1.49	2.7%	$1,134
The Rest of the World	3.62	49.9%	$17.27	31.4%	$4,768

Data Source: World Bank
Note: Consumption represents Final Consumption Expenditure in Constant 2010 US$

However, to access the markets of high-income countries, developing countries have to produce what the markets in high-income countries are asking for. Consequently, the economy of developing countries develops in tune with the needs of developed countries. They are to a very large extent dependent on developed countries, needing both access to their large markets, and being molded to the appearance of developed countries. If developed countries ask for textiles and cars, that is what developing countries will specialize in.

Of course, it is not enough to just be willing to produce what markets in developed countries are asking for. You need to also have the working force that can produce these goods and services. Developing countries gradually develop such a working force, and they work their way up along the economic food-chain. Basically, the process of economic growth and development presupposes that people get engaged in more and more sophisticated and high-value added activities. In more simple terms, countries develop only to the extent their people develop.

This process of transition to higher value-added activities is nicely evidenced by the way the economies of New EU Member Countries have evolved in recent years. From 1995 to 2015, the structure of Western European exports has remained relatively stable, with around 72% of exports being generated by three sectors: machines (e.g. computers, integrate circuits, cell phones, TVs, video displays, refrigerators), transportation (e.g. cars, vehicle parts, buses, motorcycles, planes, trains), and chemical products (e.g. medicine, cosmetics, cleaning products, pesticides, glue). Central and Eastern European (CEE) countries came out of Communism with an obsolete industrial base, producing a lot of stuff that was not demanded any more by World markets (e.g. Iron Pipes, Ferroalloys, Aluminum, or Hot-Rolled Iron). As these industrial giants went bust, the economy of CEE countries underwent a deep transformation. In a first phase, light industry facilities (e.g. textiles and food processing) absorbed some of the surplus labor force in the economy. Then, as the economy of CEE countries became more and more integrated into the common EU market, it started to look more and more like the economy of Western European countries. In 2014, New EU Member countries exported the same type of products (machines, transportation, and chemical products) as their Western European cousins.

The Economic Transformation of New EU Member Countries

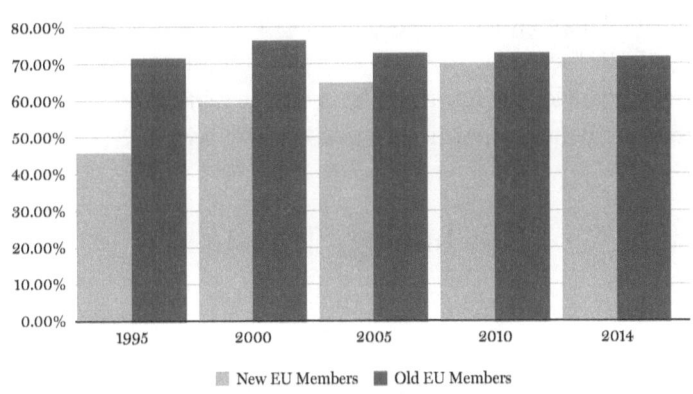

Data Source: MIT Observatory of Economic Complexity
Note: Data refers to exports (in US$) in the following three sectors: machines, transportation, and chemical products. New EU Member Countries include here: Bulgaria, Croatia, Cyprus, the Czech Republic, Estonia, Hungary, Latvia, Lithuania, Malta, Poland, Romania, Slovakia, and Slovenia. Old EU Member countries include: Belgium, Denmark, Finland, Germany, France, Greece, Ireland, Italy, Luxembourg, the Netherlands, Portugal, Spain, Sweden, the UK.

The countries that were most developed at the start of the transition (e.g. Hungary and the Czech Republic), also had an economy that looked more like the economy of Western European countries. The countries that registered the fastest growth rates between 1995 and 2014 (e.g. Romania, Slovakia, Poland) also underwent the most dramatic transformation of their economies. For example, in 1995, Romanian exports amounted to only around $8.6 billion and only 23% of these exports were generated by the three sectors dominant in Western Europe: machines, transportation, and chemical products. By 2014, Romanian exports ballooned to $71.4 billion, and around 46% of exports were generated by these three sectors. In Slovakia, the share grew from 30% in 1995 to 62% in 2014.

The implications for developing countries are quite clear. One, you need to find the biggest market close to you. This will be likely the block you will be doing most of your trade with. Next, figure out what is being consumed by the middle-class in this large market and determine which of those needs you could cover (or the sectors where you can develop a competitive advantage). Lastly, to the extent you have easy access to those markets, start trading and look to move up higher-up the value chain – i.e. strive to trade in more sophisticated goods and services.

Technology Transfers

Moving up the economic value chain is easier said than done for developing countries. To make this transition, you require the technologies that have been developed and refined over decades in high-income countries. Obviously, inventing these technologies from scratch is neither economical nor practical. It makes much more sense to enable a transfer of technologies from developed countries. Such a transfer enables developing countries to make a developmental leap-frog. And the data shows indeed that there has been a dramatic in foreign direct investment (FDI) flows. If in the 1990s, the average yearly flow of FDIs to developing countries was around $75 billion, following 2010, the yearly average jumped to around $550 billion.

We folks from developing countries like to think we are a smart lot. We are not exactly stupid, but neither are we as smart as we think we are. To be able to catch up with developed countries, all of us have to get better at what we do, and many have to start doing other things. The same way we need teachers to show us how to read, write, and reason, so too we need teachers that show us how to operate in a developed economy.

The easiest and most frequent way people in developing countries learn how a developed economy operates, is by working for a foreign company. Consequently, foreign direct investments are absolutely critical for developing countries. They don't only enable the technology transfers that enable developing countries to modernize their economies, but they also enable knowledge transfers that help people in developing countries to beef up their skills and become better at what they do. In addition, foreign companies bring with them easy access to large markets -- i.e. a network of trusted clients, which usually gets built over a long time and based on frequent interactions and the building of trust.

For example, in 2015, there were over 665,000 companies in Romania, which generated cumulated revenues of around 251 billion Euro. Of those companies, the first 100, generated around 27% of all revenues, while only employing around 8% of the people working for Romanian companies. Moreover, 72 of these 100 largest Romanian companies had foreign capital participation.[14]

Mind you that people in Romania, as well as the people in other former Communist countries were not exactly skill-less when they started the transition to a market economy. Quite the contrary. It's just that the things they were good at producing, were not things needed by the large markets of Western Europe – their new major trade partners.

Modernizing the economy requires not only a lot of foreign investments, but also several successive waves of investment. As the Eastern European examples have shown, countries have first exported the types of goods they were already good at producing (e.g. metal products). Then they moved to producing low-value added textiles, then machines, and then cars and car components.

Initially, these foreign direct investments focused primarily on the most developed cities. As the cost of labor in these large cities went up, investors gradually moved to the periphery of cities, and then to further and further locations. As the most dynamic cities in developing countries grow, they also pass a certain threshold when they start to innovate themselves and be less reliant on technology transfers from abroad.

The World Bank looked at 700 dynamic cities from around the globe, to see if there is a certain point when cities become less reliant on manufacturing and move more towards service-intensive and creative industries[15]. Empirical data showed that when cities reach a GDP per Capita of around $20,000, they start making the shift towards innovative and creative industries. This is quite relevant for the governments of developing countries, as it gives them an idea of which cities are most likely to generate the innovations that are required to sustain long-term economic growth.

Migration

Foreign direct investments are only part of the story when it comes to the modernization of the economy. Migration is the other big part of the story. If FDIs enable people to upgrade their skills at home, migration enables them to upgrade their skills abroad. Both approaches have their merits and they usually happen in parallel. However, if FDI upgrades peoples' skills in domains that are required by foreign investors, migration makes it easier for people to upgrade their skills in the areas they are interested in.

As such, migration represents the fastest way to innovation for people from developing countries. Benefits are of course split between the sending country and the host country. For example, although immigrants represent only 13% of the US population, they generate around 33% of all patents, and are 25% of all US Nobel laureates. More than half of all start-ups in Sillicon Valley have at least one cofounder who was born outside the US[16]. Steve Jobs' biological father was a migrant from Syria; Sergey Brin (Google's co-founder) was born in Russia; Pierre Omidyar (the founder of eBay) was born in France, the son of Iranian immigrants; Elon Musk was born in South Africa and grew up in Canada.

Migration is critical for development, but it is a politically and socially loaded issue. Neither sending countries, nor host countries, deal with the issue lightly. The reason the topic is so sensitive are the negative externalities migration comes with. The problem is that these negative externalities are often blown out of proportion. When doctors migrate in high numbers abroad, governments are of course scared this will jeopardize the efficiency and stability of their health-care system. When migrants commit crimes abroad, the blame often goes to entire groups instead the individuals that have done the crimes. It is always easier to blame the proverbial others for what is going wrong in your life.

Migration helps sending countries not only through the knowledge transfers it enables, but also through the capital that gets transferred. For some countries, remittances represent an overwhelming share of their GDP, while for others remittances are a larger and more reliable source of capital inflow than FDI. In 2015, remittances to developing countries amounted to around $200 billion, while FDI to developing countries was around $550 billion.

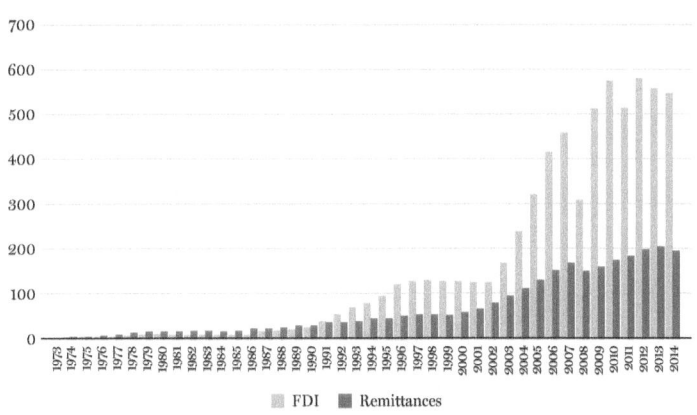

Remittances rival FDI in Developing Countries

Data Source: World Bank
Note: Data on remittances and FDI is in Billion Current US$

Migration also works to push development within developing countries, as people move from lagging regions to leading regions in search of opportunities. This enables the most dynamic cities to develop the critical mass to compete on equal footing with cities in developed countries. This type of migration is also critical for development, as it allows a more efficient allocation of resources. However, it is a dynamic that yet again does not sit well with politicians. But, it is a reality that unfolds regardless of what policy makers do.

DEVELOPED:
How to Invent the Future

"[T]hrough history we see an ironic process [...]: a dialectic whereby the success of a culture develops within itself its own antithesis. The more well-off we become, the less reason we have to look for change, and hence the more exposed we are to outside forces."
MIHALY CSIKSZENTMIHALYI

"Abundance is harder for us to handle than scarcity."
NASSIM TALEB

"We consistently fail to grasp how many ideas remain to be discovered."
PAUL ROMER

Developed countries are understood here as High Income countries (as defined using the World Bank GNI per Capital Atlas methodology) that are non-resource dependent. In 2015, around 1 billion people lived in developed countries. Developed countries usually manage to sustain growth long term, but have growth rates that are lower than those of developing countries. A particularly interesting case is Japan, which on a background of demographic decline and aging, has registered negative growth between 1995 and 2015. The experience of Japan is interesting to analyze, as it may also affect other developed countries with net demographic decline.

One thing to note early on is that while most people think that developed countries have hit the jack pot, they actually have the hardest task of all. Undeveloped countries have a clear mission to unlock their growth potential. Developing countries aim to overcome the middle-income trap. Developed countries, however, often don't have a clear mission – apart from losing their hard earned position in the world hierarchy. They sit on top of the hill, and the way they perform has an impact well beyond their borders. If developed countries do well, the whole World does well. If developed countries enter a crisis, the World does too.

Developed countries represent the large markets that the developing world depends upon for its positive performance.

On the other hand, developed countries also generate the bulk of the innovations needed to push the global economy forward. Innovations require large enough markets, where they can be tested and refined, and it is largely developed countries that have large enough markets for the testing and maturing of innovations. In fact, it is the US that is best equipped to generate and help mature innovations, and we will see in the following sections why.

The funny thing about innovations is you can't anticipate them. Innovations (e.g. the internet) have the power to dramatically change the world we live in, but we don't know what these innovations will be until they are invented and are actually taken-up by markets. And, the burden is to a large extent on developed countries to generate these innovations and to ensure that these innovations make the World a better place.

Undeveloped and developing countries have a clear aim. They have to a large extent to repeat the good lessons developed countries offer, and avoid some of the mistakes developed countries have done. Developed countries however, have to invent tomorrow. And, the only thing we know about tomorrow is that it will be different.

On the other hand, developed countries enjoy a unique advantage. By virtue of the position they enjoy in the World hierarchy, they get to dictate the pace and direction of growth and development for developing and undeveloped countries. This is both a boon and a burden – it comes both with a lot of benefits and a lot of responsibilities. As we will discuss later, it will be very difficult for developing and undeveloped countries to make a significant jump forward without the conscious effort and involvement of developed countries.

Of course, developed countries don't only have to take care of the World as a whole, they also have to take care of themselves. In what follows, we will discuss shortly how geography, institutions, and markets impact the growth and development of developed countries. We will see that social and environmental issues become increasingly important in developed countries, as the distance between the have and have-nots is widening, and as economic progress puts a pressure on nature. Sustainability thus becomes the key feature of development and growth in developed countries. On the one hand, developed countries have to identify the mechanisms to sustain long-term economic growth. On the other hand, they have to ensure that this growth does not create and/or widen social rifts, nor negatively impact the environment.

GEOGRAPHY 2.0: Winning the Lottery Does not Mean Eternal Bliss

Developed countries have already won the geography lottery. Europe has enjoyed an early advantage, which it has fully banked on. The US, not only had a geography favorable for economic growth (amenable for intensive agriculture, and with vast natural resources), but also favorable from a strategic point of view – apart from a few skirmishes with the Brits, the Canadians, the Mexicans, and the Japanese, the US has not carried a major war on its soil. Japan is an island that has managed to use the water around it as a natural moat, for much of its history. Geography has, and continues to favor developed countries. But it also poses its challenges. We will see how.

The Big Periphery

Developed countries are developed. That, most people know. They are however not developed evenly. Some parts are more developed than others. The regional discrepancies are not as large as in developing countries (the standard of living is usually uniformly high across space), but a few areas are responsible for an overwhelming share of economic output. These areas are basically the country's development engines. As we have seen earlier, the 16 largest metropolitan areas in the US generate 50% of national GDP, the primate cities and the secondary cities in the EU generate around 50%-70% of the GDP in their respective countries. Tokyo and Osaka are responsible for 33% of the GDP in Japan. Without these economic growth engines, the economy would shrink dramatically. Research by the Cologne Institute for Economic Research indicates that in most EU countries, the GDP per Capita would decrease dramatically if you would take the capital cities outside the respective countries. Only Germany would do better without Berlin, given that Berlin's economy was underdeveloped when the German reunification took place. Until the reunification, East Berlin was under the centralized planning system of Eastern Germany, while West Berlin was an enclave of Western Germany, which until 1990 was not an attractive location for private investors. While it is the most developed region in the former East Germany, Berlin still has some ways to catch up with the most developed regions in the former Western Germany.

National per Capita GDP without Capital Cities, in selected Developed Countries

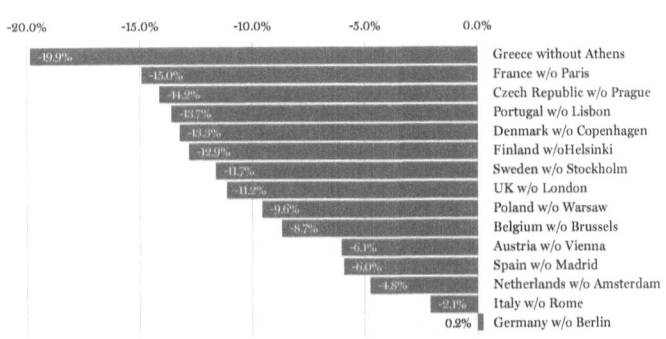

Source: Cologne Institute for Economic Research

The question that begs itself in this situation is: what happens in the rest of the country, outside the largest and most dynamic urban centers? The simple answer is: a lot. Even the less dynamic areas have a higher level of development than most areas in developing countries. They are however performing worse when compared to leading areas.

Consequently, a good deal of public policy and public investments aim to raise the level of development in these less developed areas. In the US, the coasts are more developed than the heartland; in Germany the West is more developed than the East; in France, the East is more developed than the West; in Italy the North is more developed than the South; in the UK, the London Metropolitan Area is more developed than anything else; in Japan, the southern islands are more developed than Hokkaido.

Generally, an overwhelming share of a country's economic output is generated on a relatively small piece of land. Policy makers spend a lot of time, energy, and resources trying to figure out what to do with the rest of the country. This in itself is not a bad thing, but it is important that they heed the lessons of history when trying to develop the Big Periphery.

In "The Siberian Curse", Fiona Hill and Clifford Gaddy from the Brookings Institution, do a brilliant overview of the mistakes done by the Soviet Union leaders, when they undertook the development of the vast Siberian hinterland. Driven partly by military considerations (to protect the vast southern border of the empire) and partly by the need to exploit the vast resources of the Eurasian landmass, Soviet leaders went about creating cities in places where no large communities have naturally taken hold over the years. The reason why Siberia was largely unpopulated when the Soviets started to move people there, is relatively straight forward. The place was and still is too unhospitable for people. When given the option, people do not naturally chose to be there. Neither do businesses.

Following the fall of the Soviet Union, the leaders of Russia were faced with a particular difficult conundrum: what to do with all the cities and settlements in the Siberian expanse. To a large extent, these cities now produce things that the rest of the World does not want to buy. Even if the rest of the World would want to buy those things, the shipping costs of getting them to markets are too prohibitive to make it a profitable or worth-while enterprise. The factories that employ the people living in those cities are to a large extent subsidized from oil and gas revenues, and out-migration from those regions (to dynamic cities like Moscow or St. Petersburg) has been high in recent years.

The Siberian story is of course an extreme one, but it offers a significant array of lessons that are relevant for developed countries today. One of the lessons is that a myopic focus on regions and not on people, most often leads to sub-optimal outcomes. Governments should primarily focus on enabling as many people as possible access to opportunities, rather than trying to create opportunities for people in the places they happen to find themselves at one point. It is much more efficient to enable people to move there where they have the highest probability of achieving their dreams, than trying to create a dream machine for every person in every region. This approach does not of course entail a disappearance of the importance of regions, or a weakening of the concept of regions – it just entails a paradigm shift in how governments develop regional policies.

In Canada, for example, the overwhelming share of the population is clustered in a few metropolitan areas on the Southern border of the country. There is almost nobody living in the cold and inhospitable Northern territories. A similar dynamic can be encountered in Australia, where the hot and dry interior desert remains largely unpopulated.

The Small Peripheries

A common misconception is that poor people and marginalized communities are primarily located in lagging areas. While lagging areas do indeed have a higher share of poor and marginalized people, leading areas tend to have higher absolute numbers. Almost every large city, regardless how developed or dynamic it might be, has one or several pockets of poverty in or around it. Since cities are centers of opportunity, they attract a high number of people, including poor people. Unfortunately, poor and marginalized people cluster together, forming pockets of poverty. They do so for a variety of reasons: lower housing costs, migrant communities that stick together, outmigration of wealthier and more mobile people, or misguided public policies.

One of the toughest challenges for developed countries is dealing with these urban pockets of poverty. And one would think that developed cities have all the instruments required to adequately address this challenge. Cities offer plenty of opportunities for poor people (lots of jobs, easy access to quality education, lots of people to learn from), but somehow these problems persist.

There is no country and almost no city without an impoverished community. There are poor(er) and rich(er) people in almost every country and community, although the difference between the very rich and the very poor varies from place to place.

Poverty is also a relative measure. We define poverty in relation to the wide population. Most often poor people are considered to be those with an income, or consumption below a certain threshold (e.g. below 60% of the national average income). Of course, a poor person in the US is, at least in nominal terms, better off than the majority of people living in undeveloped and developing countries. But, the cost of living in the US is also very high. Thus, the US

Bureau of Labor Statistics has identified that the bottom 30% on the income scale in the US, had average annual earnings of around $14,000, but spent around $25,000 yearly – primarily on basic needs, like food, housing, and transportation (78% of poor people's income alone went to housing; 28% went to food; and, 28% to transportation). Obviously, the difference between what they earned and what they spent indicates that these poor are to a large extent dependent on Government social programs, like social housing programs, food stamps, and/or transport subsidies.

Consequently, poor people have no/little expandable income that they can spend on up-keeping their house and their neighborhood, so they tend to live in places with a lower standard of living. In the US, schools are unfortunately funded from the taxes generated in their respective school districts, so the quality of education in poor neighborhoods tends to suffer. In essence, a vicious circle is created, with people in poor neighborhoods often getting a bad education, which lowers their chance to rise out of poverty.

Poverty is also a deeply spatial issue. Your income may afford you a good standard of living in a remote village and a very poor standard of living in a booming city. The Atlantic has looked at income gaps in Silicon Valley and saw that the ever growing incomes of IT specialists in the Valley drive up living costs in the area and price-out many other professionals, like teachers.[17] Similarly, the New York Times has done an analysis that indicates that the rising housing costs in Silicon Valley push many people, which would otherwise have a decent living on their salary in other parts of the US, into homelessness.[18] Since Silicon Valley has a large number of high earning individuals who can afford to pay high rents, the cost of living for everybody else goes up. So, the teachers, the people who maw the lawns, the barbers, the sale clerks, the cleaning people, and everybody else providing a service that would earn them a living wage somewhere else, find themselves struggling in a booming area.

Identifying targeted solutions for dealing with these pockets of poverty should be a priority for public authorities. Without the proper social inclusion measures, problems in poor and marginalized communities tend to grow over time, generating not only social problems, but also deep economic problems. Humanity's great empires have almost all fallen victim to internal strife and civil unrest, rather than crumbling in the face of external threats.

Developed countries today will not be challenged economically by the emergence of more global players (e.g. China or India). Quite the contrary – more developed countries mean a larger global market and more trade for the existent developed countries (i.e. everybody will be better off). They can however corrode from within if they don't efficiently and timely address social problems.

Clusters

Developed countries decide the pace and direction of development for the rest of the World. They are responsible for an overwhelming share of innovations that change the way the economy operates. These innovations however are rarely produced by lone geniuses. They almost always require the interaction and exchange of ideas between several smart people. In "The Geography of Genius", Eric Weiner shows how Humanity's evolution has been defined by smart people that have clustered together in certain places and have produced a joint body of work that made society as a whole better.

Much of the work of the Greek classics was produced in less than 100 years in Ancient Athens. Florence gave the World banking and the Renaissance. Detroit made us more mobile. Los Angeles gave us entertainment. And, Silicon Valley has given us the computer and has helped the spread of the internet. These clusters of smart people are essential for innovation.

The literature on clusters is quite rich, but has not evolved much more beyond the key ideas put down by Alfred Marshall in "The Principle of Economics". In essence, people move to places with a higher concentration of firms that work in their area of expertise, and they do this for obvious reasons. More companies where they can work means more options, the opportunity for a more competitive environment, and more competitive salaries. Clusters also have a higher number of people with similar skills, and as such offer more opportunities for professional and personal growth. The more people with similar skills you have around you, the more likely you are to find people you can learn new tricks from. In Marshall's own words:

> The mysteries of the trade become no mysteries; but are as it were in the air, and children learn many of them unconsciously. Good work is rightly appreciated, inventions and improvements in machinery, in process and the general organization of the business have their merits promptly discussed: if one man starts a new idea, it is taken up by others and combined with suggestions of their own; and thus it becomes the source of further new ideas.

For companies, the decision to cluster together with similar companies may seem counterintuitive. It is not. As discussed earlier, companies move closer to similar companies because they can thus take advantage of a larger and more competitive labor pool, they can more easily adopt the latest developments in the field, and they are forced to stay competitive. The companies that are not capable to continually innovate, exit the market sooner or later.

Of course, clusters look easier to put together on paper than in practice. Virtually every developing and developed country has tried, or has pondered trying to create its own Silicon Valley. None has managed this feat however – not, at least, on the scale of the original.

The reason world changing clusters are rare, has more to do with pure luck than purposeful engineering. Ingenuity and innovation cannot be concocted in a lab. Karl Popper brilliantly observed that it is impossible to predict the future because we don't know what technologies and innovations will define the World of tomorrow. If we would know, we would create these new technologies today, and not wait until some point in the future. Of the over 7 billion people on the planet, it is hard to estimate how many will generate World changing ideas – although the odds are better than a 100 years ago. Also, it is hard to estimate how many of these World changing ideas become marketable. What we know however is that World changing ideas are often generated by clusters of smart people. Moreover, innovations generated in such clusters have a higher likelihood of becoming marketable. The sheer number of experts in a cluster enables an innovation a faster path from concept to actual implementation, as input and feed-back can be collected from several sides.

INSTITUTIONS 2.0:
The Innovative State

The price we pay for independence from the whims of nature is dependence on our societies and civilizations. The more sophisticated a given society is as a whole, the less its members are able to survive on their own as individuals, without society.
TOMAS SEDLACEK

A party of order or stability, and a party of progress or reform, are both necessary elements of a healthy state of political life.
JOHN STUART MILL

Developed countries have mature and stable institutions. Following the Second World War, no developed country has seen an autocratic government come to power, although most have had to deal with different crisis situations. This relative stability was ensured through a system of national and international institutions that quickly addressed slippages and kinks in the system. Another mechanism was trade. The World is so interconnected now, and individual economies are so dependent on each other that it is almost impossible to remove yourself from this system, lest you want your economy to go belly-up. These national and international checks-and-balance mechanisms are continuously at work to address challenges and problems that might appear.

For an economy to grow and develop, it needs to have solid institutions at its foundation. As the economy grows though, it continuously strengthens these institutions, as a larger economy is a more inter-connected economy, and an inter-connected economy lowers the chance of actions that may be destabilizing. In essence, a growing economy creates its own virtuous cycle.

This does not mean however that governments of developed countries should not invest in strengthening their institutions – quite the contrary! Institutions play a role even in situations where markets seem to be all powerful. Political battles in developed countries are fought between those that would want less government intervention and those that want more – with the obvious variations across the globe. In the US, the importance of markets is a subject of almost every political campaign. In most Western European countries and in Japan, the need for government intervention is almost taken for granted.

In what follows, we will discuss three key institutions that are critical for developed countries, no matter where they happen to find themselves on a political spectrum.

Fixing the Failures of Markets

Developed countries develop not only the innovations that change the World, they also create the institutions that help address the externalities created by these innovations. The advent of the internet gave birth to a sleuth of cyber-security institutions; the advent of the car triggered the birth of the traffic police; the advent of the TV made media monitoring institutions necessary.

Governments are unfortunately not always quick to create the institutions that help address larger or smaller market slip-ups. The advent of the Industrial Revolution caught most governments off-guard. Without the proper rules and regulations in place, the first industrialists had nothing but market signals to guide their decisions. Thus, if one factory owner decided to have his workers do 16 hour shifts, as a way of cutting down costs, other industrialists would have to, sooner or later, follow suit. And many did indeed. Those that did not, had a higher likelihood of going bankrupt.

This logic applies time and time again in almost every facet of our life. In "The Darwin Economy", the brilliant Robert Frank gives a relevant example from the world of hockey. Thus, until helmets have been made mandatory for all hockey players, most players preferred to play without one, although this led to a dramatically higher number of head injuries. Although most players were conscious that without a helmet they would be more susceptible to a head injury, they chose not to wear helmets because: 1) a helmet negatively affected their agility on the ice; and 2) it does not look cool (players felt more macho without a helmet than with one). Surprisingly, when helmets were made mandatory for all, the measure was welcomed by a vast majority of hockey players. Left on their own (i.e. subject to market dynamics), hockey players widely chose not to wear a helmet. However, when helmets were made mandatory for everyone, the measure was widely welcomed. In essence, this is what institutions do: identify a fix to a market failure (i.e. intervene in cases where market outcomes are not ideal).

When Karl Marx talked about the failures of capitalism, he should have actually talked about the failure of Government to find the proper fixes to negative market externalities. Marx developed much of his work in a time when governments understood too little about the inner workings of market systems, and were too slow to respond to market slip-ups.

It took quite some time for the 8-hour day to be implemented and thus regulate the abuses of many factory owners. Since then, a sleuth of other institutions have been created to address market inefficiencies (e.g. the minimum wage, unemployment benefits, life-long training institutions).

As economies evolve and become more complex, government have to remain on their toes. The Global Crisis of 2008 made clear the need for better regulation of complex financial instruments. The advent of the computer and the internet opened the way for the reform and modernization of public administration systems. The ever-evolving needs of markets require a continuous reform of the education system, to ensure market needs are better met.

Most importantly however, institutions should guard that power in a system does not get concentrated in too few hands (either private or public). Whenever that happens, there is the possibility for a system failure. And indeed, whenever the developing world faced a major crisis, it did so because of a market failure – e.g. because the financial markets derailed as a consequence of the decisions taken by a handful of players; or, energy markets have caused an economic slowdown, because similarly, a few players took the wrong decisions.

Governments of developed countries, particularly the US Government, hide behind principles of free market capitalism to allow the private sector to misbehave. Such a lax attitude almost always ends up bad, and usually a crisis comes to reset the system. In fact, in many cases, it is the crises that trigger much needed change. One could thus argue that crises are actually a positive thing, as they force the creation of much needed institutions.

The capacity of developed countries to create the institutions required for a proper management of market economies, does not only imply an inward responsibility, but an outward one as well. The failure of developed countries to create such institutions can have negative repercussions for the World as a whole.

Social Equity

Every system, regardless if it's capitalism, socialism, communism, or pure anarchy, is divided between the haves and have-nots. This is basically part of the entropy of a system, and a key feature of all of nature's organisms – everything grows, and once they stop growing, they eventually die. To remain relevant, a system has to sustain growth – otherwise, it sooner or later loses relevance and dies (a lesson all Communist systems learned the hard way). When a system grows, it never does so evenly – there will always be some elements that will grow faster than the rest. It's simply how the World and the Universe works. If the Universe were made of parts that are the same and grow at the same rate, it would basically be a soup of basic elements, not an intricate system of galaxies, solar systems, and planets. Variation is by its definition the essence of life, and one could not imagine a dynamic system without variation.

The World Bank has computed the Gini Coefficient (a measure of inequality that looks at the gap between the high and the low earners) for 101 countries, to see where inequality posed the greatest challenges[19]. Of course the measure showed that inequality is encountered everywhere, although developed countries tend to be more equitable than developing and undeveloped countries. All of the developed countries scored below the Average Gini value for the sample (which is good), with two exceptions – the US and Uruguay. Of the 56 countries that scored below the average value, 38 were from Europe, indicating the presence of institutions and social norms that favor more social equality.

However, regardless if the inequalities are larger or smaller, when some parts of the system grow faster that the rest, a tension in the system is created. If this tension is not addressed, the system can come undone. Thomas Piketty brilliantly discusses this issue in "Capital in the Twenty-First Century". He indicates that in developed countries, where demographic decline depresses growth rates, returns above a country's economic average growth rate can primarily be generated by those who have the capital – i.e. the wealthy. He shows that if left un-checked, those who control the capital will amass more and more resources, to the detriment of the poor and the middle-class. Think of it this way. If an economy grows at an average of 1% yearly, as many developed countries do, it is hard to raise the wages of most people faster than this growth rate – it would not be sustainable. However, those that control the capital find ways to generate returns in excess of 1%, by the simple fact that they control the capital (i.e. they can purchase more real estate, can invest large sums of money in the most profitable businesses, and have the proper funds required by the most profitable financial instruments). However, if the revenues of most people grow slower than over-all economic growth, while the revenues of the rich grow faster, over time, more and more resources will eventually be concentrated in fewer and fewer hands. Empirical evidence Piketty has collected from several developed countries indicates that this is in fact happening currently.

Over the long term, such a dynamic is not sustainable. The middle-class is the bedrock of a market economy. Without an increase in prosperity for the middle-class, the well-off will eventually stand to suffer too. Rich people are simply too few in numbers to enable an economy to keep growing – they simply can't consume at a fast enough rate.

Industrialist and hard-core capitalist Henry Ford instinctively understood the importance of a large and dynamic middle-class. He offered his workers some of the highest salaries in the industry because he wanted them to afford the cars they helped produce. Ford understood that a company cannot grow if the market it targets includes only a handful of people.

However, taking care of the middle-class is not enough. Developed countries need to also pay attention to their poor. If you are born in a poor family and poor community, the odds are basically stacked against you. Chances are that you will have parents (often only one parent) struggling to make ends meet, you are likely to get a subpar education, and your upward mobility will not be exactly great. This is where public institutions should come in, and stack the odds in your favor.

We are not born equal. That is just the harsh reality. But, the fact that we are not born equal should not mean that we cannot have the same start in life. It is absolutely critical for all governments (although the task is somewhat easier for developed countries), to ensure that all of their citizens have the same start in life. This means that regardless of your condition, you should have access to quality education and healthcare, you should not go hungry for even a day, you should have easy access to knowledge, culture and art, and you should have it easy to reach opportunities.

Paying attention to the needs of the middle-class and the poor is simply good politics and good policy. An economy cannot sustain growth without a strong middle-class, and a society cannot stay healthy if a significant share of the population lives in poverty.

Climate Change

Climate change is a powerful force. I don't think you need Al Gore to convince you of that. We can see the effects of climate change with every passing year. Developed countries are responsible for a significant share of the mess we're in, so it is imperative that they come up with adequate solutions.

Part of the problem is the explosive growth of population numbers. According to estimates of Angus Maddison, there were around 230 million of us in 1 AD. By 1700, our numbers only went up to around 600 million, and to 1 billion by 1870. Fast-forward 150 years later, and our numbers jumped to over 7 billion – and our numbers continue to grow fast. This dramatic surge in population numbers will of course put a strain on the planet. However, the bulk of the population growth is now generated by undeveloped and developing countries. Developed countries have a relatively flat population growth rate, and most keep up their numbers through in-migration.

The other part of the problem is industrialization. We now have power plants, factories, millions of cars, and billions of households spewing bad stuff into the air, water, and soil. On top of it, we have dramatically cut the forests that could help mitigate the negative climate effects of industrialization. Worse-over, as undeveloped and developing countries start to modernize, these negative effects get compounded. In China alone, the number of new registered cars has grown from 4 million in 2005 to 21 million in 2015. From 1990 to 2015, China has almost doubled its greenhouse gas emissions, and now is the largest emitter of such gasses, overtaking even the US.[20] In simple terms, the situation is bad and so far it is only getting worse.

Figuring out a solution to the problem cannot be done without the involvement of developed countries and without the full participation of developing countries. Developed countries banked on good geography in their initial development phase. Climate change can wipe that advantage away. If current trends continue, there is a good chance that some cities, and even significant parts of countries will disappear, while other spots will become too inhospitable for living.

Creating the institutions and mechanisms that will address climate change, requires the concerted effort of developed countries, and it has to have a global focus. Climate does not recognize any boundaries. This will require lots of resources, lots of energy, and lots of time, and it is an area of public policy that no developed country can afford to ignore.

The fight against climate change does not have to be only about the environment – it can also be good economics. Contrary to popular belief, public institutions play a significant role in economic development. If public institutions would not build and maintain roads, then car producers would not have a raison d'etre. If governments did not build an energy infrastructure, many companies would not be able to operate. If the US military would not have invested in ARPANET, it is possible we would not have had the internet today. Similarly, governments could help develop a climate change infrastructure, and thus help the emergence and growth of entire private sectors. One could imagine a burgeoning of solar panel producers, of electric car producers, of self-powered appliances, or of energy efficient construction companies.

Climate change is here and it's here to stay. It's likely to be one of the major challenges in coming years, for institutions from developed countries. Of course, the more developing countries that make the transition to developed countries, the more people that will be working on solutions to climate change challenges, and the higher the likelihood of identifying more and better solutions.

MARKETS 2.0:
The Bedrock of the Economy

The best solution does not always come from a Nobel laureate at Harvard. It just might turn out that some kid in Romania has got a better idea worth pursuing.
ALPHEUS BINGHAM

Every leap forward is preceded by an exposure to foreign ideas.
ERIC WEINER

Markets form the bedrock of the economy of developed states. Developed countries already enjoy a favorable geography (they are overwhelmingly situated in the Northern hemisphere, between the 30^0 and 60^0 parallel), they already have strong institutions, so their economies are primarily driven by market forces.

One of the key challenges developed countries face are appropriate responses to market failures. Markets are not perfect. They represent the sum of individual choices we make, and this sum is not always positive. When markets backfire, it is important to have the proper institutions in place to generate the proper responses.

In addition to responding to market failures, developed countries should also attempt to create the proper enabling conditions for innovation – i.e. it should be easier for people to innovate and bring their innovations to market.

In what follows, we will discuss three major ways markets fire and backfire in developed countries.

Demography

The Atlantic puts out some of the best and most insightful articles of any magazine I've read. One article I have read a while ago (to my great shame, I forgot the name of the author and the title of the article) discusses an interesting dynamic in developed countries, and now increasingly in developing countries. As the population becomes more educated, more mobile, and more productive, it also becomes less inclined to make a lot of babies. Throughout the developed and developing world, fertility rates have dropped well below replacement level, leading not only to population decline, but also to the aging of the population. World Bank Indicators database indicates that High Income countries have a fertility rate of around 1.7 (i.e. 1.7 babies born on average per woman) – down from 3.0 in 1960. In fact, fertility rates have dropped below replacement level (i.e. 2.1) in 1977. In the European Union, fertility rates have dropped to 1.5, in Japan to 1.4, and in South Korea to 1.2 – the lowest value registered Worldwide.

As women have become more emancipated (in most developed countries, there are now more women in the labor force than men), as they have become more upwardly mobile, and having adapted much better than men to a service based economy, they have also changed their priorities in life. Women now want more than just being an appendage to a man. They want to live out their youth to the fullest and have a professional career. As such, they marry much later in life and have fewer kids.

The decline is much more pronounced for the middle-class than for the poor, and this has deep repercussions for the economies of developed countries. When the middle-class is shrinking, it means that markets are also shrinking, and when markets are shrinking it is hard to keep the economy on a growth trajectory. In many respects, the Crisis of 2008 is a direct result of the shrinking of markets in developed countries, and it may be a precursor to a more prolonged struggle.

When their middle-class is shrinking, developed countries have basically two major options to enlarge their markets: 1) to grow internal markets by encouraging in-migration (the US, Germany, Canada, and Australia actively do that); 2) to try to tap additional markets in the developing world. The EU strategy is uniquely powerful from this point of view, as it not only helps New Member Countries to develop, but by helping them to develop, they also grow the markets for all EU countries.

There are few sustainable interventions that stem however the decline of the middle-class in developed countries. Even generous maternity leave packages for young parents, of the kind the French Government offers, cannot sustain the growth of the middle-class over the long-term. Raising three kids, for example, is a difficult and testing endeavor when you also have a full-time job. In essence, as the economy becomes more productive, it also becomes less fertile.

From one point of view, this dynamic is positive and it represents a market response to the Malthus over-population problem (Malthus, posited in 1798 that the World population will grow exponentially, to eventually reach unsustainable levels). On the other hand the dynamic is negative because of the entropy of systems. When a system enters a phase of decline, there is usually no other way forward but down.

Developed countries have to identify ways to operate in this new reality and determine what solutions they are ready to employ (e.g. in-migration or tapping new markets) to counter the negative trend.

Large Unified Markets for Innovations

Without innovations, developed economies cannot sustain long-term growth. However, innovations require a number of enabling conditions – a large unified market being one of them. Innovations are rarely "pure creations", thought by some lone genius and taken over willingly by markets. Almost every innovation is subject to a longer or shorter trial period, until it reaches a level of maturity that either enables it to enter markets or to exit them altogether.

A large market for testing innovations can both shorten the trial period of an innovation (large markets also contain more early adopters) and increase the chance for improvement (as there are more people that can provide feed-back and useful inputs).

At this point, the US has the largest unified market for testing innovations. The EU is the largest trade block, and is indeed the largest global market for goods, but it is not the largest market for services. Due to language barriers, cultural differences, the lack of a unified patent system, and the lack of an official lingua franca (e.g. English), ideas and knowledge cannot flow freely throughout the EU. This is one of the reasons why the US is better at generating innovations than the EU is. Its more competitive higher education system is another reason. Of the 50 top World universities in the Shanghai University Ranking, 33 are from the US).

I remember the days when Apple introduced the first iPod. I was at Cornell and I could easily identify the people with iPods by their distinctive white earbuds. Apple purposefully targeted college campuses in the US, as the students at these colleges were the middle-class of tomorrow, and potential future clients. To entice students to buy Apple products, these were offered at a steep discount. Furthermore, the white earbuds were a brilliant marketing gimmick. College students are both early adopters and trend-setters. Thus, they helped to dramatically raise the popularity of the iPod among other population groups. Even I, not exactly a fan of Apple products, eventually ended up with an iPod Shuffle.

Such a marketing strategy and product placement, would be hard to be put into practice, or achieve the same level of success, within the network of universities in the EU.

To innovate more, developed countries should integrate their markets even more. Moreover, they should start using a lingua franca for innovations. If an article or a patent have to be translated first (with attention paid to the proper equivalents to technical jargon), for an idea to be shared and circulated, there is a lower likelihood of this idea ever reaching a wide audience.

Ultimately, a transition should be made towards global markets for innovations. Given that the best innovations have a global impact, but are primarily incubated in developed countries, it is imperative that people from the developing world have a say in how the innovations that will change their life will look like. The more people innovate or are involved in improving innovations, the better off the World as a whole will be.

Creative Destruction and Scalability

In practice, inventions rarely run late. They turn up at just the moment in history when it makes most sense that they do so.
MATT RIDLEY

Joseph Schumpeter, a brilliant Austrian economist, introduced the concept of "creative destruction" to describe the process through which disruptive innovations often destroy other products, or entire sectors. Cars made horse drawn-carriages obsolete; cellphones made land-lines obsolete; the cassette made LPs obsolete, then CDs made cassettes obsolete, and the internet and digital music players made CDs obsolete. I now have a music library that includes the LPs my father collected, the cassettes I collected as a kid in post-Communist Romania, the CDs I collected while in the US, and the digital music I now collect.

Innovations are disruptive, and some, are very disruptive. Consequently, both policy makers and private companies view innovations with mixed feelings. On the one hand, innovations are welcomed because they are essential to economic progress. On the other hand, they are viewed with circumspection, because of the unexpected negative side-effects they can generate. Just think how the leadership at Nokia, and the Finish Government, which openly and pro-actively encourages innovation, reacted when smart-phones virtually wiped out regular cell-phones, and forced Nokia to re-think it business model.

Innovations that are produced in rapid succession can also generate negative side-effects for the companies that produce them. For example, Intel, in an attempt to stay ahead of the competition, may put on the market a new and more powerful chip, before the previous version of the chip had a chance to reach its entire potential market. This, of course, eats its profit margin, but the overall market outcomes are positive (you get to buy a more powerful chip and maybe do work you wouldn't be able to do with a less powerful chip – e.g. digitally animated films were made possible by computers with a stronger computing power).

For a large unified market like that of the US, creative destruction is an easier pill to swallow. For the common EU market however, this is a less appealing prospect. The problem is that a disruptive innovation generated in one country can lead to the disappearance of a sector in a different country. Currently, much of what the EU innovates are marginal additions on existent products, in established fields (e.g. car manufacturing).

However, no matter how difficult creative destruction is to deal with, it is an inherent part of economic progress – a painful process, but a necessary one nonetheless. By better dealing with the side-effects of innovation, developed countries can ensure that innovations appear with a higher frequency.

The trick is to always replace a lower value-added sector with a higher value-added one. Basically, creative destruction should push the economy upward, not downward. In this sense, it is critical to encourage the development of sectors with high scalability potential. For example, if you produce laptops, for each unit you produce, you have a set of upfront costs, and you can sell it only once, However, if you produce a hit song, the upfront costs for producing the song only go up to the point the song is finished. The song can however be sold virtually endlessly to generations of people.

The tiny country of Iceland, with a population of around 300,000, has given us at least two bands of World renown (one of which I like, and have actually bought all of their albums). On the other hand, I know no band from China, a country with a population of 1.3 billion – the largest country in the World. In essence, a handful of rock-stars can generate larger revenues than an entire factory, with minimal upfront costs.

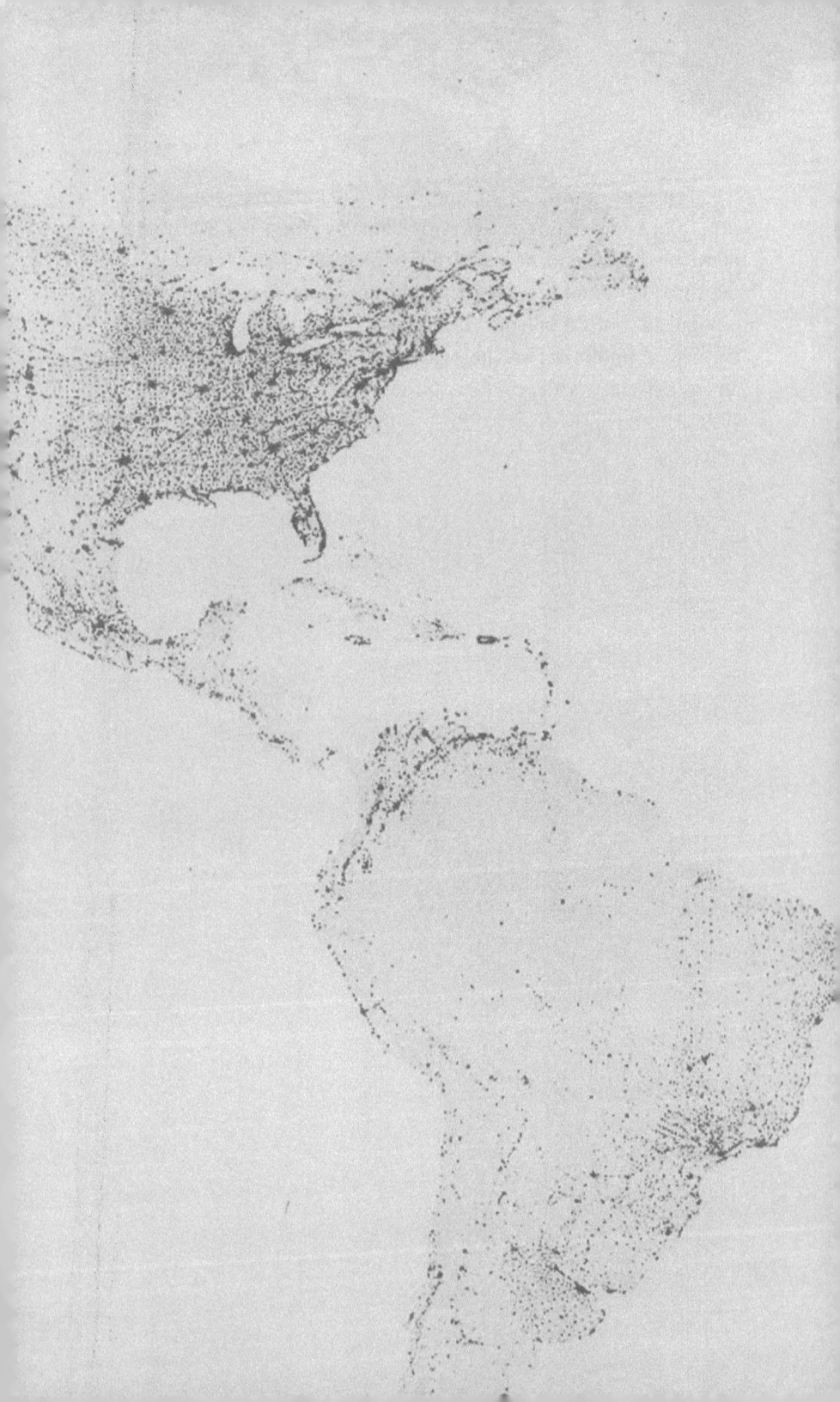

RECOMMENDATIONS
What to Do and What Not to Do to Grow and Develop

> *Don't tell me what. I know what. Tell me how.*
> MICHAEL BARBER

Simply knowing what are some of the factors that influence growth and development is of course only half the story. It is important to also determine what can pro-actively be done to catalyze and encourage the process. This obviously is easier said than done. Generations of policy makers, academics, and a motley assembly of smart people have tried to find the golden chalice of growth and development. They haven't found it, and neither did I. There are however some clues that can bring us closer to it.

One of the most important things to note is that sometimes, the best thing one could do, is to do nothing. Markets have their own logic, and outside intervention can often harm a finely tuned system. At least that is what classics like Friedrich Hayek or some of the bright minds of today, like Matt Ridley, think.

Others, like Douglas North or Daron Acemoglu, claim that strong institutions form the bedrock of growth and development. Institutions are of course critical, and their effectiveness reflects the level of sophistication of that respective country. In an ideal world, institutions should not negatively affect markets, but rather try to buttress positive market dynamics while addressing negative market externalities.

Still others, like Jared Diamond or Paul Krugman, believe geography has played a crucial role in the growth and development game, and continue to do so today.

As we have seen so far, geography, institutions, and markets are all critical for growth and development – although for different countries and communities, some are more important than others. We have seen that geography played a critical role in determining what regions of the World got an early start and managed to pull ahead. We have seen that war and conflict have been critical in giving birth to the first institutions. Europeans, being a heterogeneous group of people, more or less in a continuous state of warfare, have managed to develop better and more efficient weapons and ships, which they have used to extract value from other places. Having access to the vast resources of the World, European countries managed to pull ahead of the rest of the pack. At the time of the Industrial Revolution, the British Empire spanned every continent of the Earth, supplying the Island with bounty all the way from India to the Americas. This early advantage was solidified through the creation of strong institutions that guarded (more than in other places) individual freedom and the free hand of the market. These institutions were then exported to some of the new colonies, which, when coupled with bountiful resources, enabled those new colonies to flourish too.

Another thing we discussed in the previous chapters is the unevenness that defines growth and development – that defines in fact everything about our universe. One could say that unevenness is a key characteristic of life (it is all around us) and it is a definitive feature and intrinsic dynamic of growth and development. The data clearly shows that the World economy has only grown as fast as the World population. It is in fact population growth that has driven the growth of the economy. However, the growth of the economy has been uneven, with some groups becoming more astute at generating goods and services that many around the World were willing to purchase. More often than not, these groups are clustered in large cities, and it is these cities that are responsible for an overwhelming share of what the Global Economy generates. In essence, while the World Economy has not managed to outpace population growth, some groups of people are more productive than others, and some places are wealthier than others. Unevenness is a key characteristic of growth and development and it will continue to be so.

The next sections will focus on what can be done to help countries along the growth and development path. Initially we will discuss a number of broad themes, which apply to almost any a country, and then we will move to a set of more targeted recommendations for undeveloped, developing, and developed countries.

TOWARDS A DEVELOPED WORLD

Development is neither quick nor easy. It can't be done **by** someone **for** someone. And, it will not be sustainable unless the entire population is engaged. In what follows, I will talk about some of the ingredients required to have sustainable development and growth. As opposed to the previous section, I will not order the discussion around the three main enablers/disablers (geography, institutions, markets), but rather focus first on the issues that I consider to be most important. Inevitably, given that interventions are about what people can actually do (not about the cold rigidity of geography, or the markets with a mind of their own), the discussion will focus more on a number of key institutions and ways in which these can be strengthened.

People and the Pursuit of Happiness

I am a big fan of the US. After living there for 10 years, I am convinced the US is at this moment the greatest country in the World. Don't freak out though – I'm not doing this to get a Green Card (I could have, but chose not to). I genuinely think the US has a lot of lessons to offer to the rest of the World. My heart and my future are in Romania (or so I think now), but my education, both academic and professional, was completed on American soil.

One thing that I like about the US is that they got things right early on. There is one sentence in the 1776 Declaration of Independence that I think should serve as inspiration for every country around the World:

> *"We hold these truths to be sacred and undeniable; that all men are created equal and independent; that from equal creation they derive rights inherent and inalienable,*

> *among which are the preservation of life and liberty and the pursuit of happiness. That to secure these rights, Governments are instituted among Men, deriving their just powers from the consent of the governed"*

Brilliant stuff! Of course, when this line was written, slavery was still going strong in the US and women were only allowed to vote starting with 1920 (although individual US states established women's suffrage as early as 1896). However, the key principle that the Declaration of Independence underscored (that of people's right to life, liberty, and the pursuit of happiness) is still relevant today, and it would be hard to write a line that defines in a better way this basic axiom of growth and development. It is principles like this that have enabled the US to play a strong role internationally. As Joseph Nye rightly observed, the US is much more efficient as an international player when it uses its soft power, rather than when it uses its hard power.

A country that fails to build its economy on this basic principle, has failed from the start. If you happen to live in a country that does not ensure this basic right, you better start cooking a revolution. Democracy is a pre-requisite for a functioning market economy. If you don't have a real, functioning democracy in place, you may well give up trying to come up with solutions for making your economy work. It's the hard truth and that's all there is to it.

Why Democracy is Good for a Country

> *"Democracy can be defined as the willingness to fight, to the last drop of blood, for your right to disagree with me."*
> ION RATIU, during Romania's first televised presidential debates, in 1990

The amount of ink and brain power spent on explaining why democracy is good, can fill an entire library. I won't be able to do justice to this essential concept here. In "Development as Freedom", Nobel Prize Laureate Amartya Sen provides maybe the best defense of democracy. He indicates that no truly democratic country has seen its people die from famine – it is usually autocratic governments that fail to respond adequately to crises, focusing more on preserving the interests of the few, against the needs of the many.

However, if Amartya Sen's argument is not potent enough for you, let me propose a short thinking exercise. Let's say you are the chief of a tribe 100,000 years ago, at a time when most tribes had less than 150 people, and all had similar access to food and resources. The chief of one of those other tribes is a particularly nasty fellow and he starts a violent campaign of territory expansion and resource grabbing, entering in direct conflict with other tribes. You know that sooner or later, you will be next. Given that your tribe is smaller than that of the conquering tribe, what are your chances to defeat the bigger guy? Do you have better odds if all your people think of nifty strategy of defense, or will you be better off, if you are the only one taking the decisions?

Now, picture yourself in today's world, where wars are not fought with weapons anymore (well, technically they are still fought with weapons, but bear with me), but with ideas, and where the big tribes are the developed countries – the already established centers of power. What are your chances of competing with these guys? Are you better off if you alone dream up the solutions, or are you better off if everybody is doing it.

The Soviet Union learned this lesson the hard way. It lost the Cold War not because it did not have bigger weapons (it rivaled the US in almost every aspect of military technology), it lost it because it did not have blue jeans. In the Soviet Union, the leadership of the Communist Party set the priorities, and the arms race was one of their chief priorities. In the US however, people chose for themselves what to focus on – and that was blue jeans and rock n' roll. Funny enough, that is what the rest of the world wanted too, including people in the Soviet Union. Now, if you happened to live through those times, remember what you craved more – Russian rockets and tanks, or US blue jeans and Chuck Norris movies.

For me and the group of kids I grew up with, Chuck Norris beat Gorbatchev every day of the week, and twice on Sunday.

The US has fought the Cold War, directly, indirectly, and subliminally with its entire population. The Soviet Union assigned the task to a group of smart people. We know who won in the end.

Now, as anyone who has tried to sustain a democratic system in an undeveloped or developing country knows, this is not an easy task. Development takes time, and you need more than a 4-year mandate to show clear results. People get antsy, impatient, and disenchanted with the failures of democratically elected governments to bring about the positive changes they were hoping for. As such, they become easier pray for autocratic and/or populist regimes, which promise a tough stance on key issues and results that people can see quickly. And indeed, autocratic regimes do deliver, at least in the short and medium term. However, development is not a sprint, but a marathon, and autocratic governments seldom manage to finish the long run – they simply don't have enough runners to do it.

Keeping a democracy going is tough, but without a sustainable democratic system in place, there are really no hopes for sustained economic growth and development. While there are countries that have managed to sustain impressive growth rates over long periods of time without a true democratic system in place, none has managed to also stay at the technological frontier and dictate the growth path for the rest of the World. You need your entire population to fight to make your country and the World a better place, not just an enlightened elite.

An Economy is the Sum of Its People

An economy is only as developed as its people are. You may have enlightened leaders, you may have productive companies, but if you don't have strong individuals, you cannot sustain economic growth over the long term. Bill Easterly rightly indicates that "free individuals with political and economic rights [...] make up a remarkably successful problem-solving system".

Enlightened leaders are usually most effective in times of crisis, when they are faced primarily with binary, black-or-white decisions. In times of peace or economic expansion, they are just as clueless as the rest of us. An economy functioning in times of peace, is predicated on the decisions taken by a vast myriad of people, and it is impossible to manage all of those decisions. The best you can do as a leader in such situations is to ensure that someone's pursuit of happiness does not negatively affect someone else's chance to pursue their own happiness.

Similarly, private companies come and go. Some build a legacy that holds for centuries. Most go bankrupt eventually and make room for other companies. This is a natural and much needed process, which mimics natural evolution, but at a much faster pace.

The one thing that doesn't move when governments or companies come and go, is YOU. Private and public institutions may disappear, but you don't (OK, eventually you do, but you get the point). You form the foundation of your economy and society. An economy will only be as strong as you and your peers are.

The Good Big Brother

Becoming a developed country is not an easy feat. As we discussed earlier in the book, developed countries have benefited from favorable geography, have developed strong institutions early on (i.e. "non-extractive institutions" in the parlance of Acemoglu and Robinson), and have managed to benefit from positive market dynamics, while addressing negative market dynamics. Western European countries and the US stand out as the early good performers, with Western Europe taking advantage of a vast array of colonies, and the US taking advantage of its vast territory and resources, and its trade relations with Europe.

Virtually every country that has managed to overcome the middle-income trap has depended to a lesser or greater degree on the markets of the US and Western Europe. As South Korea, Taiwan, Singapore, and Hong Kong developed, they relied to an overwhelming extent on their favored trade relations with Western markets – particularly that of the US, the UK, and Japan. This opening of Western markets to South-East Asian goods had both geo-strategic considerations (as a way of securing friendly allies in the region), and economic considerations (taking advantage of the cheap labor in the region). In recent years, China has of course been one of the largest markets these countries depend on for their continued growth and development.

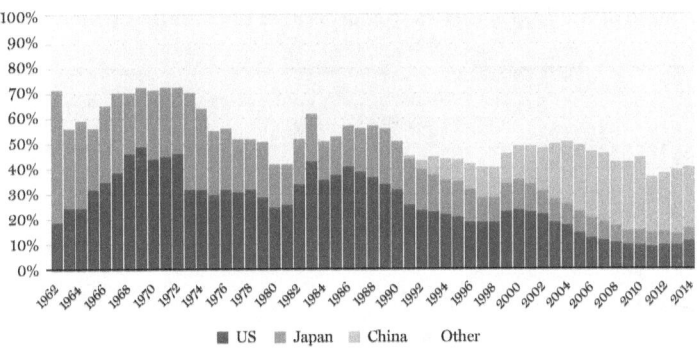

Data Source: MIT Observatory of Economic Complexity

In 1952 however, with the establishment of the European Coal and Steel Community (the precursor of the European Union), it was the first time that developed countries started to purposefully help neighboring countries develop, as a way of securing peace on the continent, and as a way of furthering their common economic interest. The EU has eventually turned into the most successful development model the World has ever seen, and it is a model that could be scaled up globally, as a way of enabling other countries to make the transition to development.

Humanity's Greatest Achievement

The US may be the greatest country in the World, but the EU is humanity's greatest achievement. The EU represents the first instance in World history when a group of developed countries have undertaken as a strategic objective to help a group of developing countries overcome the middle-income trap. Not only have they proposed to do this, they have actually achieved it.

The EU has rightfully been called "the Convergence Machine"[21]. It has managed a fantastic feat – to help 12 countries overcome the middle-income trap.

Some of the EU Countries that overcame the middle-income trap

	Year EU Candidacy Negotiation was started	Year the country became a EU member	Year the country became a high-income country
Croatia	2003	2013	2007
Czech Republic	1995	2004	2004
Estonia	1995	2004	2006
Greece	1975	1981	1987
Hungary	1994	2004	2006
Ireland	1968	1973	1986
Latvia	1995	2004	2008
Lithuania	1995	2004	2008
Poland	1994	2004	2008
Portugal	1977	1986	1994
Slovak Republic	1995	2004	2005
Spain	1977	1986	1987

The way it has achieved is more or less known, and it includes some basic ingredients we have also discussed in this book:

1. To enter the EU, Candidate Countries have to prove they have a functioning democracy.
2. Candidate Countries also have to prove that they have a functioning market economy, not one dependent on state intervention.
3. Once they get in the EU, New Member Countries have to commit to strengthen their institutions and undertake massive administrative reforms, while overhauling their legislative and judicial system.
4. New Member Countries have to fully open their markets to other EU countries, while at the same time gaining full access to EU markets – and freedom of movement and work in the EU for their citizens.
5. All Member Countries, but particularly the Less Developed ones, receive massive amounts of EU grants for various public and private development projects.

After becoming EU Members, countries quickly become part of the common market, and their economies undergo a modernization process and quick growth and development. This process of growth and development for New EU Member countries deserves some attention, as it is highly relevant for other developing countries.

The story of growth in new EU member countries may actually begin when these countries start the negotiations for EU accession. Development is inherently a compounded result of many individual choices – who invests where, who moves where, who partners with whom. Being part of the EU is likely to trigger many of these positive individual decisions, driven primarily by the knowledge that an individual's / firm's / organization's interest would be protected, should anything come to pass (e.g. the nationalization of a private company).

The figure below indicates that following the first EU eastern extension wave, foreign direct investments (FDI) in New Member Countries have gone up dramatically. The FDI growth was only curtailed by the 2008 Global Crisis. Still, in 2014 FDI in New Member Countries represented 15% of all the FDI in the EU.

Foreign Direct Investments in EU New Member Countries[22] (in billion $)

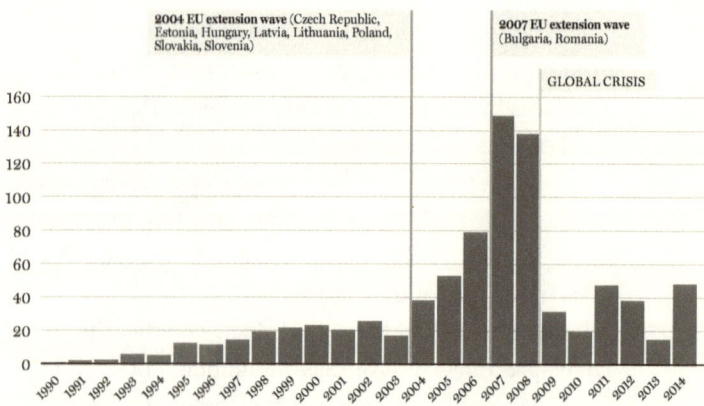

Source: World Bank

This FDI was critical for the development of New Member Countries and their regions. On the one hand, foreign companies brought with them technological advances and know-how that have been refined in the West over decades. On the other hand, these foreign companies have re-trained the staff they hired, they have raised the staff's productivity, and often they offered them higher salaries. Thus, foreign companies have helped modernize national and regional economies and they encouraged human capital development and productivity growth.

Productivity increases in New Member States have also occurred through a different venue – out-migration. People in the New Member States have sought opportunities in other EU countries, and these decisions have dramatically increased their individual revenues. Moreover, all of these people working abroad have sent money back home and many have moved back and invested in their home countries. Remittances represent for New Member Countries a significant and substantial source of revenues – in recent years it has been almost as significant as FDIs. Moreover, the remittances flow has been much more stable than foreign investments, with a smaller downward dip after the Crisis and a more reliable pattern afterward. Remittances to New Member Countries now represent around 30% of remittances in the EU as a whole.

Remittances to New Member Countries (in billion $)

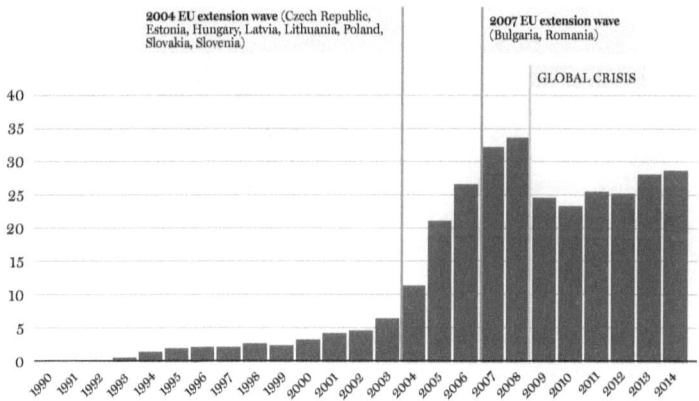

Source: World Bank

Membership in the EU has helped buttress the economies of New Member States in another, more "prosaic" way – through exports. Obviously, being part of the largest trade block in the World comes with its benefits. Thus, exports of New Member State have risen steadily over the years, and the 2008 Global Crisis was but a blip, with export growth resuming immediately in 2010. Of course, an overwhelming share of these exports go to the EU – ranging from around 60% in Bulgaria, to 70% in Romania, 75% in Poland, and 83% in Slovakia (EuroStat). In turn, companies with foreign capital were responsible for a lion share of these exports. For example, in Romania, 42% of exports in 2013 were generated by just 30 companies, the large majority of them foreign owned.

Exports of New Member Countries (in billion $)

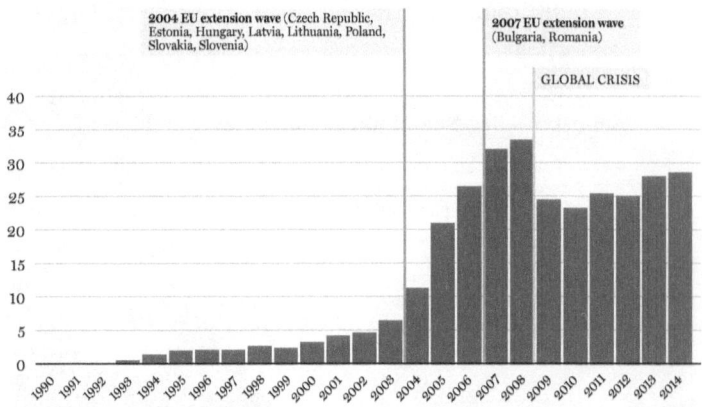

Source: World Bank

The end effect of EU Membership has been widespread economic growth – both at the national, and at the regional level. The map below indicates that between 2000 and 2013, virtually every region from New Member States has registered economic growth, with the least developed regions also registering the fastest growth. For example, virtually each of the 42 counties in Romania grew at a compound annual growth rate of over 6% This performance is almost uniform, although different regions have different governance arrangements, different economic make-ups, and different human capital endowments.

GDP per Capita (PPS) Compound Annual Growth Rate, between 2000 and 2013

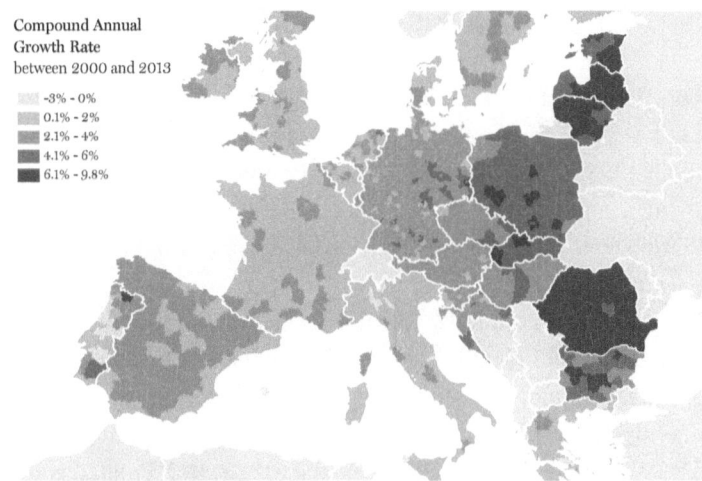

Data Source: EuroStat

Thus, one could say that being part of the EU was, and continues to be, one of the key drivers, if not the key driver of regional growth in New Member States. Of course, EU funds and the legislative and administrative changes that the EU pushes, also play a critical role. They enable a closing of the public infrastructure gap, they permit a modernization of the legislative framework and a strengthening of administrative capacity. Basically, a modernization of the private sector made possible by being under the EU umbrella was doubled by a rapid modernization of the public sector.

The implications of this analysis for other developing countries are important. In essence, the fastest and most efficient way for triggering sustained economic growth in developing countries is by deeply integrating them into larger trade blocks. At a minimum, developing countries should be allowed easier access to large markets (the way Japan and South Korea were enabled access to the US market). Further steps towards trade integration can then be taken, culminating with an economic union similar to the EU model.

Towards a World Union

The EU model works – it works exceedingly well! Entering the EU has been, from my point of view, Romania's most important achievement. At this point, it is bar-none the World's most efficient and successful development model. Thus, the question that obviously begs itself, is: how can this model be scaled-up at the global level?

The United Nations, and the family of institutions that are part of the UN network (e.g. the World Bank or the International Monetary Fund), play a crucial role in encouraging global development. But, there is only so much these institutions can do. As a point of comparison, for the 2007-2013 Programming Period, Romania received more grants from the EU (around $50 billion) than the World Bank's entire portfolio (primarily lending and technical assistance) for all of Europe and Central Asia – i.e. for all countries from Portugal to the former Soviet republics, and to Turkey. Moreover, Romania had to do wide-sweeping legislative changes and massive administrative reforms, to ensure that the basic tenants of a functioning democracy and market economy, were guaranteed. This has been no small feat, and the results were quick to show – between 2000 and 2013, Romania has registered a compound annual growth rate of around 8.5%, and has reached a level of development it never reached in its history (exports alone are now 8 times larger than what they were during Communist times).

Obviously, it is hard to imagine that the resources the EU allocates to its New Member Countries, could be allocated globally for other developing countries. But, some of the key principles that stand at the foundation of EU membership could still be considered. For example:

1. International aid should primarily target countries that have functioning democracies in place, and plenty of assistance should be provided to ensure that democracy is kept alive and well in these countries. If a country does not have a functioning democracy, it basically lacks one of the essential building blocks of long-term growth. When aid is provided to countries without functioning democracies, it is important that the aid targets communities in need rather than buttressing an autocratic government.

2. Developed countries should open their markets to products and services offered by undeveloped and developing countries, and they should primarily encourage the export of value-added products – i.e. the types of products that would enable undeveloped and developing countries to establish a foundation for a healthy economy. Ideally, regional trade blocks should be encouraged, with undeveloped and developing countries targeting primarily the developed markets closest to them. Thus, for Latin American countries, the US and Canada can become the most important trade partner. For African countries, the EU and Asia are the most advantageous markets. While, for Asian countries, Japan and China can be prime targets now – as well as India, once its economy becomes more established.

Of course, regional trade blocks are easier to establish in theory than in practice. From a political point of view, it is quite hard to convince your population that helping others is good for everybody in the long term. However, if the population is engaged actively in the establishment of such aid schemes, there is more hope for their success. In the long term, more trade and a growing global middle-class is good for everybody – especially given the aging of the population and the shrinking of the middle class in developed countries.

3. There is a higher need for institutions like the Multilateral Investment Guarantee Agency (part of the World Bank Group), backed with financing from developed countries, which could provide guarantees to investors that undertake new operations in undeveloped and developing countries. Without foreign direct investment and technological transfers from the West, it is virtually impossible to modernize the economies of undeveloped and developing countries.

Such an undertaking is also a touchy political issues, as foreign direct investments are often equivalent to the transfer of operations from developed countries to developing countries. No politician interested in being re-elected would willingly sign off on the transfer of jobs from their own country to a developing country.

Nonetheless, a reticence to potential increased trade, may in the long-term be a lose-lose proposition for all parties involved. Developing countries lose the chance to modernize their economy, while developed countries lose the chance to tap growing markets. If developing countries do better economically, developed countries benefit too, as they have larger markets for their own products and services. Also, developed countries cannot sustain long-term growth if they do not continuously re-invent their economies – i.e. moving from lower value-added activities to higher value-added ones. For example, most developed countries have long replaced lower value-added sectors, like textile manufacturing, with higher value-added ones, like manufacturing of electronics. In the most developed places, the shift has gone even further, with a focus away from manufacturing, to higher value-added creative industries, such as design, marketing, or software development.

The transfer process of lower value-added activities from developed countries to developing countries is something that now happens organically. As a higher share of the population moves into higher value-added activities, they also tend to acquire higher salaries. The general rise in salaries pushes many labor intensive industries towards countries with lower labor costs. However, many of the countries that would benefit from such investments are avoided for a variety of reasons – one of the most important being the lack of perceived stability and predictability. This is where a guarantee mechanism buttressed by developed countries could help.

4. Make migration and reverse migration easier. Undeveloped and developing countries have significant shares of their population working well below their potential. More specifically, they have people that could do more, but are stuck with the opportunities their countries have to offer. For example, you may have an excellent physicist in Rwanda, but she has no research center or company she could work for at home.

For such situations, it is important to make the movement of people easier. The top performers usually find ways to make it to develop countries, but they face significant barriers when it comes to returning to their countries of origin. The most important barrier is the fear of not being able to return to the host country if the return to the country of origin does not go as planned. Developed countries have a significant share of migrants that would be willing to return home, but they don't do it because returning to the host country is not a seamless undertaking – especially if things do not go as planned.

5. Strengthen the capacity of public administrations in undeveloped and developing countries. Undeveloped and developing countries have a huge and almost unsurmountable task in front of them. For one, they have to deal with tougher challenges than developed countries (wide-spread poverty, underdeveloped public infrastructure, weak private sector), and they have to do so with a more poorly trained staff. Most often, when developing countries grow, the private sector modernizes at a much faster rate than the public sector. This however can lead to a number of shortcomings and hick-ups. For example, a growing economy translates into growing public budgets. However, public authorities are often ill prepared to spend these additional revenues in a meaningful and productive way (e.g. for public investment projects). When faced with growing revenues, most governments do the easiest thing to do – they grow the salaries of public functionaries. While higher salaries for public officials is not a bad thing, problems can arise when the salaries and employment in the public sector grow faster than in the private sector. When it becomes more attractive to work for the public sector than for the private sector, you have the basic seed of an economic crisis. As such, it is important for developed countries to

think about ways of strengthening the capacity of public authorities in undeveloped and developing countries.

6. Encourage and finance peer-to-peer learning programs. Developed countries could undertake a concerted effort to help undeveloped and developing countries modernize their administration and their private sector. Peer-to-peer programs expose people in undeveloped and developing countries to the way things are done in a developed economy, and thus may open the door for improvements at home.

Trade Integration

A more developed World Economy is a more integrated world economy. The more countries, companies, and people trade with each other, the faster does the World economy progress, and the higher the likelihood for the generation of innovations. Increased trade is good for everybody, but it is rarely perceived as such. Almost every country has, at some point in its past, put a protectionist measure in place, and the opening up of economies is not an easy sell.

However, further trade integration is an absolute must for every country in the World, given current dynamics. For developed countries this is critical, given that their internal markets are shrinking. As such, they have to tap additional market, and it is within their own interest to have these markets grow (which basically means growth and development in undeveloped and developing countries). When you have managed to sell a car to every household in the developed world, and when the number of households in the developed world is not growing anymore (or may actually be shrinking), it is in your own interest to identify households in the rest of the World that may be interested in purchasing a car. The larger this number of households, and the easier it is to get to them, the better off you are.

For undeveloped and developing countries, increased trade integration is critical because they get access to the prosperous markets of the West. Without proper access to these markets, it is virtually impossible to sustain growth and development. It does not matter if you produce some of the best goods and services in the world, if you have nowhere to sell them.

Given the shape the World is in today, it is imperative that countries realize they are part of the same club. The more they work together, the better off they are. With one notable exception (the US), none of the countries in the World today can afford not to trade. With the exception of the US, which is a net importing country and has an internal market that could be self-sustaining, all other developed countries are net exporters and require access to external markets to sustain their growth and development.

Trade integration is not an easy political issue, but it is absolutely critical for sustaining growth and development. Governments should get better at promoting the benefits of trade integration and take bold steps in this direction, while involving the citizens and key stakeholders in the planning and decisions making process.

The Shrinking Middles Class

Developed countries and many developing countries face a difficult challenge. Their population and their middle-class is either stagnating or shrinking. This basically means that their internal markets (the most reliable ones for the national economy) are stagnating or shrinking. Over the long term, this dynamic is not sustainable. Regardless of how fast productivity increases, shrinking markets will eventually affect developed countries.

The map below shows that a large majority of developed and developing countries have fertility rates that are below replacement level. Overall, 3.4 billion people live in these countries. In countries like South Korea and Portugal, fertility rates have dropped to 1.2.

Fertility Rates

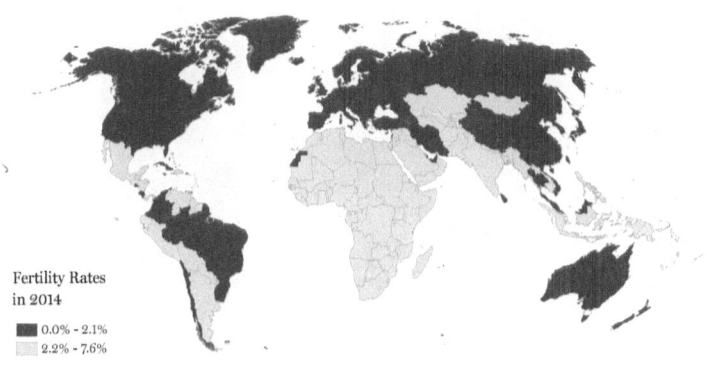

Fertility Rates in 2014
- 0.0% - 2.1%
- 2.2% - 7.6%

Data Source: World Bank

Low fertility rates have affected disproportionately the middle class in developed and developing countries. And, when the middle-class shrinks, so does overall consumption. In Japan, where fertility rates has dropped to 1.42, consumption has grown by a compound annual growth rate of around 1% between 1995 and 2015. In the EU, where the average fertility rate is 1.5, consumption growth has been around 1.6% in the same time period. The average fertility rate at the global level is 2.45.

When overall consumption is shrinking, so does the economy. Moreover, a poor performance of developed countries inevitably affects the performance of developing countries. The alternative, short of pro-natality policies, is to try to tap the growing markets of developing countries. For example, consumption in China has been growing at a compound annual growth rate of 8.2%. Although the fertility rate in China is 1.56 (and it has been lower than the replacement level of 2.1 since 1993), the country's rapid economic growth has pushed more and more people into the middle-class.

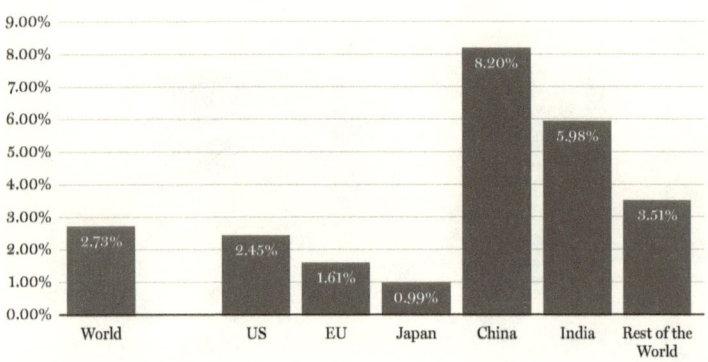

Data Source: World Bank

Unfortunately, China cannot yet compensate a sluggish performance in developed countries. While its markets have been expanding at a very fast pace, it can hardly compensate a poor performance of the markets in the US and the EU. China currently consumes around $4 trillion per year (what the US consumed around 1970), while the US and the EU each consume around $10 trillion more.

Moreover, as Thomas Piketty has brilliantly shown, a low fertility rate and slow population growth, or decline, can ultimately lead to an increased concentration of resources in fewer and fewer hands, as the return on capital tends to be higher than the return on labor in times of slow growth. Thus, those with a lot of capital will have even more of it, and those without will have less – until a disequilibrium is reached and a system reset (e.g. revolution, crisis, depression) is triggered.

Consumption Dynamics in the World's Largest Markets
(in trillion Constant 2010 US$)

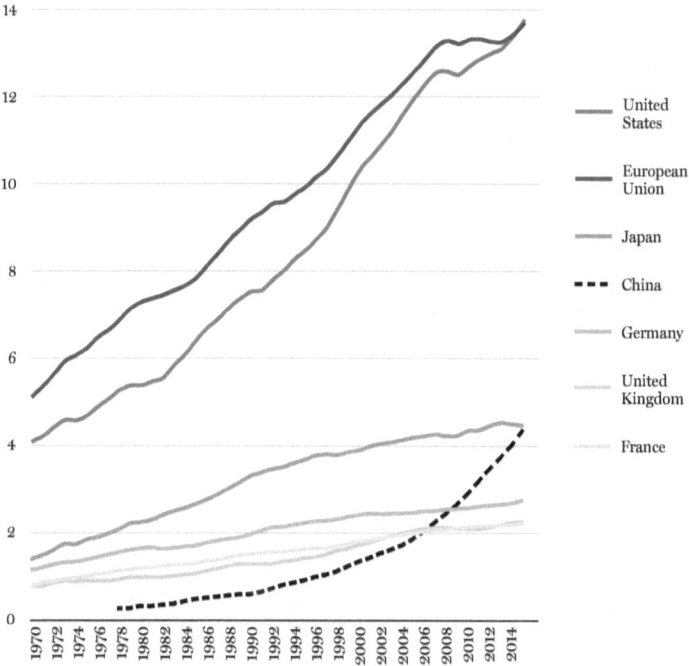

Data Source: World Bank

This basically means that unless people in the developed World start making babies again, the global economy may be in big dudu. Pro-natality policies have been used by several countries (e.g. France, Romania, or Poland) with mixed results. Public infrastructure (such as affordable and easily accessible nurseries), benefits for young parents (e.g. paid leave for raising children, subsidies for each child born), or tax incentives (lower taxes for people with more children), can help address the demographic decline only up to a point. We simply live in a new reality, where people marry much later in life and have fewer children. This means that a large majority of couples will not have more than 2 children, which inevitably places the natality rate below the 2.1 population replacement level. Conversely, people live much longer (i.e. most developed countries have an aging population), raising the share of retired people and the pressure on social systems.

In the countries where the fertility rate is quite high, people don't necessarily make lots of babies because of a lack of adequate birth control methods. They often have a lot of babies out of sheer economic interest. Particularly for farming communities, more kids mean more hands that can help tend the fields. This is in fact a practice that has been used almost everywhere around the globe. In the US of 1800, for example, the fertility rate was around 7 (i.e. women gave birth on average to 7 kids), higher than the fertility rate in any country today, and the population of the country doubled every twenty years[23].

As countries develop however, they also see more and more women enter the workforce. And, women that have a career are less likely to want to make lots of babies. I discussed with my girlfriend this issue too, and we tried to identify under what circumstances we would decide to have more than two babies. We realized, for one, that we would be facing some natural barriers, as neither of us is in their prime anymore (although she is in pretty good shape). And, throughout the World, couples make babies much later in life, and there is a higher incidence of singles and people that never marry. We also decided that no Government incentive could convince us to be prolific baby makers, given that we have jobs that provide generous salaries, and given that we put a high value on our free time.

Different Governments have tried to use different policies to encourage higher policy rates, but almost none managed to get fertility rates over 2.1. For example, for a while, the Romanian Government offered every new mother the option of a two-year paid leave, the mother receiving 80% of the her wage before giving birth. The policy was subsequently altered, to provide only one year of paid leave, and the option of a second year of un-paid leave. In Poland, the Government provides 500 Zloty (around $125) for every child within a household. Thus, a family with three children receives from the Government the equivalent of the minimum salary in the country. While such policies can make it easier for couples to take the decisions to have a baby, they are unlikely to trigger a baby boom.

As the map below indicates, in the large majority of countries, women represent over 45% of the active workforce. Raising a child is in essence another full-time job, so it is quite difficult for a woman to juggle both a career and a large household. The fact that women actively participate in a country's economy is excellent for the economy itself – more productive people translate into a more productive economy. On the other hand, a household where both parents have productive careers leaves little time for rearing and growing a big family.

Female Workforce as Percent of Total Workforce

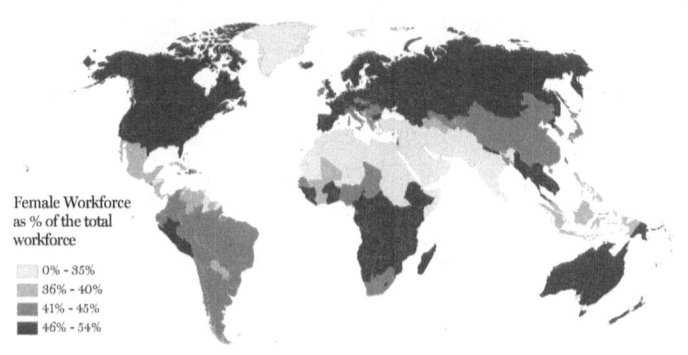

Female Workforce as % of the total workforce

- 0% - 35%
- 36% - 40%
- 41% - 45%
- 46% - 54%

Data Source: World Bank

On a background of shrinking fertility rates, the population in most developed and developing countries is shrinking, which will sooner or later lead to a shrinking of internal markets in these countries. To sustain growth rates, these countries will have to identify ways to tap growing markets (e.g. China), and markets with future potential (e.g. India and Africa). This will require further trade integration and direct assistance to helping these countries grow and develop.

The Super-Productive Companies

All this talk about productivity and growth may lead some to believe that the most developed countries also have a high-share of people engaged in productive activities. To be quite frank, I also thought that developed countries will have a higher employment rate than developing countries. Then, I decided to actually look at the data and see what the situation actually looks like. To my great surprise, I discovered that less developed countries like Tanzania, Madagascar, or Rwanda, had far higher employment rates than developed countries (e.g. around 85%).

One obvious explanation for this discrepancy is the structure of the population in these countries. All three countries mentioned above had a relatively young population, with only 3% being 65 years or older – 3% is actually the average for Low Income countries. On the other hand, in High Income countries, the share of the population of 65+ is 17%, with the share being over 20% in countries such as Germany, Italy, or Japan.[24] In simple terms, developed countries have a higher median age (most have a median age of over 40), an aging population, and a higher (and growing) share of retired people. The median age in most undeveloped countries is below 20[25].

Employment to Population Ratio

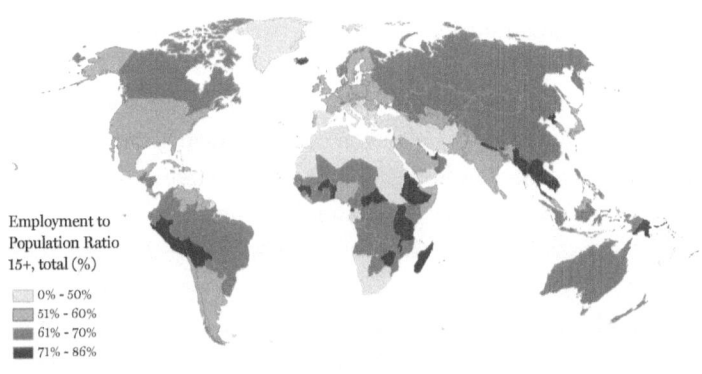

Data Source: World Bank

Still, even if 20%-30% of the population in High Income countries would be retired (assuming that not only those that pass a certain age retire), one cannot explain why only 56% of the population in High Income countries is gainfully employed. One possible answer can be given by the relatively high share of people that are self-employed – i.e. people that don't necessarily have a contract with a private company, but who work none-the-less. Another explanation is related to the fact that developed countries have economies that are powerful enough to sustain a more generous social state. Thus, developed countries have higher unemployment rates than developing and undeveloped countries, and unemployment among young people (ages 15 to 24) is particularly high – around 18%[26]. In Spain, youth unemployment is a staggering 58%; in Greece, it is 54%; Italy, 44%.

All in all, the surprising reality is that developed countries have a smaller share of people that are gainfully employed. They simply have a strong enough economy that enables the existence of a more generous social state. In essence, these developed countries have a private sector that generates enough wealth to enable almost everybody a relatively good standard of living. In fact, when one looks at the data in-depth, one finds out that a relatively small share of the private sector is the key driving force of the economy – usually a small number of large and super-productive firms.

For example, in the EU, companies with more than 250 employees, represent less than 1% of the total number of private companies, but they amass 33% of total employment, and generate 44% of total turn-over in the EU[27]. It is these large and productive companies that push the EU economy forward.

In the case of Romania, companies with over 250 employees (around 1,600 in number) are responsible for around 42% of total firm turn-over. If the analysis is pushed further, one can see that the largest 100 companies (out of a total of around 665,000 companies) employ around 9% of the labor employed by firms, and generate around 27% of total firm turnover. The 10 largest companies in Romania, employ 1.5% of the total labor force, and generate 10% of total firm turnover in the country.[28]

And, if we were to take the Romania example further, Apple, with only 110,000 employees world-wide has a higher turnover than all of Romania (with all its 20 million residents)[29]. One single company is more productive than an entire country. In fact, Apple has a higher turn-over than around 166 countries. Now, imagine what an economic boon your country could go through if Apple decided to move there. You don't need to think too much. There already is a country where a number of super-producers have moved to, turning the country from a laggard to an economic super-power. That country is Ireland. Ireland went from being one of the poorest economic performers in Europe, to having one of the fastest growing economies and one of the highest GDPs per Capita. Several smart heads have tried to explain in different ways Ireland's brilliant performance, but one needs to go no further than the list of largest companies in Ireland to understand why the country has performed so well in recent years. Among the 20 largest companies in Ireland, one finds: Microsoft, Google, Dell, Apple, Oracle, and Facebook. The 10 largest companies in Ireland generate more than the entire Romanian economy. Now, imagine if those companies were actually in Romania!

The moral of the story here is simple. There are a few super-productive companies in the World, which basically push the World Economy forward. If you are the leader of the country and are thinking about one simple way to develop your economy fast, look no further than trying to attract as many super-productive companies as possible – it may be the most efficient way of growing and developing your economy, although not always a foolproof way.

A Flexible and Motivated Workforce

Now, attracting super-productive companies is easier said than done. Private companies do not come over at the click of your fingers – you need to offer them something they need. And, private companies, especially those that are growth driven, are interested in profits and talent. More specifically, before moving to your country, a company wants to know that it will find the qualified labor force to run its business, and that it has the necessary pre-conditions for generating a profit. Among these pre-conditions, among the most important are: proximity to markets (the farther you are from large markets, the more you will be avoided by private investors); stability and predictability (if private companies think there is a high risk of their business being affected by outside forces – e.g. political turmoil, change of legislation, they will think twice before investing); the presence of competitors (as counterintuitive as it may seem, a private company will be easier to convince to move over, if similar companies have done this step before).

People are however the one thing companies are most interested in. Google, Microsoft, Apple, Dell, and Facebook came to Ireland because they knew not only that Ireland will provide an excellent spring-board to the EU markets, but that it would also offer plentiful qualified labor force – people that spoke English, people that understood the Anglo-Saxon business culture, and people with a high educational attainment (37% of people aged 20-24 go to university in Ireland – one of the highest rates in Western Europe).

One thing companies care about when looking for workforce is adequate schooling. People with basic schooling (i.e. people that are literate) can in turn be "schooled" much easier by private companies. In today's economy, people rarely come out of school with the exact competencies and expertise companies need. Most people learn the job, on the job. Of course, one of the essential pre-requisites for learning the job on the job is to be literate. Knowledge on world geography and history may not take you very far in an assembly plant, but being able to read basic instructions and do basic math will be a big help.

Trends of Educational Attainment of the Total Population Aged 15 and Over

	No Schooling			Enrollment in Tertiary Education		
Year	World	Advanced Countries (24)	Developing Countries (122)	World	Advanced Countries (24)	Developing Countries (122)
1950	47.1%	9.2%	61.1%	1.1%	2.8%	0.5%
1960	42.4%	7.7%	54.6%	1.5%	3.8%	0.7%
1970	35.5%	6.2%	45.0%	2.1%	5.3%	1.0%
1980	30.1%	5.4%	37.2%	3.1%	8.1%	1.7%
1990	25.7%	5.4%	30.8%	4.7%	12.3%	2.9%
2000	19.3%	3.4%	22.9%	6.4%	16.0%	4.3%
2010	14.8%	2.4%	17.4%	7.8%	17.9%	5.7%

Source: Barro, Robert J. and Jong-Wha Lee. 2011. "A New Set of Educational Attainment in the World, 1950-2010".

The good news is that the share of people with no schooling in the World has dropped from 47.1% in 1950 to 14.8% in 2010. The largest advances in basic educational attainment have taken place in developing countries, which also explains the dramatic economic progress these countries have witnessed in the past years.

There is however much more to do. In India, for example, 30% of the population (around 400 million people) are illiterate, making it almost impossible for them to move up quickly in the World. By comparison, only 5% of the population in China is illiterate. In undeveloped countries, more than 50% of the population is illiterate.[30]

Obviously, if undeveloped and developing countries are not able to provide basic schooling to their population, they can hardly hope to make quick economic progress. At the same time, a good education system does not necessarily translate into immediate economic growth. Central and Eastern European countries came out of Communism with a highly educated population (illiteracy was almost non-existent), but it took some time before their economies took off. Ukraine and Russia have a relatively high share of the labor force with tertiary education, but this has not translated into dynamic private sector development.

What is essential for economic growth and development, is to have the enabling conditions in place that enable a quick transition of the labor force from low value-added activities to higher value-added activities. Most importantly, it is important to create the conditions that enable a quick transition of the workforce from agricultural activities to industry and services. The countries that have managed this transitions the fastest, are also the countries that have developed the quickest.

The table below is quite powerful and telling. For one, it shows that the share of the labor force engaged in agricultural activities is quite low in High Income countries – less than 3% now. On the other hand, it shows that Upper Middle Income countries (i.e. the countries with the fastest economic growth rate), have managed a staggering transition of their labor force out of agriculture. In less than a generation, the share of the population engaged in agricultural activities has dropped from 43% to 7%. This is absolutely key for economic growth and development.

Employment in Agriculture (% of total employment)

	1994	2010
Lower middle income	54%	46%
Low & middle income	48%	24%
Middle income	47%	24%
Upper middle income	43%	7%
High income	6%	3%

Source: World Bank

Unfortunately, policy makers all over the World, tout agriculture as a strategic sector for development, and allocate lots of resources for the development of this sector, failing to grasp that while agriculture is indeed strategic (you have to be able to feed your population), it is not a growth sector. The reason why agriculture is not a growth sector is blindingly simple, but few policy makers bother to think about it. In essence, every country looks to achieve self-sufficiency in the agriculture sector, because this is a sine qua-non condition for keeping your population fed. If you cannot feed your people, you sooner or later disappear as a country. Thus, if we assume that all countries manage to cover their food needs from what their agricultural sector produces, than export of excess production is either subject to price competition on international markets, or it targets niche markets. Romania produces five times the amount of grains it needs for internal consumption. All the excess production is sold internationally at dumping prices, or stored for "better days".

As the authors of the **Atlas of Economic Complexity** have shown, when a high share of your labor force is engaged in activities that many other people around the World know how to do (e.g. plant and reap grains), you inevitably enter a price competition. And this competition is usually won by developed countries, which have a highly mechanized agriculture sector and advanced technologies that ensure higher yields per hectare. Only a measly 2.8% of global trade is done in Vegetable Products, such as wheat, corn, or soybeans.

As a consequence, there are very few countries, and almost no developed country where the exports of vegetable products represent more than 5% of total exports. When such exports are an important contributor to the national economy, the country does not have a high level of development, and exports are done in staple products that cannot be produced in developed countries (e.g. bananas, coffee, tropical fruits). An interesting exception is South America, where countries such as Brazil, Argentina, or Uruguay generate significant revenues from the export of vegetable products – primarily soybeans that are exported to China.

Exports of Vegetable Products as Percent of Total Exports, in 2014

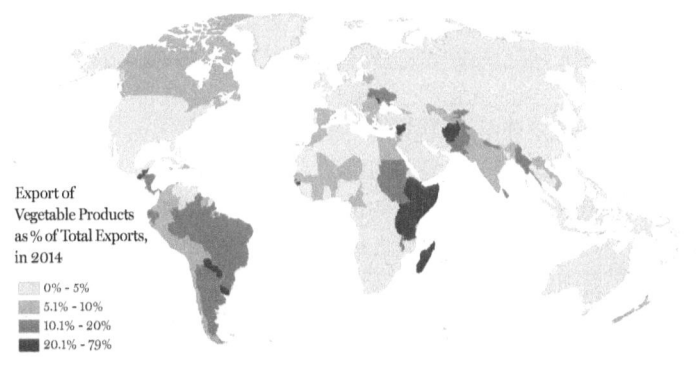

Source: *MIT Observatory of Economic Complexity*

The bottom line is that the agricultural sector cannot sustain economic growth – not when every country is endogenously covering its own food needs. In the past, agriculture was a growth sector (in 1840, 56% of US exports were in cotton, fueling the textile mills in Britain[31]), but not anymore. Not even light industry sectors, such as canaries, meat packers, or food processors, can sustain long-term growth. Whenever there is a lot of competition in a particular sector (e.g. processed food), profit margins tend to be low, and so are growth margins. Moreover, to generate a semblance of profit margin in this sector, heavy mechanization is necessary. As such, the share of people working in agriculture in developed countries is less than 3%. This is a target developing countries should keep in mind too – it's critical for ensuring both a competitive agriculture sector and a competitive economy.

A shift away from agriculture employment necessarily requires a process of urbanization. And, people move to urban areas when there is something attracting them there – most often a job. Thus, it is critical for cities in developing countries to be able to attract private investors and people. When it comes to private investments, it is ideal to focus on high-value added sectors requiring a specialized workforce. It is usually these sectors that have the largest growth potential. When there is strong competition within a sector, profit and growth margins tend to be small.

Consequently, the most efficient way to sustain long-term growth is to have a specialized, motivated, and driven population. In simple terms, it means having a population that knows how to produce sellable things that few other people on the face of the World know how to do. By and large, almost everybody on the face of the Earth knows how to plant a potato or wheat, most people can easily learn how to drive a car or operate a cashier's register, and a large number of people can learn how to assemble a car. What offers developed countries a competitive advantage, is the high share of people that specialize in things few people know how to do (e.g. software development, product design, marketing and sales, logistics, management).

LARGE UNIFIED MARKETS - Make It Easy to Move Goods around the World

The easier it is to do trade at the Global level, the better off the Global Economy is. Economic output is directly related to the ease of getting goods, services, and ideas to as many people as possible. In "The Rational Optimist: How Prosperity Evolves", Matt Ridley makes a brilliant case for why trade was critical for the evolution of human civilization, and why it is critical for the continued evolution of the World Economy.

Ridley makes a case not only for trade, but also for large trade blocks. He indicates that the more people we trade with, the more innovations we generate. Writing was developed by traders to keep tabs on all the deals they made; transport improvements across history were developed, or at least matured, by traders; the discovery of new territories and their settlement was also largely an accomplishment of traders; lastly, it is traders (e.g. the British East India Company and the Dutch East India Company) that have made the Industrial Revolution happen.

The more people we trade with, the more innovative we tend to become, because we serve larger markets (i.e. we have a larger potential pay-off) and we serve more diverse markets (i.e. there are higher chances of finding a market for something we are particularly good at producing). To bring this message home, Ridley gives a counter-example. He talks about the early colonization of the islands around Australia and New Zealand, as people have ventured out to find new and more hospitable places to settle. He indicates that the colonization of these islands inevitably required a fragmentation of population groups. More specifically, the groups that moved to those islands formed communities that were smaller than the communities they left behind. An analysis of the relics left behind by these newly formed island communities indicates not only an involution of trade, but also a dramatic involution of innovations. For example, they saw a gradual disappearance of more sophisticated fishing and hunting tools, and their gradual replacement with more rudimentary tools. Historians postulate that as the experts specialized in the production of sophisticated fishing and hunting tools migrated to these places with fewer people, they also had fewer people they could trade with – e.g. they had fewer fishermen interested in exchanging something of value for the fishing hooks they produced. Since these experts at producing sophisticated fishing and hunting tools gradually lost the economic incentives to produce these tools, they also gave up producing them and reverted to a self-sufficient lifestyle. Worse-over, they did not pass the knowledge on to others, and their expertise and their innovations, died with them.

Over time, policy makers have established miss-guided trade barriers in place, thinking that if you protect your own market from imports from abroad, you will encourage the development of your own markets. Of course, this did not happen. Every shred of evidence out there (and fortunately the quantity and quality of data gets better and better) shows that countries that trade more, grow more. Globally, trade went from being 17% of the World GDP in 1960, to being 52% of the World GDP in 2008 (just before the Global Crisis). There is basically no developing country that has managed to grow between 1995 and 2015, without also growing its exports.

Growth of Developing Countries has Gone Hand-in-Hand with Trade Growth

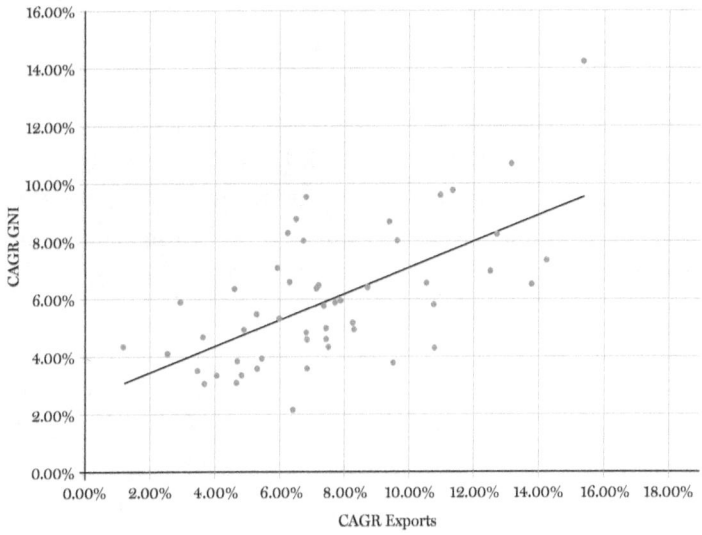

Source: World Bank
Note: X Axis signifies Compound Annual Growth Rate of Exports between 1995 and 2005. Y Axis signifies Compound Annual Growth Rate of Gross National Income (GNI) between 1995 and 2005

Trade is critical to development, and the more open the World Market is, the better off everybody is. Trade agreements are viewed with suspicion and often they require long negotiations and significant compromises. They also make however everybody better off – larger and more diverse markets are simply good for business.

A more open global economy is simply a more developed world economy. Every shroud of empirical evidence shows that countries that have opened up their economies, have managed to reap significant benefits. Particularly for undeveloped and developing countries, the access to developed markets is paramount. Their own markets are simply too small to sustain economic growth.

Remember that Indians consume by-and-large less than Italians do. Also remember that the US could not have developed in the 19th century without access to European markets. Neither could Japan and South Korea have developed without access to US markets.

It is that simple! A more open global economy is a more developed global economy. Consequently, developing countries should attempt to negotiate favorable trade deals with developed economies, and they should focus on the markets that are closest to them. For example, the countries of North Africa should attempt to become close friends with the EU – most of their exports go to the EU anyway. They should attempt to re-create the buzzing trade of the Ancient World, when the Mediterranean was one of the busiest trade space in the World. This would benefit not only North African countries, but also EU countries – particularly the less developed regions on the Southern periphery of the EU. These regions used to be booming areas when trade with North Africa was flourishing, but they have in the meantime become the lagging regions of the EU.

Similarly, European countries that are not yet part of the EU (the Western Balkans, the Caucasus countries, the Former Soviet Republics), should make it their key aim to achieve EU membership. The benefits of such a move can be seen directly in the myriad of New EU Member Countries that have grown at a break-neck pace in the past years.

Countries in Central America and northern South America, should aim to become part of NAFTA (the North American Free Trade Agreement), or a different incarnation of NAFTA. That's where much of their exports already go, and further trade integration can bring them nothing but benefits. North American countries would in turn benefit from such an integration, as their own middle-class is shrinking, and tapping growing markets will be critical for them.

Lastly, China is the new big kid on the block in the trade world, and its economy and internal markets have been growing by heaps and bounds. It has already become the main export destination for countries in the Middle East, in Central and East Africa, and in South America. Currently, China primarily imports resources, but it has gradually shifted to trade integration (particularly with other countries in South-East Asia). For example, in 2014, 8.8% of Chinese imports were integrated circuits – 92% of which came from other countries in the region.

The easier it is for goods to move around the World, the better off we all are. Populist trade protectionist policies are more than often misguided and do nothing more than protect the interests of a few against benefits for the many.

A GLOBAL LINGUA FRANCA – Make it Easy for Ideas to Move around the World

The EU is the largest trade market in the World. However, while it functions exceedingly well for the trade of goods, it is less efficient when it comes to the trade of ideas, knowledge, and innovation. Language and culture pose distinct barriers. The US market on the other hand, allows the seamless spread and maturing of ideas. This is one of the reasons why the US has been much more astute at generating disruptive innovations, and why it has developed a comparative advantage in sectors with high Research and Development (R&D) intensity.

Europe specializes in sectors with medium R&D intensity, the United States in high intensity

(relative technological advantage (RTA) indices by sector, ratio, 2007)

	Europe	U.S.
Aerospace and defense	*1.5*	*1.13*
Automobiles and parts	1.26	0.58
Biotechnology	*0.32*	*2.2*
Chemicals	1.31	0.64
Commercial vehicles and trucks	1.3	1.06
Computer hardware and services	*0.08*	*1.39*
Electrical components and equipment	1.56	0.18
Electronic equipment and electronic office equipment	0.18	0.37
Fixed and mobile telecommunications	1.53	0.2
Food, beverages, and tobacco	0.92	0.74
General industrials	0.61	1.49
Health care equipment and services	*0.7*	*1.86*
Household goods	0.84	1.6
Industrial machinery	1.84	0.24
Industrial metals	1	0.3
Internet	*0*	*2.54*
Oil	1	0.85
Personal goods	1.44	0.69
Pharmaceuticals	*1.27*	*1.16*
Semiconductors	*0.5*	*1.72*
Software	*0.51*	*2.05*
Support services	0.78	1.19
Telecommunications equipment	1.38	1.09

Source: World Bank. 2012. Golden Growth: Restoring the lustre of the European economic model.
Note: Relative technological advantage is calculated as the region's share in total sectoral R&D relative to the region's share in overall R&D. A value in relative technological advantage that is higher than 1 means that the region is technology-specialized in this sector. Japan and the rest of the world are not reported because of too few observations when disaggregating to individual sectors.

Innovation-based growth sectors are bold and in italics.

Without such a large unified market as that of the US, it is much harder to generate and mature innovations. In essence, the higher the number of early adopters an innovation can rely on, the higher its chances of survival and market entry.

A key pre-condition for the spread of ideas, is the ease with which they can be understood and analyzed by others. Finland has a high share of innovators (it is among the World's leading innovative economies), but if the ideas they generate can be easily understood by only the 5.5 million Finish speaking people, you will obviously have a lower share of ideas that can make it to market maturity.

For ideas to circulate freely and easily, it is important to institutionalize the use of a Global Business Lingua Franca – with the most obvious candidate being the English language. Most people in the business world, and most people in academia speak English, and this is the official language of most global conferences and knowledge share events. However, English should be taught to kids from early on as a second language – in essence, every child on the face of the planet should grow up knowing how to speak the business language of the World. This would not only benefit them personally (i.e. they would have easier access to global opportunities), but it would also be good for the global spread of ideas and innovations.

A global lingua franca would not only enable the spread of ideas and innovations, but it would also be a huge booster to trade, and it would be an important contributor to global peace. The easier it is for individual people to understand each other, the more likely they are to get along.

The Importance of
HOPE, VISION and TRUST

If our era and our culture and our leaders do not, or cannot, offer great meanings, great objectives, great convictions, then people will settle for shallow and trivial substitutes.

VIKTOR FRANKL

Sometimes the situation demands clear priorities and bold ambition. This is one reason why history judges war leaders as great. Lincoln's commitment to saving the Union and (ultimately) ending slavery provided a clear mission and called for unwavering ambition – literally whatever it took. The same is true of Churchill's determination first to save the island nation and then to defeat the scourge of Nazism.

MICHAEL BARBER

People will not invest in their countries if there is no hope for a better future, if there is no unified vision to guide them forward, and if they have little trust in their fellow citizens.

Far too often, culture, race, and nationality are used as proxies for explaining why some countries are doing better than others. I myself have believed in this fairy tale for quite some time. Like most Romanians, I looked up to Western Europeans like some sort of Uebermenschen – people endowed with special gifts and talents that were out of reach for me. I have spent a good chunk of my life being overly critical with my own culture, and being overly reverent with Western culture. Not that Western culture does not deserve to be revered. Quite the contrary – it serves as an example for many countries, including Romania.

Western culture is not something that appeared overnight though – it is something that has been molded over centuries. It gives people born in the Western World a definite advantage, it does not necessarily make these people better than you and me.

RECOMMENDATIONS: TOWARDS A DEVELOPED WORLD

The way Romania and Romanian culture have evolved over the past years is to me a clear example that things can always change for the better, and a culture can evolve substantially, if there are some pre-requisites in place. I will give you a brief history of Romania, the way I have perceived it. You can decide for yourself if this story is convincing enough, and if it actually has relevance for other developing countries.

Whenever I get into a pissing contest with my foreign friends on who owns the monopoly on sorrow, I tell them that I was born in worst years of Communism, I came of age in a period of tumult and tough transition from a centrally planned-economy to a market economy, and I entered the job market in the middle of a Global Crisis. Truth be told, my life has been pretty awesome despite the many hardships I encountered. I wouldn't change much about it, and I have few regrets.

I have however become keenly aware of how important hope, vision and trust are for a community. In the 1980s, Communism was drawing its last breath and Governments started to use more and more repressive measures, to compensate for the lack of economic opportunities and the continuous decline of the standard of living. As such, people were encouraged to rat on each other and there are many stories of work colleagues, friends, or family members that informed on people they cared about. This has created a society in which nobody had trust in anybody, and self-interest dominated over the community interest. A clear and visible manifestation of this lack of trust and lack of community spirit is the way apartment blocks looked. Most people invested in furnishing their own apartments, but communal spaces were most often left to fall apart, leading to the shabby appearance many of them still have. While Communism was in theory all about community, there were little true communities in the Communist Romania I grew up in.

The 1989 Revolution brought about a dramatic change in the

life of Eastern Europeans. It gave an entire generation of people hope for a better life. It was the change many have prayed for, for a long time. The Revolution has unleashed significant energies in the Romanian society, but these energies have dissipated in a million different directions in the 1990s. We basically lacked a clear direction, and a clear vision.

The direction soon took shape. The large majority of Romanians saw the West and the clear direction our country should take. Unlike other Eastern European countries, like Moldova or the Ukraine, where the population is somewhat split between the East and the West (part of them wanting to continue to have strong links to Russia, part wanting to strengthen the links to the West), Romanians chose the West almost unanimously. We hoped Romania will look like a Western European country someday.

Of course, wanting to look like a Western European country won't get you there if you don't have a plan to achieve that goal. We didn't have a plan then, and unfortunately we still don't, now. We had however two major goals that rallied together the energies of the entire country: accession to the EU, and NATO membership. These goals galvanized the nation, and thankfully we managed to achieve them – with a big, big help from our friends in the West. The fact that we joined the EU and got into NATO provided a green light for investors that were interested in Romania, and enabled our economy to grow at a very fast pace. The fact that we had full access to the EU market, enabled Romanian companies and foreign investors to flourish.

Following EU accession, the country galvanized around another common goal: the absorption of EU funds and development of public infrastructure to Western European standards. It is an issue that wins or loses elections in Romania, and it is an issue that everybody has an opinion about in the country. It has galvanized people around a myriad of public and private investments taking place all over the country.

Without this clear direction and without the hope that things will get better, it would have been almost impossible to unleash the energies of the people in Romania. And these energies are currently clustered in a couple of more dynamic cities – i.e. the cities that have benefited most from foreign direct investments. There are more and more places where hope springs up, and this is largely the result of Romania's privileged relationship with Western Europe.

It may take some time before Romania can carve for itself a Vision, the same way the Founding Fathers did for the US in the Declaration of Independence in 1776, but when that happens, Romania can embark on a growth and development path of its own. Every country needs a vision to guide its growth and development.

Concentration, Spillovers, and the Re-birth of the Renaissance Man

Each man's destiny is as large as the world he inhabits.
CORMAC MCCARTHY

Productivity growth means concentration. If there is one big take-away for you from this book, this is it. For the most part, global economic growth has gone hand in hand with population growth – the more people one can sell things to, the more things are produced, and the more diverse the economy becomes. Those that produce something that many other people want, become wealthier, and in turn they consume a larger number and variety of goods and services. The global patterns of economic growth has been one of concentration of wealth in a few areas, and the spill-over of that wealth to other areas.

The citizens of Great Britain following the dawn of the Industrial Revolution represent the World's first middle-class. They got to be a middle-class, because the British Empire extracted resources from the territories it controlled in. It got gold, diamonds and slaves from Africa; sugar from the Caribbean; cotton, tea, and silver from India; silk, tea, and opium from China; timber, whale oil, cod, and tobacco from the Americas. To run such a huge trade enterprise, the British Empire had to rely on a lot of people, and many of those people got wealthy in the process. The extra revenue they made allowed them to consume more, and they became the clients for the first industrial enterprises (primarily textile mills) that started to take shape in Britain.

The growing wealth of the British citizens turned Britain into a prime destination for exports from other parts of the World. Between 1790 and 1913, 62% to 81% of US exports went to Europe, and of European exports more than 50% went to Great Britain[32]. The US also had the advantage of having a small population with access to a great bounty – the vast tracts of arable land and natural resources of North America. Its resources and the access to European markets have allowed the US to grow it economy from around $12 billion in 1820 to around $312 billion in 1900 (a compound annual growth rate of around 4.1%), while the population grew from around 10 million to around 76 million within the same time frame[33].

Japan and South Korea have followed a similar path. Following the Second World War and the Korea War, the US opened its markets to Japanese and South Korean exports, as a way of securing their position in the region through soft rather than hard power. It worked, and it turned out to be a win-win proposition. Not only did Japan and South Korea develop quickly (between 1950 and 2000, they grew at compound annual growth rates of 5.7% and 7.8% respectively), but they also turned into markets for US exports. In 2014, around 8% of US exports (around $110 billion) went to these two countries[34].

RECOMMENDATIONS: TOWARDS A DEVELOPED WORLD

The access to the emerging rich markets in South-East Asia has allowed China and a number of other countries in the region (e.g. Malaysia, Thailand, Singapore) to grow very fast. In 1980, 50% of Chinese exports went to Japan and Hong Kong. In turn, China's growth and its growing markets, have enabled the rapid growth of other countries in the region, such as Vietnam, the Philippines, or Indonesia.

The opening of Western European markets to countries in Central and Eastern Europe, has allowed the latter to register some of the most rapid growth rates ever recorded.

Throughout history, growth has concentrated in a few areas, and then has spilled over to other areas, as these areas have become more open to trade. This global pattern of concentration and subsequent spill-over holds true at smaller scales too.

Within countries, it is a few large and dynamic cites that generate an overwhelming share of economic output. In the EU, the largest 250 metropolitan areas are responsible for around 63% of GDP output[35]. The same pattern of concentration is observed in almost every country around the world.

Within these dynamic cities, there is a further concentration of wealth, with a few larger companies being responsible for an overwhelming share of economic output. These are the super-productive companies that usually push the economy forward.

Within these companies, and generally within these cities, there are a few super-productive people, on which the good performance of private enterprises rests. It is these super-performers that generate the disruptive innovations that push the global economy forward. When such super-performers have been identified, they should be nurtured. One cannot engineer the appearance of such super-performers – one can only create the enabling conditions that permit as many super-performers as possible to appear.

And here is moral of this chapter. If you happen to be a super-performer, or if you happen to know one, make sure you expand the world you inhabit. People that are good at something, are usually good at many things. Daniel Kahneman, the Nobel Prize winner who has made behavioral economics popular, was tasked early in his career to determine what different army conscripts would be good at – i.e. who would be good at flying a plane, who would be good at riding a tank, or who would be good at leading an army regiment. What he found after testing thousands of soldiers is that the good people were usually good at more than one thing. If they were given the opportunity to excel, they usually did. They were in effect, most often unbeknownst to them, Renaissance men.

And indeed, the Renaissance Men of Medieval times intuitively worked on more than one thing (Leonardo da Vinci being but one example), many managing to achieve excellence in fields as varied as arts and science. It is important to nurture Renaissance People in our time too, particularly since the number of super-performers has grown exponentially since medieval times. The larger and more varied is the universe these super-performers inhabit, the more innovations and progress they are likely to generate.

Unfortunately, we live in times when people narrowly specialize in a particular field, and seldom venture in uncharted territory. That has to change, and it all starts from ourselves. We can design the universe we want to inhabit, and we can subsequently proceed to populate that universe with whatever animates us.

The Importance of CONNECTIVITY

One of people's most basic needs, is to be connected to other people. That is why people congregate in cities, even when they could very much live and work from anywhere. Normally, the more an economy develops, the more people congregate in cities or functional urban zones. When an economy contracts, an opposite dynamic takes place. For example, in the 1990s, a significant number of people from Romania's cities moved to the country side, as a response to the decade-long recession and transition period the country underwent. The large majority of them lost their job in the city and moved to rural areas where they engaged in subsistence farming.

Cities make it easier for people to meet other people, but connectivity (e.g. transport, communication) still is critical. A large share of what is produced in the World has to do with connectivity (e.g. cars, fuel for cars, roads, airplanes, buses, trains, airports, railway lines, telephones, computers, TVs, TV stations, the press). And, funny enough, the more connected we become, the more we crave connectivity. When I grew up, a four hour car ride was almost an odyssey. Now, almost every city in Europe is just a short budget airline ride away, and I spend more time on the road and more time communicating.

In 1817, to get from New York to Chicago, took around 43 days. At that time, one could only travel via stagecoach (at a pace of around 12 kilometers per hour). Subsequently, canals have been built all over the North-East, at a pace that seems impressive by the standards of today. The map below shows the impressive engineering marvel that the US managed to achieve in the 1800s – a network of connective waterways that brought the bounties of the heartland to the ports of the East Coast. Such a network of canals is hard to achieve by most countries today with technology that is much more evolved than what these guys had at the time. Following the water canals, came the railway lines, which made many of the active canals obsolete. Between 1860 and 1890, the total mileage of new railways developed west of the Mississippi increased from 2,175 miles to 72,389 miles (around 115,000 km)[36]. The total mileage of railways covering all of the US was 163,597 miles (around 263,000 km) – more than the mileage of railways constructed by any country in this World, to this day[37]. Let that sink in! The US managed to connect the continent by railway, in the 1900s, with the technologies they had to their disposal at that time – a feat that is outside the realm of possibility for most countries today. Of course, after the railways came the road, highways, and air travel, which made many of the railways obsolete. Why a majority of inland freight in the US is carried by rail today, most people use other means of transportation to get from place to place.

The US System of Inland Navigable Canals

Major Canals Built in the 19th Century, American Northeast

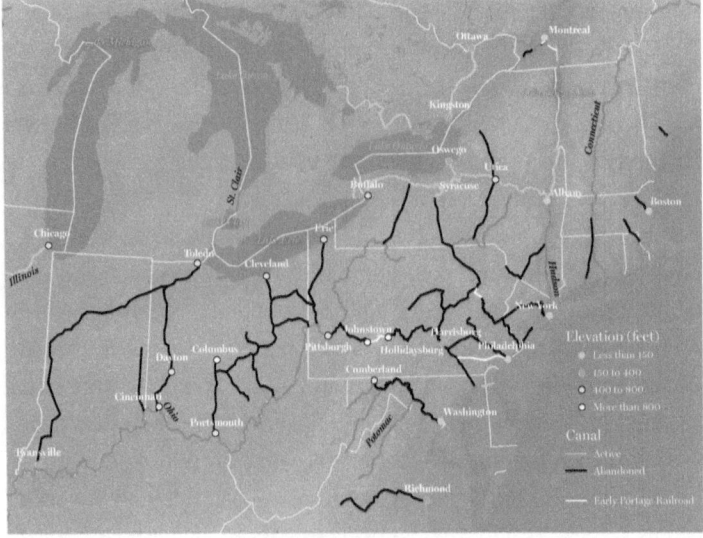

Dr. Jean-Paul Rodrigue, Dept. of Global Studies & Geography, Hofstra University

Source: https://people.hofstra.edu/geotrans/eng/ch2en/conc2en/map_american_canals_19th.html

Connectivity is the one thing that governments today spend an overwhelming amount of resources on. For many public governments, both national and local, expenditures on connective infrastructure represent more than 50% of all public infrastructure investments. Most developing countries however, have a significant infrastructure gap, and they have to undertake ambitious investment programs to catch up with the developed world. Without the proper connective infrastructure in place (transport, internet, communication), an economy cannot function at an optimum.

Now, while the development of connective infrastructure should be a priority for every developing country, it is also important to know when to stop, and to the extent possible, to foresee advances in transportation and communication. For example, following the successful completion of the Erie Canal in New York State, the government in Pennsylvania decided they will also build a system of canals to make their state more competitive. However, by the time they finished this canal system, freight transport by train had become much easier, faster, and economical than transport by canal barges.

Similarly, countries like Spain and Hungary have taken advantage of EU funds and have aggressively extended their highway network. Spain has one of the highest highway densities in the World, but its economy is not exactly booming. Hungary has five major highways that connect Budapest with every corner of the country, but none of Hungary's secondary cities has a population higher than around 100,000.

It is also important to note that public infrastructure has to be maintained. A highway needs to have the snow removed, to have the potholes filled, to have damages addressed after accidents occur, and to be periodically repaved. This takes a lot of resources, and many governments have found themselves in an incapacity to maintain the infrastructure they had, because they built such infrastructure at a faster rate than the economy could actually cope with.

The Importance of ACCESS TO FINANCING

To say that you need connective infrastructure is one thing, to actually build it is another. Governments of developing countries often lack the necessary funds to build such infrastructure, and even when they have the funds they lack the tools and capacity to actually bring such projects to completion.

I was part of a discussion with a bunch of smart heads in Romania, and the topic of discussion was how to create additional financing instruments to help cover the large infrastructure gap (around $88 billion in 2016) in the country. Infrastructure bonds were named among the "innovative" financial tools that could be used for such projects. It didn't matter that such bonds have been in use since the early 1800s, in 21st century Romania, they were a novelty. To a significant degree, new public infrastructure in Romania is built either through annual allocations from a public budget, or with the use of EU funds. Bonds remain a mystery to a significant share of people in the Romanian public administration.

Mind you that the lack of money is not the actual problem in Romania. Romania has been growing at a very fast pace, and the national budget grows every year. There is however a lack of long-term thinking and careful planning of infrastructure investment projects. This means that every year, funds are allocated from the budget for individual projects, but in the absence of clear prioritization, some projects receive funding one year, and no funding in the next year. For example, a highway project started in 2002, had only around 20% of its length completed, because of intermittent financing and repeated contract negotiations. If a special bond would have been issued for this project before the project commenced, the funding would have been insured from the get-go, and the repayment of the bond could have been scheduled over a longer time-frame. It's a simple financial instrument that ensures focus on projects and their delivery, and provides the necessary funding upfront. Unfortunately, simple financial tools like bonds for critical public projects are seldom used by developing countries.

Proper access to financing and financing tools is of course needed not only for public authorities, but also for private entities. People have to be able to access mortgages, companies need to be able to borrow, and NGOs need to be able to generate funding for their operations. This type of financing is however quite easily provided by the private sector. If there is a profit to be made, than the market will usually fill the gap – unless there is something preventing its proper functioning.

Most countries, developing and developed, are trying to identify ways of developing venture capital systems that can finance start-ups and innovative companies, but most, have not managed to replicate the success of the US in this field. The reason is quite simple. Venture capital firms will likely take hold anywhere if there is a market they could take advantage of – i.e. if there were enough innovative start-ups making it big on the market. At this point, only the US provides the conditions that enables a high number of innovative firms to make it big on the market, which makes innovative start-ups a target market for venture capitalists. When you know that a certain share out of the companies you finance will register explosive growth, you are more likely to take the risk of financing them. When you know that only few new companies register explosive growth (which is the case in most of the other developed countries), you will be more guarded about financing start-ups.

In sum, the private sector can usually take care of itself when it comes to financing – most of the times. However, the public sector is less astute at accessing financing – particularly for ambitious investments projects. At a bare minimum, public authorities should be better equipped to finance large infrastructure projects through the issuance of government bonds.

Help People to Educate Themselves

Something that was once learned can become an instinct.
MATT RIDLEY

Undeveloped and developing countries have relatively weak institutions that seldom manage to cope with the significant challenges they have to deal with. In no sector is this lack of capacity more visible than in the Education Sector. Most parents want their children to have a good future, and they know that a good education is an important stepping stone to a better future. However, education systems in undeveloped and developing countries are usually overwhelmed, and there are a significant number of people (particularly in rural and remote areas, and in urban slums) that get no or poor education. It is important that these people are provided with the tools that allow at least some of them to get a better education.

And given that education means access to information, governments around the world should ensure that everybody has access to cable TV and internet. This may involve subsidies for poor people to access such services, or it could involve transforming these services into public goods. Most countries already have national TV channels that broadcast nationally for free, and many cities experiment with offering free WiFi to a significant share of their population.

I myself have benefited immensely from access to cable TV and internet. Before 1989, the only TV programs we had access to in Communist Romania were two hours of propaganda every night, and one hour of cartoons on Saturday, at 1:00 PM. That was it. Following the fall of the Communist Regime, my dad got a satellite dish, with which we managed to receive TV channels from all over Europe. The Germans were the most prolific and offered the largest variety of channels, and particularly a lot of cartoons on week-ends. While I spoke no iota of German, I gobbled up every cartoon I could get my eyes on. And, over time, I realized that unbeknownst to be, I actually learned German. Without ever going to Germany, and without any formal German teaching, I learned the language. And I didn't only learn the basic stuff. With my cartoon German, I managed to get a university scholarship to study one semester at the Free University in Berlin. Not only did I get to study in German in Germany, but I also did quite well (although before starting the program I was scared shitless and considered myself somewhat of an impostor) – I was first in a class of 300 in Mathematics, Microeconomics, and Macroeconomics. Not bad for someone with no formal education in the German language.

The internet then allowed me to prepare myself for my graduate education in the US. Given that libraries in Romania did not really excel in the availability of good books on economics, I relied almost exclusively on information readily available on-line to prepare myself for university life in the US. Of course, the internet cannot replace a methodologically rigorous educational curriculum, but it can offer people easy access to information and it creates and environment conducive to the exchange of ideas. Moreover, it enables people to self-educate themselves when a formal education system is missing or is poorly developed.

Easy access to cable TV and internet can have another important fringe benefit. It can help strengthen good social norms. For example, cases of domestic abuse have dropped dramatically in rural communities in India once households got cable TV. By watching their favorite soap operas, both women and men learned about social norms that guide the life of couples around the world. Similarly, the incidence of rapes has dropped dramatically in regions with access to internet, as the internet provides men with plenty of ways to release their sexual frustrations.

Lastly, easy access to cable TV and internet can help diminish global violence and conflict, by enabling people to learn about the things we humans have in common. Empirical data actually shows that as the world has become interconnected, the incidence of violence has gone down – despite an exponential population growth, which normally would trigger more violence and conflict.

Create Big Data Storage

Humanity has an uncanny ability to periodically reset itself. Whenever a certain dominating civilization reaches its apex, a period of recess and soul-searching follows. The fall of the Roman Empire was followed by the Dark Ages in Europe; the Chinese are only now starting to recapture some of their past glory; the Egyptians never managed to achieve the might they once possessed. The way people, communities, countries, or empires managed to weather tough times is strongly correlated to how they manage to store and prize data.

The book "The Swerve" brilliantly describes the tragic loss of data and information that the Dark Ages triggered. We have no way of knowing how much of the knowledge generated before the Dark Ages is lost to us forever, because no proper storage of this data/information was available.

We will likely face more periods of recess in our glorious journey through the universe. It is important however that we will be prepared for these moments. And, it is of utmost importance that we store all the ideas we have generated over time.

To a certain extent, we can say that big data storage is already happening – on the millions of hard drives and folders that people around the World manage. And this is a good thing. The more people have access to information, the better. However, an individualistic and organic way of storing data may lead to a situation where vital pieces of information may be lost.

It is important to have data stored in a more systematic way – ensuring that obvious information gaps are filled. Such a database is important not only for a post-doomsday scenario, but also for the way the world functions today. We know for example that strong institutions have been fundamental for the performance of developed countries, but we have not always managed to properly codify and put on paper how these institutions work. For example, Romania used the Belgian Constitutions to elaborate its own Constitution after 1989, but it has been slow and/or incapable to import the institutions that would enable its cities to develop in a sustainable way. When local administrations are preparing a terms of reference for the rehabilitation of a road, the development of a bike path, or the modernization of a park, they most often have an unclear or incomplete idea about what they should ask for.

While just a hopscotch away, local administrations in Austria, Germany, or Italy, were managing to revamp their cities following clear guidelines, local authorities in Romania were groping for ideas on what to do.

Playing with the Status Syndrome

No matter how developed a country is, it will always have a set of problems to deal with – even Switzerland. This has a lot to do with how people's minds operate. If we wouldn't have something bigger to strive for, we would soon lose our drive to push forward. As Panait Istrati said, "if you don't have something to fight for, you don't live, you vegetate".

And the one thing that seems to drive people more than anything else is the drive to be better than those around us. In "The Status Syndrome", Michael Marmot indicates that people judge where they are in life based on how others around them are doing. If people perceive themselves as being higher in the pecking order, they are generally happier than those that perceive themselves to have a lower status. And given that we are complex creatures, there will always be someone that is better at something than we are – some people are better lovers, others better at making friends, some are smarter, others more driven, some know how to thrive in an organization, others are better at coping with life's challenges. We are perfectible and we spend a good part of our life trying to figure out how to best others.

This is good news for economists and business people. Given that every person has a lower status in a particular field (even a Renaissance man can't do everything well), it means that everybody has basically a never ending set of needs, wants, and desires. When basic needs are covered, people will strive to achieve higher status through the things they own (e.g. house, car, TV, fridge). When people achieve a certain level of material welfare, they often seek to get the approval and respect of other people – which explains why so many rich people dabble in politics. When you have the approval and respects of other people, you often look for ways to leave a mark behind, and higher level pursuits (e.g. writing a book that will change the world) become more important. We are all unfinished products, to the day we die, and what drives us is also what drives an economy.

In developing countries, the achievement of material wealth is what drives the economy forward. People want bigger houses, fast cars, and flat screen TVs. In developed countries, material wealth is within the grip of a large middle-class, and people care more about social connection and interaction, and personal growth.

From a social point of view, what is important to note about status, and this goes back to Thomas Piketty's argument, is that a system faces significant challenges when a significant share of the population does not see an improvement in its status over a long term. If you have been poor for 20-30 years, and your situation has not improved dramatically in this time-period, you are likely to be open to any type of change that can shake things up. This opens the door to populists, nationalists, and extremists, and it challenges the foundation of democratic institutions.

As Piketty has argued, demographic decline will lead to a concentration of wealth in fewer and fewer hands, leaving more and more people worse off. For those at the bottom of society, such a perpetuating situation pushes them to crave any change that may shake the system up, and thus allow them to maybe rise up. For them, there is no upside to perpetuating the status-quo (they are already at the bottom), but there may be an upside to a challenge to the status-quo – although this change may affect the foundations on which a free market society has been built.

Thus, every Government should heed Piketty's advice and ensure that the gap between the have and have-nots does not widen too much. A system that perpetuates stark inequalities will sooner or later face significant challenges from within.

How Can We Achieve More of Our Dreams

The only way to save yourself is to fight to save others.
NIKOS KAZANTZAKIS

We have an endless set of need, wants and desires, and we will never get to satisfy all of them. And that is OK. While we can only achieve few of our dreams in a lifetime, there are small tools we can use to achieve more of them. These tools are used quite efficiently in developed countries, where people are strongly vested in the future of the country. These tools are important to developing countries to, in their quest for better economic performance.

As I have repeated ad nauseam throughout the book, an economy is the sum of its people. Each of these people have a certain set of dreams they want to achieve, but are conscious they will only achieve a few. However, nobody is an island, and the dreams we have are usually shared by many other people. Thus, if we cannot realize a certain dream, we can help others do so. This is what makes strong communities, and strong communities are good for the economy.

We may not realize our dream to become a soccer star, but we can go cheer a young local hopeful. We may not have time or courage to start our own business, but we could buy a stake in a new and promising company. We may lack the talent to generate beautiful art, but we can buy the art of those that are good at it.

The more we give, the more we get back. Crowdfunding platforms like KickStarter, which enable usual people to finance the dreams of other usual people, have been growing in recent years, and they will become more important in the future. The capacity to help others achieve their goals as a means of achieving your own goals is a defining feature of developed countries. A country in which most people, preferably all, have the means of achieving their dreams, is a country where power cannot be grabbed and controlled by a few people – it is a country one can believe and invest in.

Ultimately, helping others achieve dreams that we also believe in may be just as satisfying as the achievement of these dreams on our own.

The Iceland Response to the Renaissance Man

Iceland is a tiny country. At a population of around 330,000 it is smaller than the neighborhood of a large city in Asia. The country's primary exports are aluminum and aluminum products, and fish and fish products – that's about it.

For a country that is so tiny however, Iceland manages to create periodic ripples. It has produced artists (e.g. Björk or Kaleo) that have reached international acclaim and have sold millions of albums. During the 2008 Global Crisis, three of its banks managed to raise to infamy as important players and major victims of the unfolding events (Michael Lewis provides a wonderful account in "Boomerang"). And, in 2016, Iceland managed to write soccer history.

Europe boasts a number of tiny countries like Iceland. These countries, being part of the Union of European Football Associations (UEFA) regularly participate in qualifiers for the World Cup or the European Cup (which usually take place 2 years apart). Up to 2016, countries like Iceland did not manage to do more in these qualifiers than make the other teams look good. A win against a country like Iceland, or Andorra, or Liechtenstein, were more or less guaranteed.

Iceland never managed to qualify to a World Cup or European Cup. Until 2016 that is. Its qualification to the 2016 European Cup group stages, was a small miracle in itself. What followed was a tsunami. It not only managed to get outside the group, beating Portugal and Austria (in the qualifiers it managed to best the Netherlands and Turkey), but it plowed through the England team, to get to the quarterfinals, where it was finally beaten by France.

While this Icelandic team included players that were active with professional clubs in mainland Europe, it also boasted players that had regular full-time jobs (e.g. butchers, dentists, drivers). With this team, picked from a male population aged 15-34 of less than 45,000, Iceland managed to take on some of the best teams in Europe.

The lesson that the Iceland Soccer team teaches us is that performance is possible in the unlikeliest of places. All it takes is a handful of people committed to a specific goal and being willing to take steps towards achieving those goals. Friedrich Hayek quipped, looking at the state of play in the field of economics, that "the person who actually does things" will usually be better off than "the economist [who is] the odious individual who sits back in his armchair and explains why the well-meaning efforts of the former are frustrated."

WHAT CAN COUNTRIES DO?

> "Even the smallest creature can change the course of the future."
> SRDJA POPOVIC

We got to this point and we have discussed some of the critical ingredients for growth and development. We know that geography, institutions, and markets matter. We also know that people are at the center of any development efforts. A country/region is only as developed as its people are. An enlightened leader, or a competent government can only do so much. Without the entire population working to pull the economy forward, you can't really go anywhere. To have the entire population on your side, you need to ensure that everybody has a stake in the future of the country/region. This means that everybody has to have access to opportunities, and following this logic, it means that a functioning democracy is an essential pre-condition for growth and development.

Another important lesson that comes out of this analysis is the importance other countries have in our development. The more integrated World markets are, the better off everyone is. For undeveloped and developing countries, access to the rich markets of developed countries is critical. For developed countries, it is paramount to have access to the growing markets in developing countries, given that their own markets are shrinking.

Data shows that while the World population has been growing by around 1.5% in recent years (and registering an overall downward trend), consumption has been growing by around 3% and exports by around 5.2%. Thus, the average person on the globe is consuming more and more, while countries trade more and more with each other to fuel this consumption growth.

The more integrated a country is in global trade flows, the better off it tends to be. In what follows, we will discuss how countries can better connect to these trade flows, as well as a number of concrete proposals that can help individual countries, and the World as a whole, sustain long-term growth and development.

Solutions for Undeveloped Countries

"Poverty is not intrinsically a trap, otherwise we would all still be poor."
PAUL COLLIER

Overcoming Distance to Markets

Undeveloped countries share a common geographic trait. They are almost all some distance away from large markets. Basically, there is no undeveloped country bordering a developed country – with the exception of quasi-autarchic systems like that of North Korea. Bordering a developed country almost always entails some positive spill-overs from the latter to the former.

Consequently, one of the key things that can help unlock growth and development in undeveloped countries is decreasing the distance to developed countries. Unfortunately, geography is a bitch! So, overcoming geography is easier said than done. The situation is not hopeless though – geography does not have to be destiny!

Transport advancements make it easier nowadays to overcome physical distance. For example, Botswana has managed to sustain relatively stable growth rates through the exports of diamonds. The one chief advantage of diamonds is that they pack a lot of value in a small package, and can thus be easily be exported by plane (foregoing the need for extensive and expensive road or rail networks, and over-coming the land-locked country problem). The chief disadvantage of diamonds is the fact that it is a depletable natural resource, it does not encourage human capital development, and it negatively affects all other economic sector (particularly the real economy). In Botswana, diamonds make-up 62% of the country's exports, and this share has grown continuously over the years.

It is more sustainable for undeveloped countries, particularly those that are landlocked, to build a competitive advantage in products (particularly agriculture and maybe light industry, which don't require a highly qualified labor force) that can be exported by cargo plane. This will enable them to only depend on their own infrastructure (e.g. airports, and their own road and rail networks) for international trade. For example, Kenya has developed a competitive advantage in the export of cut flowers, tea, and coffee. Rwanda is a land-locked country that has developed a competitive advantage in the export of tea and coffee. Ethiopia exports a lot of coffee, cut flowers, and sesame seeds.

Another option is to develop road and rail connections to the nearest port. This is also easier said than done. For one, such infrastructure is very costly – both to build and to maintain. For another, less developed countries most often lack the capacity and expertise to build such infrastructure. Even in my beloved Romania, which is on the cusp of becoming a high-income economy, the development of the national highway network has been very slow, despite the availability of significant EU grants for such investments.

A third option is a lighter version of Paul Romer's "Charter City" concept – in essence, a rip-off of the Singapore and Hong Kong development models. This is even less easy to put into practice, but an example to take into consideration none-the-less. What this model would entail is the creation of a free industrial zone within and around one, or several major ports, and allocating the management of this industrial zone to a private enterprise. Such a logistics and industry hub would enable the diversification of regional exports, and may also attract foreign direct investments.

Finding Alternatives to Resource Exploitation

Resources may seem a boon for a country, but as was discussed earlier in the book, they rarely are. Once resources have been discovered in an undeveloped country, it is difficult to stop their exploitation. From a social point of view, it is hard to postpone the exploitation of resources when much of the population has a long list of unmet needs. From a political point of view, it is suicide to postpone the exploitation of resources, as it is almost a guarantee for losing the next elections. In addition, there is likely to be a significant outside pressure from mining companies that want to make a quick buck.

There are no good models for how to deal with the resource curse. It is counter to human nature to throw away a winning lottery ticket. Not even Norway has the solution – if you strip away oil exports from the Norwegian economy, you soon see that the rest of its economy is not as performant as one might think.

There is one possible solution, which comes from an unlikely place – the former centrally planned economies. The leaders of the less developed communist countries realized that one way to modernize their economy was to barter the resources they had for technology from the West. Since they held the reins of the economy, they managed to finalize these transactions in a more or less seamless fashion.

Undeveloped countries could attempt a similar approach, and condition the exploitation of their resources on transfers of technology and investments in sectors with higher value-added than mining. In this way, concrete steps could be taken towards the modernization of their economies.

One thing that I have learned during Romania's transition

to a market economy, is that governments are not the best financial managers. As Romania's economy grew in anticipation of the EU accession, so did the revenues of the national budget. These additional budgetary resources could have been used for strategic infrastructure investments, but were instead used to grow employment and salaries in the public sector. In fact, salaries and employment in the public sector grew much faster than in the private sector, making the public sector more attractive for job seekers. The 2008 Global Crisis, thankfully put an end to this dynamic. If it would have continued, it would have been possible to get to a point where a disproportionate number of people worked for the public sector – a situation that is anything but ideal for a market economy.

In fact, this is what happened in most resource rich countries. They have become rentier economies, where the state uses revenues from resource exploitation to take care of the population. This is a trend that is not sustainable, for a variety of reasons (e.g. the depletion of the resources, a drop in global prices, a drop in the demand for that particular resource).

That is why, a solution to this conundrum is to require that resource exports be not only paid for in hard currency, but that for part of them, investments are made in other fields. For example, if a country exports legumes, some of the proceeds from resource extraction could go to the development of a canary. This way the country could export products with higher value-added. Similarly, if the country produces cotton, some proceeds from resource exports could be used for the development of textile factories.

Obviously, it is hard to get the private sector to act on a government recommendation, and investments in production facilities done by public entities rarely succeed (unless they have a monopoly on a particular service or good provision – e.g. water supply). But, it is imperative to create alternatives to a rentier economy. One of the worst aspects of the resource curse, is the gradual erosion of people's skills. Over time, people simply get complacent to make an easy salary and they fail to develop the competencies that would make them competitive on a global market. And, as discussed earlier, the strength of an economy lies in the strength of its people. The more people you have that know how to do something that few other people in the World know how to do, the better off you are. If these people furthermore know how to do things that many other people in the World want, you are in the money. The car, the TV, the computer, the software program, the smart phone, are things that few people in the World know how to do. The countries that have the people that know how to do these things, also are the most developed.

You Can't Choose Your Neighbors, but You Can Choose to Be Friends

There are no easy solutions to bad neighbors. Countries don't choose their neighbors, unless they happen to be on a conquering spree. Throughout history, countries and individual communities have been in a continuous state of conflict. Moreover, even when countries are not in conflict with each other, problems in one country (civil unrest, famine, natural disasters) can, and usually have reverberations in neighboring countries.

Undeveloped countries cannot do much on their own to offset the challenges that bad neighbors bring with them. When there is a civil war in a neighboring country, they take on a significant share of refugees. When there is a famine, they are among the first to provide aid and food. When there is a natural disaster, they are among the first to come and help. These good Samaritan deeds, however, come at a cost – both a real pecuniary cost, and a direct and indirect negative impact on the economy.

Organizations like the UN, intervene in such situations,

and often they play a critical role in lightening the burden for undeveloped countries, but there is much more that can be done. One option would be to have an international insurance system for countries. We don't know when lightning will struck, but we can do something to offset its negative consequences.

Just as the World Bank was created to have a global lender to the poor, a global insurance company could be set-up, with the assistance and financial help of developed and developing countries. The global insurance company could provide packages to undeveloped countries to help them cope with unexpected challenges, and aid to countries could be conditioned on being insured or not. For example, countries could insure against conflict in neighboring states, thus potentially having access to quick funds for setting up refugee camps. Similarly, insurance could be provided for natural disasters, like floods, droughts, or earthquakes.

Another solution to the bad neighbor problem is increased trade integration. The EU is as much a peace project as it is an economic project. By creating a common market for Member Countries, the EU has not only allowed increased prosperity in these countries, but it has also decreased the likelihood of conflict between them. When a significant share of your trade is done with neighboring countries, the performance of your economy is directly dependent on the performance of your neighbors' economy. This creates the proper incentives for the establishment of a climate of trust and cooperation.

Lastly, regional stability and order cannot be ensured without decisive action and the proper institutions in place. Currently, the UN, the US, Russia, or Western Europe, intervene in an ad-hoc manner to solve global, regional, or local conflicts. UN forces are far too small and badly funded to cope with the variety of challenges the World is facing. It may pay to develop a mechanism through which developed and developing countries commit a certain share of their standing army (e.g. 1%) to serve as Global Peace

Keepers. Such a standing army could ensure that armed forces can be quickly deployed, when an armed civil conflict like the one in Rwanda takes place. This does require a significant monetary effort on the part of developed and developing countries, but it is an effort that is well worth while when one considers the negative global consequences of conflict.

Moreover, ensuring and maintaining regional stability for undeveloped countries, can help open up the markets of those countries for investments, and can ultimately lead to the creation of new markets that developed and developing countries can take advantage of. A stable world, ultimately means prosperity for everybody.

Bridging the Teacher Gap

Historic data from the first half of the 19th century shows that while 40% of children in the south of the US went to school, around 80% of adults could read[38]. This suggests that a lot of people acquired rudimentary reading skills at home, without access to a functional education system. Nonetheless, a good education system is important for encouraging and sustaining growth and development, and teachers are essential for achieving a good education system. Unfortunately, undeveloped countries (particularly those without any natural resources), do not have enough teachers, nor is there any easy way to help them fill the existing gap. The one saving grace for them is technology.

Technological advances now permit a number of solutions for overcoming the teacher gap. For one, digital media allows the development of standardized course material, which can be translated and deployed in different countries. For example, a child in Zambia and one in Gambia, could learn basic mathematics following the same course material.

In areas where there are not enough, or no teachers, classes could be taught digitally if the right infrastructure is in place. For example, it may be enough to have a TV with an USB port, and with individual teaching material saved on an USB. A community representative could be tasked with ensuring that pupils follows the proper teaching material, and could help students with homework and questions that might arise.

This is of course a poor substitute for a real teacher, but it is much better than the alternative – no teacher and no formal education for the children whatsoever.

Another option are programs like "Teach for America", which could encourage young graduates in undeveloped countries to spend a few years in underserved areas, teaching the next generation of pupils. Developed countries could pool together capital to at least ensure a dramatic decrease in the level of illiteracy. Furthermore, efforts could be undertaken to raise computer literacy and access to the internet through much of the developed world. A young person that knows how to read, use a computer/pad/smartphone, and has access to the internet, is instantly better off because she/he has the basic tools for self-education.

In fact, international efforts to improve education outcomes should focus on ensuring that children are literate, can use a computer, and have the basic skills to use the internet. These outcomes could be achieved even if not enough teachers are available.

At a bare minimum, children in undeveloped and developing countries should have free access to the internet and cable TV. While acquiring a computer or a TV may be outside the means of a lot of people, governments could set-up simple community centers that provide people with free access to the internet and news about the outside world. When people have easy access to information, they can more easily teach themselves. In fact, the internet and the TV become surrogate teachers. I myself have managed to learn to languages (English and German) watching Chuck Norris movies and Transformers cartoons, and I have prepared myself for graduate school in the US accessing the vast library of the internet.

Cable TV and internet should be considered to be public goods, and provided freely to everybody in the country, the same way education is provided. In fact, many analyses of slum areas around the world, indicate that even people with very modest means will strive to gain access to TV and internet services, and often are also willing to pay for these services. In "Arrival City", Doug Sanders indicates that the entities that have the best census of people living in slums are Cable TV providers, as they are the only ones that provide public services to some of these slums, and they respond to a concrete demand.

Of course, being able to watch Cable TV is a very poor substitute for formal education, but it is much better than no education. It provides people with access to the outside world, and prepares many of these people to function in this World.

Leadership for the Leaderless

Oppression is a crime of opportunity. If you can do it, and you can get away with it, you will do it.
BILL EASTERLY

The road to autocracy has been paved by leaders with good intentions. Development is not easy, and a desire to do good can easily be supplanted by a thirst for power, or the simple fear of losing one's status and position. Great leaders, those that have defined the history of humanity, are by and large leaders that were faced with binary decisions (e.g. enter or not enter a war; oppose or not oppose a foreign oppressor; fight for human rights or remain idle) and a simple purpose goal. None were perfect people in real life, and none managed to maintain a track record of high achievements throughout their entire life.

Great leaders are rare worldwide, and they are even rarer in undeveloped countries, where the struggle of day-to-day living makes it really hard for most people to focus on lofty goals. Moreover, the job of developing a country is not the job of one person, but the job of the entire population. Unless there is a critical mass of people with a stake in the future of their country, one cannot sustain progress long-term.

Thus, leadership is not a quality that should be expected of someone in charge of the government, but a quality that all citizens should be endowed with. And this can be achieved quite easily. All it takes is to set up the proper goals.

One of the tragedies of coming of age in post-communist Romania, was the lack of true leaders in the country. We did not grow up with role models we could look up to. We did not have a Vaclav Havel or a Lech Walesa to inspire a generation of young people. We did have however a goal that almost everybody in the country shared – to become part of the big boys club of the West. Gaining NATO membership and the accession to the EU have been to clear goals that almost everybody in Romania shared, and that have emboldened leaders to appear throughout the Romanian society. These are largely unsung heroes that have built up the country in relative obscurity. They are leaders that no books will be written about, but they have been critical for the transformation of Romania.

The lessons offered by New EU Member Countries are relevant for undeveloped and developing countries alike. They show the importance of setting clear goals for a country, goals that can encourage the emergence of leaders and leadership throughout society. A goal that everybody believes in, is a goal that many people will be fighting for. A goal that everybody believes in, is a force that transcends electoral cycles and personal ambitions – it gives people hope and raises trust in a better tomorrow.

Undeveloped countries have to set simple, measurable, achievable, realistic, and time-bound goals (SMART goals) that can animate everybody in the country to fight for positive change. Ideally, such goals should be shared among a group of neighboring countries, to encourage friendly competition and peer-to-peer learning.

For undeveloped countries, as well as for developing countries, one of the key goals should be to become part of the "big boys club" – i.e. have access to the large markets of developed countries. Access to the US market has enabled Japan and South Korea to blossom; access to the Western European markets have enabled countries in South Europe and East Europe to perform better; access to the Chinese market enables now a number of countries in South-East Asia to grow fast.

Access to large markets is one of the surest ways to growth and development, and a stable and predictable system with access to markets is one of the biggest incentives for investors. Thus, undeveloped countries should set clear goals on trade integration and the strengthening of the rule of law. Furthermore, they should work on strengthening democratic institutions, ensuring that as many people as possible, preferably all, have access to opportunities and a stake in the future of the country. These three goals (access to large markets, stability and predictability, and easy access to power and opportunities for citizens) are the bedrock of a functioning market economy. Focusing on these three goals can help leaders in the undeveloped world to unlock the energy and creativity of the entire citizenry.

Fostering Global Human Capital

An economy is the sum of its people. This deserves repeating over and over again. However, the fact that an economy has a lot of people with great potential, does not mean that the economy would automatically do well. People have to first achieve their potential before the benefits can spill to the rest of the economy. Unfortunately, undeveloped countries rarely manage to offer the proper opportunities for their most qualified people. So what should undeveloped countries do?

I will argue here, and this will be an unpopular argument with many, that public authorities should enable their people to achieve their full potential, wherever that may be. It would be a significant loss for these countries, and for the World as a whole, if these people would wallow in relative obscurity.

Now, the free movement of people around the World is a beautiful pipe-dream, with few chances of becoming reality anytime soon. It would be an uphill battle, both in the receiving and the sending countries. However, there already are a number of programs in developed countries that enable qualified people an easier access to opportunities. For example, the US makes it easier for students and employees in the hard sciences (e.g. engineering) to receive a study/work visa. And such a program does indeed pay off, as a higher share of immigrants generate innovations than the native population.

Such a program should be extended to all developed countries. The benefits for them are quite clear – they thus manage to attract the brightest in the World, and have a higher chance of generating innovations that could push their economies forward. The benefits for the people that would get such a visa are also quite clear – they manage to access opportunities that would likely be impossible to access in their home countries.

The benefits for the sending countries are less obvious. The common argument is that undeveloped countries pay a lot of money to train their people, only to see some of their best snatched away by developed countries. This argument is fallacious though. It is true that any person that leaves is a significant loss for the sending country, but in the big scheme of things, this is a significant gain for the World as a whole. Think only of the great number of innovations that have been generated by immigrants. For example, we Romanians pride ourselves that one of our own has invented insulin. But, he did so in a research lab in Canada.

Sending countries also stand to benefit from potential reverse migration (i.e. people returning home after some time abroad). When people return after having spent some time in a developed country, they also bring with them capital, knowledge, business ties, and a different mentality and way of doing things. These are all assets that are critical for developing countries.

Of course, reverse migration only pays dividends in certain situations – i.e. when the country has embarked on a substantive growth path and when there is a large enough pool of qualified people that the economy can rely on. By and large though, the World as a whole stands to benefit when as many people as possible have access to the means to achieve their full potential.

Giving the Poor Access to Capital

Undeveloped countries will not become developed over night. Development is a long and cumbersome process that requires changes in productivity on a massive scale. In essence, a large number of people have to become more productive and thus push the economy forward. The problem is that an overwhelming share of people in undeveloped countries are engaged in subsistence farming. These people will not become software engineers from one day to the next. They can become better however at what they already do.

To become better at what they do, and thus raise their productivity, subsistence farmers need access to capital. Capital is needed if you need a new machine for plowing the field, a new tool for the manufacture of craft products, or a sewing kit. Poor households often lack the capital required to kick-start a business. Consequently, a way has to be found to fill this market gap.

It turns out that this market gap can in fact be filled by the private sector. The experience of the Grameen Bank in Bangladesh, demonstrates that the poor are not only eager to access lending, but they are also good customers, with very few of them defaulting on an accessed loan.

The Grameen Bank business model should be exported to as many undeveloped countries as possible. It is important to assess what are the conditions that would encourage private enterprises to enter this market, and identify ways in which undeveloped countries could be encouraged to create those conditions. In addition, developed countries could contribute to the capitalization of those banks, and also have representatives on those banks' boards.

Easy access to financing would not only allow people to purchase things that help them become more productive (e.g. a spinning wheel or a tractor), but also things that could help them improve their education (e.g. TV and internet) and things that could improve their overall standard of living (e.g. cookers and washing machines). When banks in Romania have started to offer credit for the purchase of everyday appliances, consumption in Romania went through the roof, not only enabling people to improve their standard of living, but also consolidating economic growth.

Credit basically allows people to enjoy benefits today that they normally could only afford to pay for at some point in the future. It is a critical element of a functional economy. Every country should strive to have a functional credit system in place. Such a system enables people to help themselves, rather than relying on government handouts.

Becoming Masters at Selling Cheap Labor

Without modernizing their economies, undeveloped countries stand no chance at sustaining growth. And, the modernization of their economies is virtually impossible without technology transfers from developed countries.

Capital cannot be attracted however without offering something in return. About the only competitive advantage of undeveloped countries is the cheap labor they can offer. However, having cheap labor is not a guarantee that investors will rush in. In fact, this rarely happens. The reason for this are relatively well known. For one, undeveloped countries do not offer the stability and predictability that investors require. For another, the available labor often does not have the necessary training that foreign investors are looking for.

Stability and predictability are hard to guarantee in undeveloped countries – especially in those with a functioning democracy. However, as was discussed earlier, a global insurance company could help cover the risks that private investors assume when going to underdeveloped countries.

As far as the training of the labor force is concerned, an essential pre-condition is a functioning basic education system (assuring literacy, basic computer skills, and the aptitude to use the internet). The most likely investments will be those in sectors that are labor intensive, but do not require a highly qualified labor force (e.g. textiles, food processing, canaries, assembly). Ideally, investments should be sought in the production of goods that are high in value but small in size, and which can be easily be transported by cargo plane. Given that undeveloped countries are usually some distance away from large markets, the cost of shipping goods by ship or road are too prohibitive (with the exception of goods that are place specific – e.g. avocados). Unless they receive a direct subsidy from developed countries for the export of these products, they simply are not competitive enough.

The need to train the labor force in the production of goods with high value in a small package, is in itself a clue with respect to how school curricula could be designed. It also helps public authorities be more focused in the type of investments they are trying to attract.

Creating Large Regional Markets

The experience of developed countries shows that trade is most efficiently carried with one's neighbors. The more developed the neighbors, the better off you are. Unfortunately, undeveloped countries have as neighbors other undeveloped countries – i.e. countries with small markets.

Nonetheless, even undeveloped countries have markets that can be tapped. Consequently, undeveloped countries stand to gain from trading more with each other. To enable as much intra-regional trade as possible, trade agreements should be encouraged whenever possible. This, as almost anything that involves less developed countries, is easier said than done. The governments of less developed countries simply lack the capacity to draft and negotiate such agreements.

This again is where developed countries could come in and provide agreement templates, as well as the proper venue and conducive environment for the negotiation of such agreements. Such trade agreements, would not necessarily be an immediate boon for the economy, but over the long term they would bring these countries closer together. If your economy depends to a significant degree on trade with your neighbors, you are more likely to be on friendly terms with them. Of course, conflicts most often have emotional origins rather than rational choice and calculated decisions, but close commercial ties can indeed function as a deterrent.

The more autarchic a country is, the more closed it is to global trade, the less developed it tends to be. Unfortunately, populist rhetoric often demonizes trade integration. Misguided, or ill-intentioned politicians, push for a closing of the economy in an attempt to protect national capital and investors. They don't realize however that by shutting off national capital from international markets, they basically doom it to sub-development and retardation. Without agile and dynamic economic sectors, no economy can develop. It does not take a brilliant mathematician to realize that when your markets are small, you have no chance of growing your economy by relying only on those endogenous markets. India has a lower consumption than Italy, and it cannot hope to grow its endogenous economy without trying to tap external large markets, the way China has done. Unlike China though, India has a functioning democratic system, which will pay dividends further down the road.

Bringing it All Together

Triggering sustainable economic growth in undeveloped countries is not an easy task. Neither is it however an impossible one. All developed countries have been at some point in their past undeveloped, and they have managed to make the transition.

For undeveloped countries, a number of strategic actions could prove useful in unlocking their growth potential:

- Shortening distance to large markets by focusing on the production of compact high value products, which can be easily exported by cargo plane.
- Enabling regional trade integration and the

establishment of partnerships with neighbors.

- Ambitious reforms of the educational sector and ambitious investments in educational infrastructure to ensure basic literacy (reading, computer, internet), for as many people as possible.
- Enabling access to credit for as many people and companies as possible.
- Attracting foreign investors to modernize the economy.

Solutions for Developing Countries

[I]t seems safe to say that some form of representative government based on the principle of popular sovereignty and some form of market economy fueled by the energies of individual citizens have become the commonly accepted ingredients for national success throughout the world.
JOSEPH J. ELLIS

With bad laws and good civil servants ... one can still govern, with bad civil servants even the best laws cannot help.
OTTO VON BISMARK

Bringing Large Markets Closer

Having a developed country as a neighbor puts you in a very good position; being part of a trade union like the EU is like hitting the jackpot – it is one of the most efficient ways of growing your economy.

Geography is a bitch though, and if you happen to be far away from developed places, you have to learn to efficiently play the cards you've been dealt. If you happen to be somewhere in Central Asia, your options are limited. If you are however somewhere in Eastern Europe, the future is a bit brighter. For example, the Ukraine is some distance away from Western Europe, but it shares a border with four EU countries (Poland, Slovakia, Hungary, and Romania). Of these, three have in the meantime become developed economies, and one is on the way to achieving the same. This basically means that the Ukraine will soon border countries with relatively large and growing markets and would be able to trade closer to home. More regional trade means higher growth, which in turn will spur even more trade, in a virtuous cycle that benefits all parties involved.

Of course, the best thing for countries like the Ukraine and Moldova is to become part of the EU, but this is not an easy process and it requires the buy-in of a large majority of stakeholders in the country, as well as in the EU countries.

The Ukraine and Moldova are in fact among the more fortunate developing countries. But, what are the options for countries like Georgia, Armenia, Tajikistan, or Kyrgyzstan? The prospects are less rosy for them, but the situation is not hopeless.

Trading with developed countries means having interconnected economies, which in more technical terms means trading back and forth in intermediary products (predominantly) and final products. The trade of intermediary products requires proximity, good infrastructure, good logistics, and predictability of trade policies. Unfortunately, most developing countries lack one or more of these assets. Generally, countries that trade in higher value-added intermediary products have stronger economies than those that trade in unprocessed agricultural products.

To better understand how developing countries could bring large markets closer, it helps to see who they are trading with now, and what they are trading. For example, developing countries in South-East Asia, primarily export to large markets in the region

(China, Japan, or South Korea). The developing countries that are closer to those markets trade primarily in intermediary goods (e.g. Thailand, Vietnam, or the Philippines). The countries that are further out (e.g. Indonesia), primarily export natural resources.

In Latin America, exports are similarly guided by geography and geopolitics. Much of the exports of Mexico, Colombia, or Venezuela go to North America – but none from Cuba. Brazil, Peru, and Chile primarily export to Asia – largely natural resources and unprocessed agricultural products. Argentina, Uruguay, and land-locked Bolivia largely export to other countries in South America.

Kyrgyzstan and Tajikistan in central Asia primarily export to Europe and Asia, and they largely export natural resources. Pakistan and Bangladesh primarily export textiles to Europe and Asia, while 80% of Mongolian exports go to China.

There is no magic wand to deal with unfavorable geography, and countries that are far away from developed markets, have a difficult task ahead of them. However, it is important that they do the best of what they got, and to the extent possible, they should look to establish trade agreements with the countries with the largest and closest markets to them. In addition, they should look to specialize in easily tradable services (e.g. software development) and goods that can be traded via cargo-plane (e.g. cell-phones, computer parts).

If your geography is favorable, and you are close to a developed market (e.g. Mexico close to the US, the Ukraine close to the EU, or Vietnam close to China), try to further trade integration as much as possible. The larger markets you have access to, the better off you will be.

For leaders of developing countries this message is critical: you cannot grow your economy by relying solely on your markets – not even China managed that feat. India with its 1.3 billion people exports less than Belgium, which has a population of 11 million."

Encouraging Density

A country's performance is inexorably linked to the performance of its largest cities. If these cities do not perform well, neither does the economy as a whole. But, what cities deserve more attention? Obviously, lavishing all cities with attention is neither practical nor economical. Empirical data that has mounted over the past years provides some clues in this respect.

In countries that have developed organically, the distribution of cities follows a strangely uniform pattern. Known as the Zipf Distribution, or the Rank Size Rule, this pattern applies almost universally. In essence, the Zipf Law indicates that if you plot the log of a city's population and the log of its rank in the national urban hierarchy, you get a uniform pattern. The figure below highlights this distribution for six countries. In lay-men's terms, the Zipf Law posits that in countries that develop organically, you usually have one, and only one, primate city, followed by 1-2 cities with around half its population, then 2-3 cities with around a third of the population, and so on... to finally produce a distribution like the one in the graph below.

When you analyze the Zipf Distribution over several decades, another pattern emerges. For one, primate cities seem to be quite resilient in their leading position. The early advantage they enjoyed over other cities, they seem to hold over the long term. New York was the largest city in the US in 1790, with a population of only around 33,000, and it holds that position to this day, with a population of around 8 million. The same can be observed for every current primate city in the World, such as London, Paris, or Istanbul. Even when a primate city was obliterated off the face of the Earth, as Warsaw was, or obliterated off the face of the Earth, then partitioned in 4 sections, then divided for over 40 years by a wall, like Berlin was, they still stay strong in their leading position.

Zipf Distribution in Selected Countries, for 2010

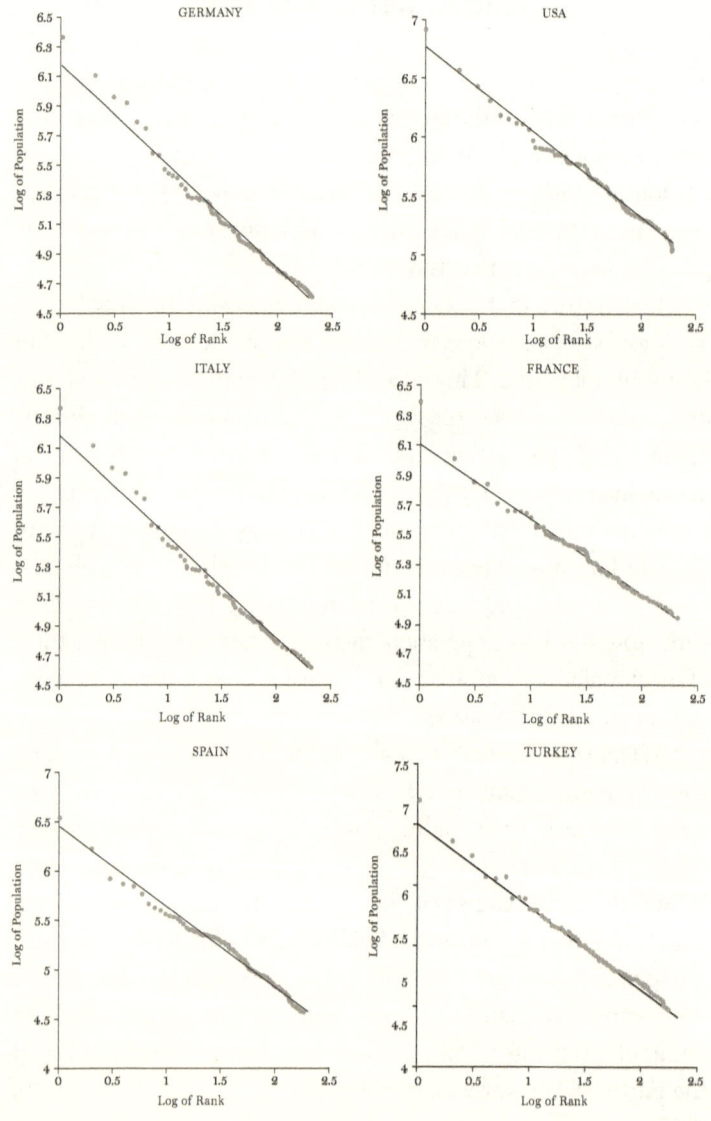

Source: World Bank. 2013. Competitive Cities: Reshaping the Economic Geography of Romania

Primate cities are consequently quite resilient not only to war and geopolitical maneuvering, but they seem to also be resilient to bad governance. The question is whether something like this is desirable or not.

Another pattern that is observed when looking at a country's Zipf distribution over several decades, is that the distribution holds. Cities change in size, secondary cities may change their position in the hierarchy, but the distribution does not budge. More concretely, there will almost always be 1-2 cities with a population around half that of the primate city (although not always the same), 2-3 cities with a population of around a third that of the primate city, and so on. These are basically market forces and statistical laws working together in a weird way. Thus, in the US, cities like Salem, Charleston, or Providence used to be in the top 10 largest cities. Large cities like Baltimore, Boston, St. Louis, Buffalo, Pittsburgh, or Detroit, used to be among the 10 largest cities in the US, but their place has been taken by cities that were barely on the map a few decades back. The dynamic with regards to city size and national rank is less pronounced for cities in Europe, largely because people are not as mobile as they are in the US.

Often times, the source of a country's competitiveness comes from these secondary cities. Primate cities can become complacent with their leading position, and secondary cities always have something to prove. The industrial revolution in the US was driven by cities like Detroit, Philadelphia, and Pittsburgh. Chicago has established itself like a logistics and trade hub. Los Angeles is a media mecca and the film capital of the World. The IT and biotech revolution is now driven by cities like San Jose, San Francisco, San Antonio, or San Diego. In Europe, a lot of the innovation is generated in places like Wolfsburg, Ingolstadt, Espoo, Nantes, or Uppsala.

Primate cities most closely resemble the overall structure of the economy and their performance directly influences the way the economy as a whole performs. If these primate cities don't do well, neither does the economy as a whole. Secondary cities provide the competitive edge and innovation required to drive the economy over the long-haul. However, the performance of secondary cities varies over time (influenced by factors such as proximity to markets, size, presence of a university, governance, global shifts, or sheer luck), and there are no reliable tools to predict which secondary city will do well and when. Nonetheless, once a secondary city has started to perform well, it is important to identify ways for ensuring the added value it generates spills over to the economy as a whole.

Data from New EU Member States shows a very interesting pattern. Thus, the primate cities in these countries, are already competing head-to-head with the primate cities in the Old Member Countries. They basically have relatively similar productivity levels. However, secondary cities in New Member Countries are much less competitive than secondary cities in Old Member Countries. It is these cities that most stringently require assistance to become more competitive. As the development cup of the primate city is getting full, development starts to spill over to secondary cities. This dynamic should be encouraged, as an economy cannot be competitive if its main cities are not competitive.

In the EU, primate cities in developing countries compete head-to-head with primate cities in developed countries

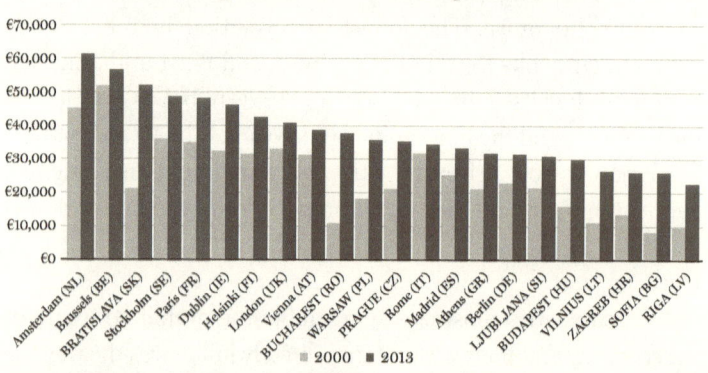

Source: EuroStat
Note: Data represents GDP per Capita (PPS)

Consequently, policy makers that want to put and keep their country on a long-term growth path, cannot think an economic development policy that does not take the primate city and the key secondary cities (i.e. the country's leading regions) into consideration. The following sub-sections discuss a number of concrete measures that can help primate and secondary cities become more competitive.

Shorten distance to large markets
Cities that have large endogenous markets, or are close to large to markets are attractive to investors. A large city is not necessarily equivalent to large markets. Many of the metropolises of the World (e.g. Mumbai, Lagos, or Tehran) are not necessary attractive places for investors. For one, they lack a large enough middle-class (i.e. people with large enough incomes to buy what the investors produce) and they are often quite a distance away from markets in the developed world. While the US is not the largest country in the World, it has the largest national market.

As recent research has shown, as transport costs have gone down, trade has not become more global, but more regionalized. Countries now primarily trade with their neighbors, and the largest share of this trade is represented by sub-components. More specifically, countries and regions have become increasingly specialized in the production of certain components rather than having vertically integrated production chains.

To shorten distance to large markets, cities have two options: 1) create large markets of their own, by attracting high-value added investments, which provide higher salaries to the people there and make the city more attractive to other investors (another oddity of real life economics is that companies prefer to settle close to their competitors rather than settling where there are no competitors); 2) invest in connective infrastructure that shortens the distance to large markets – ideally large markets that are close to home.

Some of the largest markets in the EU are large metropolises like London, Paris, or Bruxelles, and an area smack in the middle of the EU (spanning North Italy, Austria, South Germany, East France, and Switzerland), which is more-or-less at the cross-road of European trade routes.

Enable the emergence of functional urban zones
Dynamic cities do not function in a vacuum – they are most often part of functional urban zones. On its own, Bucharest amasses around 10% of Romanian's population and around 28% of the GDP. However, the one hour drive area around it amasses 25% of the national population and generates around 50% of national firm revenues. If the Bucharest metropolitan area would actually function like a metropolitan area, with an integrated metropolitan transport system, an integrated spatial planning system, and integrated planning and project implementation, then more people in its vicinity would have access to the opportunities it has to offer, and the companies in Bucharest would have access to a larger labor force. Local public administrations that are part of a metropolitan area have to come and plan together. This will allow them to be more efficient in attracting people, investors, and tourists.

Invest in quality of life
A World Bank study of over 700 global cities, shows that once cities have passed a certain development threshold (a GDP per Capita of around $20,000) creative and innovative industries become more dominant. As these industries become more dominant, cities enter a competition for highly skilled human capital. Primate cities usually compete for human capital with other global primate cities (they usually already amass the largest national pool of human capital), while secondary cities compete with other national and global secondary cities. In this competition, the quality of life cities provide plays a crucial role in how successful they are in

attracting qualified people. The most skilled people usually don't have problems finding a job in most cities, so when they decide where to locate, they also look at other things, such as: good urban design; green areas and parks; good night-life and entertainment opportunities; bars, pubs, restaurants, and clubs; and, of course, other like-minded people. Consequently, investments in quality of life can go a long way in making developed cities more attractive to qualified human capital, and, by extension, to high value-added investors.

Enable the flow of people and ideas between cities

Especially for secondary cities, which often generate a significant share of innovations in a country, it is important to have a highly mobile population. Increased mobility, means that people with similar skillsets can form clusters and give the cities where they settle a competitive edge. The EU has from this point of view a disadvantage to the US, given that population is the EU is less mobile across state boundaries than the US population is within the US. Language and culture provide some obstacles to higher mobility.

Shortening the Distance to Density

Density matters, and so does proximity to density. As a country develops, it is propelled forward by its largest cities. The growth of these cities inevitably spills over to surrounding areas. Usually, the suburban and peri-urban areas of dynamic cities are among the fastest growing in the country.

The trick to enabling a country to develop fast is to enable these spillover effects to reach an area as large as possible. In practice, this means to allow as many people as possible access to the opportunities dynamic cities offer, while at the same time allowing private companies access to a labor pool as large as possible. Achieving this desiderate requires the proper regional transportation investments, metropolitan planning, and improved governance structures.

Investments in developing countries are most often done in and around dynamic cities. As almost everything in life, these investments follow the path of least resistance. Investors want access to cheap land, good infrastructure (road, rail, air), qualified and plentiful labor, and good governance. Given that developing countries largely depend on industry to propel their economies forward, they have to identify ways to accommodate new industrial plants. Given that new industrial plants most often locate on the outskirt of cities, where land is cheaper and more easily available, it is important to make this land more easily accessible (i.e. to have functioning land markets), and to develop the proper connective infrastructure. Of course, this new connective infrastructure will raise the value of the land it connects, but it also makes more land available to investors.

In addition to connective infrastructure, it is important to develop public transport networks for the larger functional urban zones. This will enable people in the area to more easily reach the opportunities offered by dynamic cities, while enabling private companies to reach a larger labor pool.

Ensuring Stability and Predictability

Providing stability and predictability is one of the key tasks of any government. This is easier said than done though, especially when one has a democratic system with free elections and frequent changes of government.

The alternative to democratic governance are autocratic systems. Such systems are quite efficient in the medium term, but by their own design, they cannot maintain stability long-term. The experience of Communist countries highlights this well. A system that is predicated on offering stability and predictability has to do so long-term, if it is to survive long-term. This also means that it has to maintain or increase welfare and development. If it fails to do so, sooner or later there will be dissent in the system, and there will be a growing chorus of people asking for change. People invariably blame their mishap on others, and the country's leaders are frequent scapegoats.

Without giving as many people as possible preferably all, access to power and opportunities, it is hard for a country to maintain long-term growth. A country is better off when all citizens have a stake in its future, as it has a higher likelihood of identifying solutions to the myriad of development challenges it has to face. Autocracies are not very good at this. Even when they have enlightened leaders at their helm, it is hard to always have the perfect solution for all the hoops life is throwing at you.

Few countries have managed to sustain long-term growth without encountering some hick-ups, and subsequent government changes along the way. The most successful case is of course the US – the longest running democracy in the World. An analysis of the US success model is beyond the scope of this book, but the key ingredients are more or less known. For one, you need a clear separation of powers: the executive; the legislative; and the judicial. Moreover, it is important to ensure that there is a balance of powers. In many developing countries, the executive reigns supreme over the legislative and the judicial, which most often renders the latter two ineffective.

In addition, mature democracies like the US have a system of other institutions (e.g. a strong media, a strong civil society, NGOs) that ensure the proper checks-and-balances for all the power structures in the country – both public and private.

Ensuring the Proper Checks-and-Balances

A system, no matter how stable and predictable it may be, cannot sustain long-term growth without a proper system of checks-and-balances in place. A system of checks-and-balances increases the likelihood of course correction when a system has gone astray.

A key pillar is a free and dynamic media – also called the fourth state power. In developing countries, the media is often controlled by the state or a few private interests, and it tends to cater to those interests. A free media is critical in ensuring that the other three powers are kept in check.

Of course, an active media is not always enough, as it can cover only so many subjects and it is not immune to outside influence. An active civil society is critical for a healthy economic system. An active civil society is equivalent to a society of watchdogs, ensuring that when the other four powers are sleeping, someone else is left guarding the flock. Governments can do a lot in encouraging or suppressing an active civil society.

For example, in Romania, a Canadian mining company had planned to undertake a massive gold exploration, which would have wiped out four mountains of the face of the Earth, while leaving a huge cyanide lake behind. The Romanian Government, in its infinite wisdom, decided this is a good idea – all in the name of creating a few temporary jobs.

The mainstream media was, for the most part, favoring the project, because they were receiving large advertising deals from this Canadian company. Only a handful of citizens complained about the potential environmental, social, and economic negative effects such an investment might have. These handful of citizens staged protests in Romania's largest cities, and their number steadily grew, as more and more details about the project came out.

The moment the protests got too big to ignore, the media

started to pay more attention. In fact, the protesters have complained about the media's complete silence on the issue. As soon as the media blockade was broken though, the issue started to be analyzed more carefully by the Government too. Eventually, the site was declared a protected cultural heritage site (it includes kilometers of ancient Roman and medieval mines) and an anti-corruption investigation was started. Without the involvement of this handful of citizens early on, it is likely that things would have progressed differently.

Other institutions are also important to maintain a proper checks-and-balance on the key powers in the state. This may include anti-corruption agencies, integrity agencies, anti-monopoly agencies, competition councils, and so on. The key role of those institutions should be to ensure that power does not get concentrated in too few hands – either public or private. The concentration of power in a few hands is the surest way to system atrophy and eventual decline.

The Highway to Happiness

The key role of government should be to ensure that all of its citizens reach their potential, have easy access to opportunities, and are free to pursue happiness every way they see fit – as long as their pursuit of happiness does not impede the option of others to pursue their own happiness.

Consequently, it is critical for governments to identify the proper tools that allow as many people as possible, preferably all, to pursue their happiness. For starters, governments should ensure that all people have the same start in life. This means access to quality education, quality healthcare, basic services (electricity, internet, piped water, and wastewater), and easy access to opportunities – wherever these opportunities might be.

An economy is the sum of its people, and it will always be only as strong as its citizens are. A country cannot grow and develop if its citizens do not first grow and develop. The more people have access to growth and development opportunities, the better off the country is.

Governments often have a murky definition of what their role is or should be. They often see themselves as the providers of happiness (e.g. they consider it their obligation to provide jobs, housing, and a good life), where they should actually be enablers. A Government can offer free education, but cannot do for the people the work required to obtain a degree; it can attract investors, but cannot do the shifts required to holding a job; it can enable access to art and culture, but it is up to us to enjoy them.

Smart Specialization

The EU has introduced a policy of smart specialization for its Member Countries, starting from the premise that countries should specialize in the sectors whey they have a competitive advantage. The basic premise of this policy is correct. The way it is implemented in practice is not. For one, the global economy is evolving faster than economic theory, and as new sectors pop-up, others are wiped out. A few years back, Finland had a strong competitive advantage in mobile technology. Then Apple introduced the smart phone and Finland's mobile-phone industry went bust – and with it, its competitive advantage in this field. In 2005, around 20% of Finland's exports included telephones and broadcasting equipment. By 2014, this share dropped to 2%. Obviously, countries have to identify the tools to respond to such rapid change – which most often is enabled by a diversification of the economy.

In addition, to the rapid changing global economy, one has to add the dependance of developing countries on the markets of developed countries. In essence, developing countries will largely specialize in what is sought after in developed countries. Thus, if developed countries consume lots of cars, TVs, and computers, this is what many of the developing countries will produce. Developed countries basically set the pace for developing countries. Those who have the markets, control the pace of development.

Trade specialization is critical for developing countries, and it has to follow, and usually follows, the pattern of specialization of your main trade partners. Thus, if you trade a lot with Germany, there is a high likelihood that you will specialize in the production of automobiles and automobile sub-components. If you trade a lot with Japan, you probably specialize in the automobile sector or electronics.

Also, critically to understand is that developing countries do not hang on to a trade specialization for too long. As they develop, they move from lower value-added sectors to higher value-added ones. Romania, for example, relatively quickly moved away from the old and uncompetitive industrial plants, to light manufacturing – primarily in the textile sector. However, it did not keep a competitive edge in textile manufacturing for too long. As the economy developed, there was an upward pressure on salaries, and textile manufacturers could no longer stay competitive in Romania. Consequently, there was a shift from textile manufacturing to the manufacturing of automobile sub-components. This dynamic mimicked quite closely the dynamic in other Central and Eastern European countries.

Consequently, the key policy advice for developing countries is this: 1) study very closely what your key trade partners (usually the developed countries closest to you) are producing – you are likely to specialize in one or more of their key sectors; 2) study very closely what the more developed countries in the region are producing – there is a high likelihood that you will follow a similar path (e.g. Romania should look at what Poland, Hungary, Slovakia, and the Czech Republic are doing); 3) determine what interventions (e.g. education system reform; tax incentives; infrastructure development) are needed to encourage a quick development of key strategic sectors (discussions with companies in these sectors are critical for a better understanding of their needs); 4) do not get hung-up on one particular sector – the World changes faster than any of us can fathom; 5) focus instead on ensuring that the people in your country are prepared to weather these fast and sudden changes.

Instead of having a population that is good at producing cars, it is better to have a population that can quickly and flexibly adapt to change. The focus should not be on the accumulation of knowledge, but on creativity and problem solving. And, ultimately, one should eventually move from a follow-the-leader approach to a leadership approach – when the economy has reached a certain level of maturity.

Modernizing the Economy

There is one and only one clear-cut way of modernizing the economy of a developing country – through the transfer of technology from developed countries. Most commonly, the transfer of technology happens through foreign direct investments. There is also the option of using foreign technologies to spur new endogenous industries. This was the option used by most Communist countries, as well as by a number of countries in East Asia (e.g. Japan and South Korea). During Communism, Romania adopted technology from Renault to build its Dacia car manufacturing plant, technology from Citroen to build the Oltcit car manufacturing plant (now an extinct brand), French technology to build its Allouette and Puma helicopters, and Russian technology to build its fighter planes.

Japan and South Korea went the way of vertical integration – i.e. large companies, tooled with technologies from abroad, that produced an end product from start to finish, rather than having many smaller companies producing sub-components and then assembling them. They did so largely because they did not have anybody around them to trade with freely, not necessarily because of the local culture. In the EU, where markets for goods are well integrated, it is easy to produce a steering wheel in Bulgaria, a spark-plug in Poland, the upholstery in Romania, the car frame in Hungary, and assemble the whole thing in Slovakia. Japan and South Korea did not have this luxury when they started on their economic growth path. Things have of course changed in the mean-time, and the growth of economies in East Asia, has led to more and more market integration.

Both foreign direct investments and the modernization/creation of endogenous companies have their merits. Foreign direct investments have the advantage of quick economic growth, and the creation of capital for further investments in the economy. Endogenous investments have stronger local roots and are more resilient to sudden global changes.

Public authorities have tools to encourage both. For one, it is critical to have agencies that think of ways to attract investors and respond to investor's needs. Just as the best private companies have strong marketing departments, so should national governments. However, few countries/cities are actually good at marketing themselves – most don't even have dedicated units dealing with these issues.

Of course, being good at marketing only takes you so far – you also have to offer investors what they want. Good packaging will only take you so far. What investors are looking for is more or less known: stability and predictability; available cheap land and/or office space; access to a large enough pool of qualified labor force; good connective infrastructure (airports, highways, rail, roads, public transportation, ports); an efficient public administration; the presence of other similar companies locally. For national companies/entrepreneurs that are looking to expand/open a business, it is important to enable easy access to capital.

In addition to a transfer of technology it is also critical to ensure a transfer of know-how. Attracting foreign investors is the easiest way of transferring both technology and know-how, but often times investors fail to come despite a country's best efforts. In those situations, a high price should be put on the transfer of know-how. In "The Company: A short History of a Revolutionary Idea", Adrian Wooldridge Micklethwait indicates that when Japan embarked on its modernization path, it spent over 2% of its budget on foreign experts that brought know-how and tacit knowledge with them.

Enabling Citizens to Achieve Their Dreams

> *Leadership, true leadership, is not the bastion of those who sit at the top. It is the responsibility of anyone who belongs to the group.*
> SIMON SINEK

A developing country, especially the smaller ones and the less developed ones, can only offer so many opportunities to their citizens. Even developed countries don't offer the full range of opportunities people are looking for – I'm sure there are quite a few Germans dreaming of becoming Hollywood stars. Rather than trying to keep these "dreamers" at home, public authorities in developing countries should think of ways of enabling these people to reach their potential wherever they may desire.

In practice, this requires the free movement of people across the Globe – a luxury that only a relatively small share of people in developed countries enjoy right now. This, of course, is neither an easy political sell, nor an easy social sell (if all the doctors or teachers in a country would decide to leave, the country would be in a pickle). Nonetheless, it is something that can pay significant future dividends and force government to reform – when people vote with their feet (i.e. when they leave because of the lack of opportunities), there is a higher incentive for governments to come up with the right policies (this is of course predicated on having a democratic system in place).

Making it easier for people to travel elsewhere, requires strong diplomatic efforts and strong arguments to convince developed countries to open their borders. Given political and social restrictions in receiving countries (few people are open to immigration, especially in large numbers), this is a task that looks much easier on paper than in practice.

In addition, it is important to invest in the skills that makes people more mobile and enables them better upward mobility in other places. Education is paramount in this respect – the more educated a person is, the better it tends to adjust to varying conditions in other places. It is also important to encourage foreign language training from early on (ideally, everybody in the country should be fluent in the World's lingua franca – English), as well as cultural sensitiveness. The more understanding people are of other cultures, the easier it is for them to adapt abroad.

Bringing it All Together

Policies of utmost importance for developing countries include:
- The encouragement of a sustainable urbanization process;
- Shortening the distance to large markets and strengthening ties with these markets;
- Creating a stable and predictable environment for investors, and a system of checks-and-balances that prevent the concentration of power and capital in a few hands;
- Encouraging the modernization of the economy through technology transfers from abroad.

Solutions for Developed Countries

Throughout history, the vast majority of geniuses have come from middle and upper-middle classes. They had enough money to pursue their passions, but not so much that they lapsed into complacency.
ERIC WEINER

Dealing with Lagging Regions

No country has managed to develop evenly – not one! Growth and development are inherently uneven. Some regions will always do better, while other will others will have a poorer performance. Over time, performance of regions shifts. India used to generate the highest share of World output a millennium ago. In the US, the current Rust Belt used to be the most productive region in the country half a century ago. The Ruhr Region used to be the economic heart of Germany.

Addressing the challenges faced by lagging regions is something that almost all national governments undertake. They do so for various reasons, and sometimes those reasons are not necessarily sound. Quite often, the drive of lagging region policies is the eradication of the economic gap between lagging and leading regions. I will argue here that this task is a futile one, often leading to a senseless waste of resources.

To address the challenges faced by lagging regions, one has to first understand some of the key characteristics of such regions. More often than not, lagging regions are far away from markets (and, of course, they lack a large market of their own), they tend to have few dynamic urban agglomerations, and a significant share of their population works in agriculture (usually subsistence farming).

For these regions to develop, it is absolutely critical that agglomeration forces kick in and drive in these regions a process of sustainable urbanization. No region has managed to develop without having a dynamic city to help it along. And city growth is a process that goes hand in hand with individual productivity growth.

Vernon Henderson has pioneered brilliant work on the sources of city growth, and ingeniously shows how city growth is intimately intertwined with individual productivity growth[39]. Henderson indicates that as cities grow, so does the cost of living in those cities. Getting around the city gets more cumbersome and costly, which drives a rise in land and rent prices in central city locations, which in turn leads to a growth in prices for the supermarkets, restaurants and pubs operating in those areas. To offset these costs, both firms and individuals have to become more productive. When productivity increases are unlikely in such a location, firms may choose to re-locate – and they often do in search of cheaper labor.

This in itself explains why there are no agricultural metropolises in the World, or, for that matter, why there are almost no industrial metropolises. Neither the agriculture sector, nor the industrial sector provide the kind of salaries, or rather the salary growth, required to offset the continuing growth in the cost of living in growing cities. In almost all metropolises around the World, regardless whether in the developed or the developing world, an overwhelming share of the population works in the services sector. In fact, these metropolises tend to concentrate a high share of high value-added businesses in the country.

Thus, for lagging regions to catch up with leading regions, they have to build up a high concentration of productive individuals (assuming relatively high mobility of people) and high value-added businesses. This is of course easier said than done. And here is why.

In almost every country around the world, the primate city

also represents the most developed region in the country. Catching up with the primate city is a difficult task, given that these cities not only concentrate the largest population in the country, but also concentrate a high share of high value-added businesses. Catching up to a secondary city is an easier task, and in countries with high population mobility, such as the US, secondary cities switch ranks quite often (this is a less frequent occurrence in Europe and Japan). However, the Zipf Rule that we have discussed earlier, indicates that a city may grow in rank (and by extension grow its economy), but it always does that at the cost of another city. San Jose, San Antonio, or San Diego are now booming cities in the Sun Belt of the US, but their rise was paralleled by the decline of the Rust Belt cities, such as Detroit, Philadelphia, or Cleveland.

Given the importance of urban agglomerations why doesn't everybody simply cluster in such a large agglomeration? The simple and simplistic answer is that each large urban agglomeration generates forces that attract people (e.g. higher salaries and more opportunities), but also forces that push people out (e.g. a high cost of living and congestion). You only have to visit one of the metropolises around the world to understand how these forces work in practice.

What is important to understand for the argument here, is that a country will almost always have a panoply of human settlements – some larger, some smaller. Those regions with the smaller settlements will tend to also have more economic difficulties – i.e. those will usually be the lagging regions in their respective countries.

Thus, a lagging region policy is in many respects a defeatist policy, because a country will never be rid of lagging regions, no matter how developed it might be. There will always be regions that do worse than the rest, and there will always be individuals that are worse-off than the rest of the population. Thus, a lagging regions policy will rarely be successful – even if it helps some regions to do better, it can make things worse off somewhere else.

To properly address the challenges of lagging regions, one has to shift from a focus on space to a focus on the people inhabiting the space. The task is to identify ways in which the needs, wishes and desires of the people living in the lagging regions can be addressed, and to enable them the same start in life and the same access to opportunities that people in leading regions enjoy. Some of the tools that will be used will be similar to the tools presently used (e.g. the modernization of existent and development of new infrastructure), while some will be harder to accept (e.g. making it easier for people to access opportunities elsewhere).

Addressing the Challenges Faced by Marginalized Communities

Every developed country, no matter how well it is doing, will be divided between the haves and have-nots. While a significant share of the population will be doing well (the middle-class and the rich), there will always be a group that is less fortunate. The have-nots may be victims of discrimination by the majority (racism, xenophobia, elitism), or they may simply be in a situation that pushes them at the margin of society (e.g. single parents earning minimum pay, working on-and-off jobs, or being recipients of social security).

Generally, marginalized communities (e.g. racial minorities, immigrants, the poor) represent a higher share of the population in countries that are more market-oriented and have fewer social intervention tools. For example, almost every major US city has one or more socially excluded groups. In countries with stronger welfare systems (e.g. countries in Western Europe), the incidence of marginalization is less pronounced, but it is still there.

No country is free of social challenges, not even the most

boring ones, like Switzerland. And, unless these challenges are addressed head-on, they risk growing into bigger and bigger issues, and risk spiraling out of control (e.g. social clashes). A lack of attention to the challenges faced by marginalized communities can have not only social and political repercussions, but also economic ones. Marginalized communities are often in a position to work below their productive potential, because of forces that are outside their control (e.g. racism, elite capture, xenophobia). This is of course a loss for the economy as a whole. For example, a World Bank report[40] estimated that if the Roma minority in Romania would achieve the productivity level of the average Romanian, the country's GDP would be boosted by 3%.

While many people think that poor and marginalized people deserve the fate they have, reality is a bit more nuanced. Study after study shows that poor and marginalized people face challenges most of us have never had to deal with. One of my favorite such studies is written by George Orwell – "Down and Out in Paris and London". Orwell did what few advocates of the poor ever do – he actually spent a few months with the homeless in Paris and London, to better understand the challenges they faced. He indicates that the constant lack of food, and the lack of human interaction, empathy, and compassion, leaves these people with little energy to pursue anything else. Life becomes a fight for survival, and existence becomes merely a fight for the next meal.

Dealing with the challenges poor and marginalized people face is neither easy nor straight forward. Even the countries with a strong social net haven't managed to eradicate marginalization. Social inclusion tools will almost always have to be tailored to the specific community they are targeting. Moreover, they have to be designed in a bottom-up way, requiring the involvement and ownership of the communities in question. Development almost never works if it is done **for** a community, rather than **by** the community.

It is important to note though that proportionally, marginalized communities tend to be over-represented in lagging areas, while in absolute term, it is large urban areas, often the economic engines of the country that concentrate a significant share of marginalized people. Consequently, policies targeting marginalized people are often urban development policies, targeting specific districts or neighborhoods (e.g. improved connectivity, affordable housing, rehabilitation of public infrastructure, development and rehabilitation of educational and health infrastructure, the provision of social services).

Enabling the Emergence and Functioning of Clusters

No economy can sustain economic growth long-term without innovating. Innovation is required to respond to a growing panoply of needs of the world population, in a cost-effective and efficient way. Innovations have a higher chance to occur if more people try their hand at it, and people have a higher likelihood of innovating if they interact with more like-minded people. Clusters have the benefit of bringing together people and firms that learn from each other, and that generate a higher innovation output.

Of course, clusters cannot be engineered. This is a lesson that many country governments have learned the hard way. Innovation does not happen by fiat – it requires the interplay, cooperation, and competition of a myriad of actors. What public authorities can do is to enable as many of these actors to come together.

Several tools are available in this sense. For one, developed countries can make it easier for people from all over the World to come over. There are higher chances of innovating if you are drawing on a global talent pool, than if you are only relying on a national talent pool. A good transport infrastructure and logistics are key for enabling the most efficient distribution of global talent across space. It makes more sense to have three IT specialists clustered together, than if you have them spread across the World.

If it is easy for people to move from place to place, it should also be easy for them to settle down. This requires functional land and housing markets. More specifically, it should be easy and cost-efficient to build housing, and easy and cost-efficient to find rent.

It is also important to have access to large homogeneous markets. Such markets translate into larger numbers of early adopters of innovations, and these early adopters are critical in the life of an innovation – from idea to market success. At this point, only the US offers such a large homogeneous market, and this is likely one of the reasons it produces a disproportionate share of disruptive innovations.

Lastly, it is important to have in place the proper legislation and business norms that enable upward mobility of young people. Innovation requires fresh thinking, energy, and a new way of looking at things, and young people are prolific generators of innovations.

If it is difficult for young people to get promoted in an organization, or if it is difficult to get easy access to financing for developing an idea into a marketable product, it will also be more difficult to generate ideas that will change the World.

Adjusting to Market Changes

For the most part, developed countries already have the institutions in place that ensure a smooth functioning of their economies. These institutions have been created and improved over decades. What developed countries don't have are the institutions that will respond to the market changes that are about to happen. For example, if individual air travel is made possible, one would need to have the proper rules and regulations in place to ensure that flying cars don't crash into building and into each other. Such institutions have to be created quickly to keep with the pace of innovations. Without broadcasting licenses and the proper monitoring of broadcast content, TV channels would likely broadcast whatever brought them a larger audience.

It is also important to have the flexibility in place to quickly respond to market failures. The financial crisis of 2008 represents in many respects a failure of institutions to respond to a market failure – i.e. opaque, largely unregulated financial instruments, which turned out to be part of a major Ponzi Scheme. The financial crisis also brought to the fore the problem of having a few large financial corporations play such a large role in the well-being of the World Economy, and by extension the well-being of regular people. As discussed earlier, the concentration of power in a few hands, regardless if public or private, is never good for an economy.

Thus, the challenge for developed countries is not so much to perfect existing institutions (although the DMV in the US does need some tender, love, and care), but rather to create the proper mechanisms to respond to sudden market changes. Just as the private sector innovates, so does the public sector. Developed countries don't only develop the technologies that help modernize the World, but they also develop the institutions that ensure the proper management of these technologies.

Consequently, the failure of developed countries to quickly develop the institutions that rapidly respond to sudden market changes, can have global repercussions, not just local. This requires a pro-active, rather than reactive approach from public authorities. They have to have the proper mechanisms in place to monitor market dynamics and detect irregularities in a timely fashion.

Promoting Social Equity

A society that does not know how to take care of its weakest members can hardly be called a developed society. In almost every country (developed or not), a significant share of government spending goes to social programs – pensions, unemployment benefits, food stamps, social assistance, etc.

However, social expenditures are not enough. One has to also address the inequities in a society – especially when these are large and growing. Thomas Piketty brilliantly argues that a large share of capital in a society is owned by a few people, and when the return on that capital is higher than the overall growth rate of the economy, more and more capital ends up being concentrated in the hand of a few rich people, to the detriment of the large majority (the middle-class and the poor), whose revenues usually grow slower than the overall growth rate of the economy. In practice, those with a lot of capital almost always manage to get a higher return on capital than the average economic growth rate, for the simple reason that an economy needs access to capital to fuel its growth, and it is the already rich that provide this capital. And, naturally, they are only inclined to offer the capital if they get a return that is attractive enough.

To address social inequities, Piketty proposes a progressive taxation scheme, with higher tax rates applied to people with high incomes, but also with a proper taxation of capital to avoid a situation in which capital gets concentrated in only a few hands. Whether such a solution is enough to solve inequity problems is a matter of continuous debate in academic and policy circles. What is known however is that allowing inequities to grow, sooner or later leads to a meltdown and a reset of society around new principles.

The reasoning is quite simple. For people at the bottom of the barrel there is no upside to maintain the status-quo. And, when a significant share of the population finds itself in a rut (i.e. without prospects of a better life in the near future), populist and extremist politicians become more appealing. Such politicians offer the potential for a system reset. More specifically, the can shake things up and when a system is shook up the benefits tend to be higher for the have-nots than for the haves. There are few downsides for those that are already at the bottom, but significant downsides for those that have achieved a certain level of comfort. When enough people are doing poorly, there usually is a significant change around the corner.

Create Global Climate Change Institutions

Climate change is not a localized problem and it will never be. The fact that a country spews pollution in the air can have repercussions halfway around the globe. Developed countries are responsible for an overwhelming share of the climate change mess we're in, and they should take responsibility for leading the fight against it.

After the Second World War, institutions like the World Bank were created to help lead the reconstruction of war-torn countries, and to help the fight against global poverty.

The time has come to create a similar global institution dedicated to fighting climate change. It is critical to have a global system of rules, regulations, and instruments focused on this area – a system that does not impede the growth and development of undeveloped and developing countries, while still addressing head-on the problems caused by green-house gas emissions.

Some of these global instruments (e.g. carbon trade schemes) are already operational, but climate change requires efforts commensurate with the posed challenges.

Most countries would be all too willing to respect global

rules if these rules were clear and properly enforced. As long as these rules are missing, everybody is doing what is ultimately in their best interest. The same way early industrialists abused their workers because there were no institutions mandating the eight-hour workday and prohibiting child labor, similarly countries abuse the environment in the absence of rules that everybody has to follow.

Grow New Markets

The decline of the middle-class in developed countries is likely the most important economic challenge these countries are facing. Without growing markets, it is difficult for an economy to sustain long-term growth, and a system that enters a phase of decline, takes some time to recuperate from the decline – if ever. Growth is an essential characteristic of most systems and living organisms.

When your markets are shrinking there are only a few options you have to grow them again: 1) allow in-migration from developing and undeveloped countries; 2) grow and tap markets elsewhere. The first solution is a politically and socially charge issue, but it is used widely by most developed countries. The second solution has been used with a significant rate of success by the EU. The EU has not only enabled the growth and development of its New Member Countries, but it has also created new markets for its older member Countries.

Thus, the new middle-class in the Czech Republic, Poland, Hungary, or Romania, is a growing market for producers from Western Europe. And indeed, most New Member countries have a negative trade balance with Western Europe – importing from them more than they export. This is a win-win situation that allows all parties involved to profit – New Member countries develop their economies and grow their middle-class; older Member Countries manage to tap new and growing markets. For example, in 1990, Germany exported goods of around $8 billion (or 2.2% of total goods exports) to the countries from Eastern Europe that would eventually join the EU; by 2000, the exports to these countries grew to around $39 billion (or 8.3% of total goods exports); and, by 2014, exports grew yet again to $176 billion (or 12% of total goods exports). Basically, around half of Germany's total good exports in 1990, are now exported only to New EU Member countries.

This model of trade integration can be scaled up globally, with developed countries strengthening ties with developing and undeveloped countries, for mutual gain.

Of course, the obvious question is, what do you do when population growth has stopped world-wide and most countries have achieved a relatively high standard of development. The answer to that question may come faster than many of us anticipate, but it may be too early to speculate. What is clear though, is that developed countries have to switch from an inward looking growth model, to an outward looking one. Developed countries will soon realize that helping other markets develop abroad, is ultimately good for business at home.

Integrate Markets for Innovation

The cycle of innovation is well-known and abundantly discussed. It is known, for example, that innovations rarely follow a straight shot from idea to market product. For ideas to actually make it into marketable products; even fewer become profitable products. For the few lucky ideas that make it to the market, a group of people is of particular importance – the early adopters (i.e. the few of us that get excited about anything new and different... I myself am not one of those).

If early adopters find a particular innovation interesting, they disseminate that information to others – the next wave of adopters. If these new wave of adopters finds the innovation interesting/useful, they then disseminate the innovation further.

Of course, the best innovations are those that: 1) have relatively low up-front costs, but unlimited scalability once they have been generated (e.g. a piece of software, a book, a piece of music, a movie, a design, ideas in general); 2) have a global market and remain interesting for future generation (e.g. people still pay for Beatles songs); 3) have a short time from conception to market maturity (i.e. they are quickly adopted by people).

Now, while every innovator would be interested in reaching a global market, before getting to the global market, it needs the early adopters. And, the more early adopters it can reach, the better the chances for that innovation to reach market maturity.

At this moment, the largest unified market of early adopters is in the US. Think only of the US' higher-education system – over 20 million students (the equivalent of the entire population of Romania) were enrolled in 2016, and these students do not only work to define the future, but also welcome it when it comes.

If it is in the interest of developed countries to help developing countries develop, so they can access additional markets, it is also in their interest to unify their innovation markets with those of other developed countries. This way, they can tap a larger pool of early adopters, and can generate more successful innovations.

This is also relevant for trade unions like the EU, which function well when it comes to the trade of goods, but less well when it comes to the trade of services and knowledge. Language, cultural, and policy barriers (e.g. different patent systems) make it difficult for an innovation generated in one EU country to reach early adopters in another EU country.

Embrace Creative Destruction

Creative destruction is absolutely necessary for an economy, but it is a difficult pill to swallow – both from a social and from a political point of view. Lower value-added sectors have to make space for higher value-added sectors, if an economy is to grow. If this fails to happen, an economy eventually becomes stale, stagnates, and finally enters a period of decline. This is what happened in Communist countries. The political leadership simply did not allow inefficient industries to go bankrupt, and they lacked the market understanding of what other industries to put in their place. They produced everything under the sun, but they did not produce many products competitive on global markets.

Creative destruction however can be a counter-balancing force to trade integration. If a country develops an innovation in a field that destroys another field in a different country, it is easy to see how the country that got the shorter end of the stick would not be too excited about the trade partnership

However, a country that does not continuously innovate, and an economy that fails to modernize, does not have good future prospects.

Many developed countries deal with "Too Big to Fail" situations, when private companies, with a large number of employees, face financial difficulties, and the state comes to the rescue. The reasoning for such an action is sound and easily justifiable. However, the negative impact from the bankruptcy of a large company can be long-lasting and difficult to reverse.

It is important for developed countries to put legislation in place that avoids "Too Big to Fail" situations, and ensure the economy has the resources to continuously renew itself. Obviously, it is not sound social and economic policy (at least for the short and medium term) to let a large employer go bankrupt. But, it is important to avoid a situation in which a number of large employers end up keeping the labor market, and the economy at large, hostage. Anti-trust legislation has been used in the US ever since the dawn of the 20th century, as a way of addressing the enormous sway industrialists like Andrew Carnegie, John D. Rockefeller, or J.P. Morgan. Similar legislation could be employed to ensure that companies don't get too big to fail.

Bringing It Altogether

The key policies for developed countries include:
- Identifying and growing markets in developing countries, to balance out the shrinking home markets.
- Addressing social and equity challenge in society, as well as negative market externalities.
- Tackle head-on global climate change challenges.
- Integrate with other innovation markets, to increase the emergence of new technologies and innovation.
- Embrace creative destruction and create the proper levers for a continued modernization of the economy.

MUSINGS on the ECONOMY of TOMORROW

The only thing we know with certainty about tomorrow is that it will be different. There is a multi-billion dollar industry attempting to figure out how the world of tomorrow will look like, but there are way too many variables to be taken into consideration to make a foolproof assessment. In one of the best philosophical treatises of our time, "The Black Swan", Nassim Taleb shows that history has been, and will be defined by freak events that few people, if any, saw coming. Karl Popper also brilliantly indicates that the future will be defined by the technologies yet to be invented, and we don't know what these technologies would be – if we would, we would invent them now rather than wait for some point in the future.

Nonetheless, not knowing what the future will look like, should not prevent us from imagining it. Indeed, some dreamers like Jules Verne imagined technologies, like the submarine or the TV, decades before they were actually invented. This is also the scope of this chapter. While I am far from the visionary that Jules Verne was, I will add a few thoughts to the global market of ideas, and, who knows, maybe some of these will stick. Often, imagining the future ends up defining it.

Furthermore, there are key global trends and dynamics that are simply too powerful to overlook. The following sections will introduce some of the key issues that, in my opinion, will define the world of tomorrow.

Limits to Growth or Space the Final Frontier

The entropy of every system or living organism requires continuous growth. Once a plant, animal, or a system stops growing, it usually enters a decline phase and eventually withers away. The population of the Earth has been growing continuously over the years, and the Industrial Revolution has triggered an explosive growth. However, fertility rates have dropped below replacement level in most countries, and global population growth rates have been steadily falling – from around 2% in 1979 to 1.2% in 2015. If current population growth trends continue, then the World's population will likely stop growing somewhere around 2070. The demography will also change very quickly, with a rapid increase of elderly and retired people. While less and less babies will be born, there will be more and more people above the retirement age, as life expectation has been going up across the World.

For the most part, people have conquered every spec of inhabitable land on the face of the Earth and have spread wherever they could make a living. The most fertile areas have been the first destinations for the early migrants, and these areas also house now the largest population densities. When you compare a map with the most fertile lands and one with population densities, the correlation is clear. This dynamic is more potent when one compares the population changes in Western Offshoots, such as Australia, Canada, and the US. For example, around 1700 AD, Australia had a population of around 450,000, while the US had a population of around 1,000,000, and Canada a population of around 200,000.[41] Now, we know that the US has a larger area that is friendly to people than Australia (where much of the land is uninhabitable desert) or Canada (where much of the land is frozen throughout the year). Consequently, the US has grown to around 320 million people, while Australia is hovering at around 23 million and Canada at around 35 million. Much of the population growth in these three countries has taken place in already established urban centers. In Canada, 50% of the population lives in a few large urban agglomerations, such as Toronto, Montreal, Calgary, Vancouver, Quebec, and Edmonton.

Wherever people could move on this Earth they did, and wherever they could thrive, they did. There still are a few areas where population continues to grow naturally, such as India, Africa, and parts of Latin America, but otherwise much of the rest of the World has fertility rates below replacement level. In fact, the average fertility rate at the Global level has more than halved in the past 50 years, from around 5 births per woman in 1965 to around 2.45 in 2014, and it will likely fall below the 2.1 population replacement level in the next years (somewhere around 2025).

This is good news for the Planet and its environment, but not so good news for the Global economy. Without population growth, an economy, like any other system, cannot sustain growth either. This means that sooner or later it will also enter a period of decline and potential extinction. The main option will be to transform other areas of the Earth into hospitable places (e.g. Siberia, the Norther Territories in Canada) and/or to start conquering space. Most Sci-Fi movies talk about a future where humans conquer space, or where space comes to conquer humans.

An economy without sustained population growth, cannot itself sustain growth. As shown, earlier, the economy has throughout history grown in tandem with the population, and global productivity growth has never managed to outstrip population growth. This makes intuitive sense – without more people to sell goods, services, and ideas to, an economy will eventually run out of steam.

Thus, humanity should soon start thinking about conquering space – it will be the new frontier not only for mankind, but also the human economic system. The global economy will eventually have to make the transition to the universe economy. Word!

The End of Countries

People love to be around similar people, and community gives us a sense of security. Countries are basically large communities, comprised of more or less homogeneous groups of people, with the intent purpose of protecting group interests.

The most successful groups have been those that have managed to attract the most people – usually the most developed countries in the World. While in the past it was countries that were strongest militarily that have attracted the most people (a strong military meant protection from outside groups), it is now the strongest economies that are most attractive to people. People are willing to take on significant risks, and do so every year, to get to one of the World's developed countries. The main destinations are North America and Western Europe.

As the rest of the World will continue to develop, other places will become more and more attractive. Eventually, development gaps will disappear and it will be a number of super-productive cities that will compete with each other for talent from all over the World.

When the World will be endowed with equally good infrastructure and public services, when living standards will be roughly the same everywhere, when travel will be free and open to any place on the face of the Earth, nation states will lose some of their raison d'etre.

Things are already converging in that direction. The European Union, with all its faults and hiccups it encountered along the way, has provided and will continue to provide a model for countries around the World. To me, the EU is humanity's grandest achievement, and we should learn to build on the EU development model.

Global agreements, such as trade and climate change agreements, are already moving the World in a parastatal direction. For the World to function better, barriers between countries and between people will have to be reduced, and the nation state will become a less prominent – and "the world will be as one", as John Lennon has quipped in "Imagine".

Mayors will Rule the World

Urbanists say that the 19th Century was a century of empires; the 20th Century was a century of nation states; and, the 21st century will be a century of cities.

We live in an urban and quickly urbanizing world. Cities are the growth engines of the World and they are of paramount importance for the global economy. Increasingly, these cities will compete with each other for global talent, and as such, the ones that are best managed will also get the cream of the crop. This means that mayors will have to get better and better at what they do. And, strong mayors will also want a bigger chair at the World table.

The competitiveness of countries is already closely linked with the competitiveness of a country's major cities, and this link will get stronger in the future as countries become more urbanized. Mayors will thus have more clout to influence national policy, they will manage to secure a larger share of a country's resources, and they will likely undertake the most important infrastructure projects. City Halls will likely have to become more entrepreneurial, and better at attracting people, businesses, and tourists.

Mayors will not only have to become better at attracting global talent, but they will also have to be better at collaborating and cooperating with other public administrations; they will have to design and plan across jurisdictional boundaries; they will have to compete with cities from across the globe; they will command the World's largest economies.

Strong Universities will be a Critical Success Factor for Cities

New EU Member Countries are an excellent research subject for people interested in economic development dynamics, as the analysis benefits from an abundance of data, and one can study development and growth as they happen, unadulterated by past theories and insights. An analysis of migration data in Poland and Romania shows a number of very interesting dynamics.

For one, an overwhelming share of people move to a handful of particularly successful cities. This concentration of people and resources in a few places is a dynamic that is already well known, and it has been discussed at length in this book.

Overall, the cities that have been most successful in attracting migrants are primate cities, secondary cities with a good geographic location (i.e. close to developed markets), and university cities. This last dynamic is particularly important, and with significant consequences for the competitiveness of cities in the future.

On a background of overall demographic decline and aging, the most competitive cities will be those that will manage to attract young people. University cities have one significant advantage – they manage to concentrate a lot of young people in one place, and as such make the city more attractive for other young people. We always like to congregate with people like us.

Not only do university cities attract young people, but they also attract a higher share of high value-added private companies, which want to take advantage of the plentiful well-educated workforce. As more and more people and companies settle in these cities, they generate a virtuous circle, attracting even more people and companies. Data on Poland and Romania shows that it is the strongest university cities (not necessarily the strongest economic centers) that have managed to attract the most people in recent years. They are also the places with the highest share of young people and well qualified people. Large industrial centers, like Katowice in Poland, or Galati in Romania, have received a disproprotionately lower share of migrants, and will likely not fare too well in future years if they don't re-invent themselves.

The Transport Revolution

There is no Sci-Fi movie, or book, at least none that I know of, that does not try to imagine how people will get around in the future. From the "mundane" space travel ships, to being beamed to different locations, and wormhole riding into different galaxies, transport advancements capture the imagination of people. Given the sheer vastness of the unexplored universe, it is easy to understand why advances in transportation will be among the key defining innovation of the World of tomorrow. Transport advances (e.g. ships, the rail, highways, air travel) have been critical to pushing the World economy forward and will continue to be critical in the future.

But we don't have to get to space travel to show how the transport revolution will define the World of tomorrow. There are rapid changes that are profoundly transforming the World now.

Cheap Air Travel

Romania is not exactly on the technological frontier. While it is a relatively small country (it takes around one hour to fly from one corner to the other), getting around the country has not been easy as I was growing up. We had no real highways, the road system was underdeveloped and in a continued state of disrepair, the trains somehow managed to get slower and slower as the rail infrastructure was falling apart, and air travel was a luxury afforded by a handful of people.

In the meantime we have managed to build a few extra kilometers of highway, we have rehabilitated a few railways lines (although the trains continue to be slow as shit), and we have a passable road network. We have witnessed however a revolution in air transport. In a largely deregulated air traffic market, with a national airline company that is about to go bust, a number of budget airlines have started to operate a number of external routes. Servicing initially the diaspora hotspots (i.e. the major cities where the around 4 million Romanian emigrants have chosen to settle), these budget airlines have quickly realized that there is a buck to be made in air transport in Romania. Thus, they have quite quickly moved from servicing only external hubs to also operating internal flights. Thus, you can now fly from Bucharest to the major urban hubs in Romania for less than $10, and under an hour. By comparison, a similar train ride would cost at least double and would take around 13 hours.

Budget air travel will likely give rise to a globally more tight-knit World, enabling almost everybody to travel between major urban hubs – in turn making those major urban hubs even more attractive for people. It is already easy for Romanians to have a city break in most major cities in Europe. Most likely, it will soon be quite easy and cost-efficient for an Indian from Mumbai to fly to any other major urban center in India. This will enable not only the services sector to grow, but it will also make it easier for ideas to go from place to place.

Integrated Metropolitan Transport Systems

We now live in an urban world. In the years to follow, it is likely that more and more people will reside in large metropolitan areas and conurbations. All of these people concentrated in a few spots around the World will need a way to get around. This means that extensive connective infrastructure (e.g. roads and rail) will have to be constructed.

Moreover, public transport systems will have to be coordinated across administrative boundaries, requiring integrated policies that promote spatially compact development patterns rather than sprawl. Many of the metropolitan areas in the developed world have grown in an unsustainable manner, but cities in the developing world have an opportunity to do it right.

Most of the day-to-day travel done by people is done within metropolitan areas, and it is critical to enable people to spend as little time as possible travelling, so they have more time for personal pursuits.

Empirical data on migration to the largest functional urban zones in Romania and Poland indicates that over 50% of migrants move to the outer areas of the core city. In developed countries, much of economic activity happens in such large functional urban zones. It is important for these functional urban zones to work as cohesive wholes, making it easier for people to move around and access opportunities, and making it easier for private companies to access a large labor force.

It is likely that the personal car will become less and less used as means of getting around metropolitan areas, and they will gradually be replaced by public transport and non-motorized transport means (e.g. biking, walking, skating). Cities like Copenhagen, Stockholm, or Vienna, which consistently score high on quality of life measures, are already quite advanced on their shift away from cars. Over 50% of people in Copenhagen already commute by bike every day, and the trend is ascending. Moreover, the number of pedestrian only areas and car-free zones are growing every year. Soon, only electric cars will be allowed in the historic center of the city. Cities like Copenhagen will set the trend for the other cities of the World.

Para-statal Infrastructure Development

We live in an increasingly inter-connected World. That is a fact. No economy can sustain long-term growth and development if it is not connected to global trade networks. As I have discussed in the book, these trade networks are often regional in nature – i.e. most of a country's trade happens with its neighbors. As trade between neighboring countries grows, so will the need for better and more integrated connective infrastructure. This in itself will also require a better coordination of major infrastructure projects (e.g. highways, ports, airports).

The need to coordinate large infrastructure projects across national borders will likely witness a higher share of joint-national projects, and the involvement of para-statal institutions in the implementation of such projects. For example, it is likely that the EU will eventually become involved in the implementation of projects of continental importance.

Similarly, the African Development Bank may finance multi-country road development projects, which would enable land-locked countries in Africa an easier access to a port or cargo airport. Some countries may end up using the port infrastructure of a neighboring country (e.g. some Bulgarian producers may decide to ship their goods from the *Constanța* Port in Romania), while people in some countries will use the airport hubs of a neighboring country, as many already do.

Such para-statal infrastructure projects will also help connect communities from across the globe, and will reduce the importance/need for national governments.

The End of the Tower of Babel

In an analysis of the Chinese economy and its prospects for the future, Lee Kuan Yew (the former visionary Prime Minister of Singapore) sees the Chinese language as a key barrier to the sustained growth of the country. Chinese is a language that is very difficult to learn and master by a foreigner, and it will make it difficult for the Chinese to attract global talent in the way America is currently doing. Moreover, without the Chinese mastering English, there is a high likelihood of them missing on good ideas and business opportunities. Lee Kuan Yew indicates that English is "the lingua franca of the leaders in science, technology, invention, business, education, diplomacy, and those who rise to the top of their own societies around the world"[42]. He further explains why, as a Prime Minister of Singapore, he pushed to have English as the first national language[43]:

> *While Singapore shares with China many of the core philosophical tenets of Confucianism, we worked over the past 40 years to establish English as our first language, and Chinese as the second. Why? Certainly not by accident or without provoking strong opposition. We did so to open ourselves to the world and allow ourselves to engage and embrace the main forces of discovery and invention and creativity that occur not only in the language but also in the mentality of English.*

The economy of tomorrow will be the economy of ideas, and the easier you will make it for ideas to reach you and be sent further, the better off you will be. English already is the lingua franca for the global elite. It is time for it to also become the lingua franca for the common man. More and more countries will realize that the easier it will be for their people to communicate at the global level, the easier access to opportunities they will have.

The World Currency and the Disappearance of Banks

> *Finance [is] the only way to make money when you have no idea how to create wealth.*
> PETER THIEL

A large share of the global trade is completed using either the US Dollar or the Euro. These are the currencies of the two largest trade blocks in the World, and as such are the currencies that provide the most stability and predictability. The problem with using another country's currency for international payments lies in the difficulty of controlling the performance of your own currency. When your economy is expanding and you do a lot of trade, the value of your currency usually goes up. The opposite happens when the economy is contracting. In addition, making payments in a different currency than your own involves significant transaction costs.

The Euro is the first experiment with a common currency for several countries, and while this experiment had its good share of hick-ups, it may also pave the way for a global currency. Such a global currency does not have to be a classical currency emitted by a Global Treasury. Few countries would be willing to give up control of their capacity to mint money. A global currency could however take the form of Special Drawing Rights devised by the IMF as an alternative for the US Dollar for trading and foreign reserves. Special Drawing Rights is a virtual basket currency tied to several traded currencies (in 2016 these currencies were the USD, the Euro, the Chinese Yuan, the Japanese Yen, and the British Pound), and with an exchange rate adjusted to the exchange rate of composite currencies.

A global currency would not only make international trade easier, it would also make it easier for individuals to purchase goods and services from anywhere, at a fair price. Thus, the days of expensive tourist trips, with bad conversion rates, may be forgotten. At the same time, easier international payments can also make capital markets more fluid. It will become easier to access financing from a variety of sources, not just the classical banks.

Banks act more or less as intermediaries. They bridge the gap between those that have capital to spend and those who need capital. As such, banks hold a large sway over an economy, without necessarily providing a lot of value added. I rarely visit my Bank and do most of my transactions on-line. For many run-of-the-mill wage earners like myself, banks may well become obsolete. There already are a number of pure on-line banks. Opening an account and having a salary wired to it does not require a physical entity and a person to process the bureaucracy. Most of these steps can be done on-line, while the savings themselves could be directed to on-line deposit pools.

In turn, these deposit pools could be designed so they respond to the myriad of needs people have. Some can simply function as a simple savings account, some may be administered by a team for lending and investment operations. The best performing deposit pools will also likely attract the largest number of depositors.

The same way a large number of repetitive manufacturing and agriculture jobs will be replaced by machines, the same way travel and real estate agencies were replaced by on-line sites, so will banks be replaced by a more direct interaction between people with capital and people that need capital.

The Death of Intermediaries and Repetitive Jobs

If we are to follow one major trend with respect to the transformation of the World economy, this is the dramatic shift from manual repetitive jobs to automated processes, and the replacement of intermediaries with direct interactions between service providers and receivers.

This process will not always be sudden or rapid. The cost of labor in some parts of the world are low enough to compete with machines. There still are people who weave by hand, despite the fact that textile mills have been existence since the mid-18th century.

In some cases however, the process is fast and brutal. Real estate agents and travel agents are by-and-large an extinct species. The proliferation of on-line platforms that allow anybody with basic computer skills to buy a plane ticket, a holiday package, or a new home. Blogs, Facebook, and Twitter, and not the traditional newspaper, is how most of us stay abreast of the latest news these days. Artists can reach potential listeners directly on YouTube, and writers can reach potential readers directly on Amazon.

We are quickly learning that the brain is capable of phenomenal feats. Kids today acquire more knowledge today than most learned people in the past. Once we learn how to do a thing, it is hard to unlearn it. In addition to our regular jobs, each of us also is a travel agent, a real estate agent, a broker, a financial specialist, a trader, a diplomat, a writer, a barista, and, occasionally, a taxi driver.

Global Cadaster

Functional land markets are essential to a dynamic economy. The easier it is to purchase and develop land, the easier it is to invest. Unfortunately, land markets are dysfunctional in most countries, even in developed ones. This is because of clunky cadaster systems that impose significant transaction costs to those who want to learn about who owns a particular plot of land (and whether the owners are interested to sell).

Given the rapid advances in technology, it is likely that we will soon have access to globally integrated cadaster systems, which will enable not only the uploading of land plots outlines for most countries, where this information is available, but also a real time update function. The same way Google Maps has made it impossible for people to get lost around the World, we may soon have a global land management system that will enable the easy purchase and selling of land everywhere around the World.

Global investments will be simple endeavors that could be completed with the click of a button.

Faster and Faster Knowledge Acquisition

A kid today has a wider body of knowledge than most people just a century ago. We are getting better and better at producing and acquiring knowledge. And, the easier it is to acquire knowledge, the easier it is to generate development.

Even now, there are simple schematics on the web that allow

to quickly learn just about anything. It is likely that in the future, the diffusion of information and knowledge will become more and more efficient. The rate at which knowledge is generated every day, and the rate at which we are bombarded with information every day have grown exponentially in recent years. Consequently, it is likely that better and better methods of information dissemination will be invented, which will allow people to acquire knowledge at faster and faster rates.

Moreover, people will likely become better at doing a lot of things. Ikea has already transformed a lot of us in furniture assemblers, and Dell has enabled us to become computer wizzes (you can ask Dell to produce a computer that fits your specifications). The mind has a great capacity to acquire and store a lot of knowledge, and once you learn something, it is relatively difficult to unlearn it. I was a master on the skis when I was little (I used to live close to a ski resort and spend most of my childhood winters on the slope), but then had a 20 year hiatus. Recently, I took to the slopes again. To my great surprise, although I'm big and fat now, and my center of gravity has changed substantially, I could ski almost as well as I used to when I was younger. My mind seems to have stored somewhere the ability to do slalom and pirouettes.

We have not come close to test the full capacity of our brains, but the rate at which we have adjusted to acquiring larger and larger volumes of information hints to a large untapped potential. Moreover, we are getting better at imparting knowledge (you can nowadays learn how to build a car from a Pinterest sketch), and better and better at disseminating and accessing knowledge.

Instead of Conclusions

The story of economic development is still very much unfolding, and we are very far from writing the conclusions section. Economic development is just as important today, as medicine was in the Middle Ages. But just as people in the Middle Ages were susceptible to "wonder cures" and often did things that worsened their situation, so do people today do things that worsen economic outcomes, although the opposite was intended.

While economic development is a complex endeavor, there are some basics that are easy to get right. This book discussed some of these basics, such as:

Be friendly with others – particularly those bigger than you. For an economy, particularly an undeveloped or a developing economy, access to large markets is an absolute critical pre-condition to development. If you don't have access to large markets, you don't develop – it's as simple as that. And, although this sounds simple, there still is a myriad of national administrations that run protective economic policies. The thing is, protective policies doom your economy to underdevelopment. You cannot expect other countries to open their economies to your exports, while you get to protect your economy from imports. Protectionism never works – absolutely never! So get busy making friends.

Foreign investments are the fastest and most efficient way of modernizing an economy. Foreign investments are critical for developing countries. A foreign company does not only bring with it capital for investments, state-of-the-art technology, and new knowledge, but it also brings with it an already developed distribution and logistics network and access to markets. This is one thing that is often discounted when economic development strategies are hashed out. To access large markets you need to have access to large clients, and a relationship with such clients is built over many years. To get a large client to buy the things you produce, you need to develop trust, and this takes time and many interactions. Foreign companies come with an already developed client network. Endogenous companies need many years to build the same level of trust and strong client relationship.

Geography matters. If you are far away from developed markets, you are starting in the economic development game with an in-built handicap. A geographic handicap (e.g. distance from markets) is difficult to overcome, but it is not an impossible endeavor. You just have to identify the proper tools (e.g. connective infrastructure, such as airports or high-speed internet) to overcome it.

Institutions matter. Few companies will invest in a country where their investment is not guaranteed, and few people will invest in the future of a country if they are not vested in that future (i.e. if they feel their road to success is hard to find). The purpose of institutions is to ensure that as many people as possible, preferably all, have access to power. An economy has many more chances to succeed when it has more people invested in its future.

Markets matter. Markets represent the power of collective decisions over individual decisions. Institutions represent the work of a handful of individuals, whereas markets represent our collective effort. While a few smart people behind powerful institutions, can take a lot of smart decisions (for example, centrally planned cities have features that make them more efficient than cities predominantly shaped my market forces, such as higher density and development around public transport networks), markets are in the long run better decision takers. A lot of people can come up with better solutions than a handful of people. Strong institutions can help engender fast change (e.g. autocratic governments are better at building highways), but strong markets are a critical pre-condition to long-term performance.

Finally, it is critically important that regular people become more fluent in the language of economics. It is not a complex language (it is only made to appear so by insecure economists), and it is critical to understanding the world we live in. The more fluent people will become in the language of economics, the more astute they will be in asking the proper things from their politicians, from the companies they buy products and services from, and from themselves. And this is the ultimate goal of this book, to make as many people as possible, more fluent in the language of economics – it is more important than English these days.

NOTES

1. The international Organization of Motor Vehicle Manufacturers: http://www.oica.net/

2. Samuelson, Paul. 1970. Economics, 8th ed. McGraw-Hill.

3. North, Douglas C. 1991. "Institutions". The Journal of Economic Perspectives, Vol. 5, No. 1 (Winter 1991), pp. 97-112.

4. Popper, Karl. 2002. The Logic of Research: On the Epistemology of Modern Natural Science. Routledge

5. A detailed explanation of the methodology can be found here: https://datahelpdesk.worldbank.org/knowledgebase/articles/378832-the-world-bank-atlas-method-detailed-methodology

6. van Zanden, J., et al. (eds.). 2014. How Was Life? Global Well Being since 1820. OECD Publishing, Paris.

7. The Economist Intelligence Unit. 2016. *Democracy Index 2015: Democracy in an age of anxiety*.

8. Doemland, Doerte and James Trevino. 2014. "Which World Bank Reports are Widely Read?" World Bank Policy Research Working Paper 6851.

9. World Bank. 2009. "World Development Report 2009: Reshaping Economic Geography".

10. Ahrend, R. et al. 2014. "What Makes Cities More Productive? Evidence on the Role of Urban Governance from Five OECD Countries." *OECD Regional Development Working Papers*, 2014/05.

11. World Development Indicators

12 OECD.

13 International Labor Organization.

14 Data source: www.listafirme.ro

15 World Bank. 2015. *Competitive Cities for Jobs and Growth.*

16 Eric Weiner. 2016. *The Geography of Genius.* Simon&Schuster

17 http://www.theatlantic.com/education/archive/2015/07/silicon-valley-housing-tough-on-teachers/399071/

18 http://www.nytimes.com/2000/02/20/us/many-in-silicon-valley-cannot-afford-housing-even-at-50000-a-year.html?pagewanted=all

19 World Bank. 2016. *Taking on Inequality.*

20 https://www3.epa.gov/climatechange/EPAactivities/economics/nonco2projections.html

21 World Bank. 2012. Golden Growth: Restoring the lustre of the European economic model.

22 Bulgaria, Czech Republic, Estonia, Hungary, Latvia, Lithuania, Poland, Romania, Slovakia, Slovenia

23 Howe, Daniel Walker. 2009. *What Hath God Wrought: The Transformation of America, 1815-1848.* Oxford University Press

24 World Bank

25 CIA World Factbook

26 World Bank

27 EuroStat

28 www.listafirme.ro

29 Fortune. Global 500. Retrieved October 24, 2016

30 UNICEF

31 Howe, Daniel Walker. 2009. *What Hath God Wrought: The Transformation of America, 1815-1848*. Oxford University Press.

32 Lipsey, Robert E. 1994. "U.S. Foreign Trade and the Balance of Payments, 1800-1913". National Bureau of Economic Research Working Paper Series, Cambridge, Massachusets.

33 Maddison, Angus. 2003. *The World Economy: Historical Statistics*. OECD Publishing.

34 MIT Observatory of Economic Complexity.

35 EuroStat. 2016. *Urban Europe – Statistics on cities, towns and suburbs*.

36 http://www.cprr.org/Museum/RR_Development.html#2L

37 CIA World Factbook

38 Howe, Daniel Walker. 2007. *What Hath God Wrought: The Transformation of America, 1815-1848*. Oxford University Press.

39 See, for example: Henderson, J. Vernon. 1974. "The sizes and types of cities". The American Economic Review 1974/9/1.

40 World Bank. 2014. *Achieving Roma inclusion in Romania: what does it take?*

41 Madisson, Angus. 2003. *The World Economy: Historical Statistics*. OECD Publishing

42 Graham, Allison and Robert D. Blackwill. 2013. *Lee Kuan Yew: The Grand Master's Insights on China, the United States, and the World*. The MIT Press, Cambridge, Massachusets.

43 Ibid.

www.ingramcontent.com/pod-product-compliance
Lightning Source LLC
Chambersburg PA
CBHW031609210526
45464CB00004B/1500